P9-CWE-364

MADAME
DREAD

MADAME DREAD

A Tale of Love, Vodou,
and Civil Strife in Haiti

KATHIE KLARREICH

NATION BOOKS
NEW YORK

MADAME DREAD
A TALE OF LOVE, VODOU, AND CIVIL STRIFE IN HAITI

Published by
Nation Books
An Imprint of Avalon Publishing Group Inc.
245 West 17th St., 11th Floor
New York, NY 10011

AVALON
publishing group incorporated

Copyright © 2005 by Kathie Klarreich

First printing September 2005

Nation Books is a copublishing venture of the Nation Institute and Avalon Publishing Group Incorporated.

All rights reserved. No part of this publication may be reproduced or transmitted in any form or by any means, electronic or mechanical, including photocopy, recording, or any information storage and retrieval system now known or to be invented, without permission in writing from the publisher, except by a reviewer who wishes to quote brief passages in connection with a review written for inclusion in a magazine, newspaper, or broadcast.

Library of Congress Cataloging-in-Publication Data is available.

ISBN 1-56025-780-6

9 8 7 6 5 4 3 2 1

Book design by *Maria E Torres*
Printed in the United States of America
Distributed by Publishers Group West

In Memory of my father Harold, in Honor of my mother Susan, in Tribute to Jean Raymond, and in Celebration of Kadja

Acknowledgments

To my family, whose love and support gave me the confidence and courage to follow my dreams: Susan, Karin, Betsy, Beth, Walter, Gary, Steve, Julie, Amy, Adam, Sarah, Emily, Katie, Spencer, and Buddy.

To Gisele and Jacques, who guided me unconditionally. To my de facto sisters: Françoise, Martine, Anne, Maggie, and Loune. To Sergo, whose companionship was my salvation, and his embracing family: Botine, Vanessa, Valerie, and Valeo. To my Haitian family: Agnes, Eric, Guy, Yolette, Prosper, Bernard, and Adjaline. To Ritva, Aboudja, Chico, Pascale and Pierrot, Richard and Lounise, Nancy and Patrick, Ira, Rose Andrée, Choupet, Faika, Taina, Adrien, William, Isabelle, Andre, Pierre, Erisma, Jonas, Marie-Carmel, Alrich and the boys at the Clos, and the streetkids. To my colleagues Marvel, Venel, Herold, and Rothchild, and a special tribute to my fabulously fun and witty universal compatriots Sophie, Andrew, Mike, and

Harold. Appreciation to Sandra, Victoria, Jane, Michelle, Medea, Kirsten, Kevin, Mary, Tomi, Marcia, and Susie.

In memory of Marc Fleurant, Hugo Triest, Yves, Racine, Batala, Wowo, Jean-Marie, and Elsie. Also Ayiti, Ti David, Fatil, and the nameless streetkids who never had a fighting chance.

I am extremely grateful to those who read various forms of this manuscript, especially Mike, Diane, Susan, Marie, and particularly Dan Wakefield, who pushed me through my toughest impasse. Faye Bowers, Mark Abel, Joe Alicastro, Andrea Mitchell, and Elizabeth Farnsworth demonstrated the difference between a mediocre story and a memorable one. Thanks to the many fabulous journalists I worked with, including Peter, Greg, Sato, Linda, Larry, Howard, Joanne, Tim, Kerry, Brian, Jeffrey, and Pete. I am particularly grateful to my wise and worldly agent Janell, and my sharp and humorous editor Carl.

I am forever indebted to Jean Raymond for his love, support, and pursuit of truth. Above all, I thank Kadja, who never once complained about the countless hours of an absent or distracted parent, and who each day reminds me of all that is good and possible in the world.

Contents

MADAME
DREAD

Chapter I

A New Way of Life

Lavérité se tankou lwil nan dlo, li toujou anlè.
Truth is like oil in water; it always comes to the surface.

I registered the sound as gunfire but it was several seconds before I realized that it was live, and coming in my direction. A second, third, and fourth round of shots followed in quick succession, each one increasing in volume and proximity.

Suddenly a blue pickup truck burst through the northern gate of the Haitian National Palace, careering straight across the street toward the National Snack, where my friend Shari and I were sipping a glass of freshly squeezed grapefruit juice. Uniformed soldiers stood upright in the back of the vehicle, swaying in unison, a mass of blurred camouflage; weapons like lightning rods propped them up as the truck swerved around the tight corner in front of the picture window where I sat. Despite the rust, the guns reflected the sun's rays in our direction. The men were tossed like Pick-Up Sticks as the truck sped west toward the water. They were so close I could have identi- fied the color of their eyes if not for the oversized olive green helmets that flopped toward their noses, giving them a cartoonish look. But nothing was funny about this, particularly since I had no idea who was doing the shooting or why, or even where it was coming from. The only thing I knew for certain was that I had picked the wrong spot to take a respite from the burning heat outside.

The gunfire overpowered the usual street noise. The blasts were deafening and without thinking I dived under the table like everyone else, sending plates of french fries flying, ketchup and ice-cream cones splattering. Coke and Sprite bottles crashed alongside the mango and passion-fruit juices that pooled on the floor. Above the background noise of shooting, screeching tires, honking horns, and cries of terror was the squeaking of the side door as people stampeded out.

Minutes later there was an eerie silence. There were no more gun- shots, nor were there sounds from the street or snack bar, except for one lone Coca-Cola bottle rolling on the cement floor. When it finally came to a stop it was deathly quiet, which was far more frightening than the chaos of the last few minutes.

"Shari, we're the only ones left," I whispered in near hysteria. Peeking out from under the table the only movement in the now- empty restaurant was steam rising from the food under the heat lamps, food that was never going to be served. "Let's get out of here."

We untangled ourselves from the mess around us and made a bee- line toward the door, our adrenaline racing faster than our feet. "This way," Shari said as she grabbed my hand. "My office, it's that building on the corner—right there. Run. Run hard."

I'd met Shari one week earlier through a mutual acquaintance— she was an intern at Catholic Relief Services (CRS), where she received a stipend for her commitment to help out with several social-service projects. We'd just come from downtown Port-au-Prince, where we'd been perusing the streets for artwork. Just minutes before, Shari had been thinking of buying a painting with four oddly colored hens. Now we were running for our lives.

"Pierre!" Shari shouted to CRS's skinny caretaker, the lone figure visible on an otherwise empty street. He was just pulling down the heavy metal security gate by the front entrance when he heard our unexpected cry, an eerie shriek cutting through the moment of calm like a bolt of lightning. We squeezed through the small opening before Pierre reached with what little strength his scrawny, weathered arms could muster and clanked the iron bars together. Then he clipped the heavy lock in place and followed Shari and me as we bounced up the stairs, a nervous laughter resounding in the tight stairwell. "In here," Shari motioned toward her office, and I joined her at the window. The only thing we could see was the deserted square facing the palace, which was hidden from our view. "What the hell is happening?"

I shook my head, reeling to catch my breath and slow my heartbeat. My shirt was soaked from perspiration, first from the heat, then from nerves. It clung to my bra, and I gave it a self-conscious tug. My mouth was dry, parched from angst and fear. Splotches of dried, crusty ketchup peppered my sandals.

Outside, the only movement was military. We watched the silence, startled when intermittent shots rang out, rattling the windows with their vibrations. Then silence again. Then more shooting. It was really frightening, and I had no context for this kind of overpowering fear. I was the manager of a handicrafts store in San Francisco, and I'd come to Haiti on a three-month trip to buy handicrafts. My initial plan was to take intensive Creole lessons in Haiti's capital; my high-school French wasn't going to get me far in a country where less than 7 percent of the population spoke it. Then I planned to travel to the countryside to meet artisans and learn about their crafts until my money ran out. I'd been thinking wooden trays, painted metalwork, and papier-mâché, not machine guns, armed thugs, and military takeovers. That I was in the midst of gunfire just minutes earlier made me wish, for a brief second, that I'd listened to the skeptics who'd told me I was nuts for thinking of going to Haiti at all, let alone for three months.

Shari and I had no information; no way to get any and no idea what was going on. The phone line worked, but neither of us had been in Port-au-Prince long enough to think of a single person to call.

"Whatever it is, it can't be good," I said to Shari. I knew just enough about Haitian politics to know that anything was possible. Shortly before my arrival in Haiti, armed gunmen stormed the Catholic church of a popular priest they thought too radical, hacking to death more than a dozen parishioners. "Do you think this is connected to the incident at St. Jean Bosco Church?" I asked.

"No way to know, but I wouldn't be surprised. Everything here is connected," said Shari, visibly shaken. Her fair complexion, which had been rosy from our walk in the sun, was now flushed with fear. Tall and stately, her lean body seemed to have shrunk in the last half-hour, and her shoulder-length black hair lay plastered with perspiration against her neck. "How long do you think we'll be here?"

"I have no idea." I didn't want to think about the possibilities. "What a nightmare. We don't even know who is shooting at whom. Do you think President Namphy is in the palace? Is there a radio?"

"Broken," Shari said. "We'll probably be the last in the country to find out what's going on. I can just see the headlines when they find us next week: Two White Women Found, Bodies Paralyzed from Fear."

"Come on, it's not that bad." I poked her with my elbow. "Think of how much mileage we'll get out of this story later on." It was a tactic that I was familiar with in real life, replacing fear with humor, but I couldn't think of a single example in my thirty-three years where I had been in a situation as intense as this, with real guns and real danger.

"Rather not," Shari said, settling down in a desk chair. "At least we have water, and there's a supply closet, with things like toilet paper and cups. No food, but at least we won't die of dehydration."

I hadn't thought of that. Why would I? Things like this just didn't happen in my world. The closest I'd ever come to being stranded was when I was traveling in Nicaragua several years earlier and I'd been robbed of all my personal documents—passport, traveler's checks, plane ticket. I was in emotional distress then, but not physical danger. I'd anticipated having some adventures in Haiti, but nothing like this, and it was only the first week.

"Don't plan on being here that long." I pulled her from the chair. "Come on, let's go see if there's a better view from another window." We went from room to room looking for clues of what might be going on outside, but the only view was of the deserted streets below and National Snack, its doors still open. Wooden crates where street vendors had been sitting outside lay toppled on the sidewalk, various goods scattered on the side of the road. All the traffic, congestion, and bustle of people that filled the block when Shari and I first arrived at National Snack seemed to have melted into the blazing tarmac without a trace.

The stretches of silence eventually outlasted the periods of shooting, but we didn't believe that meant it was safe to go outside. It did give me time to reflect on the seriousness of the situation, and I began to draw on reserves that I didn't know I was capable of.

"We have to make a plan," I said. "We could make a run for your car."

"But to get there we have to run through the square," Shari said. "Are you really willing to do that?"

"No." I stated the obvious. The adrenaline of the moment had dissipated and it was no longer exciting to be in the center of whatever it was that was going on. I was unnerved and scared—not so much that I'd be the target of a stray bullet or get caught in the melee—but frightened in a distressed way, similar to how I felt as a child when I was thrust in the middle of a playing field, ignorant of the rules or even which game was being played. If Shari felt the same panic that I felt she didn't share it with me, perhaps out of the same sense of courtesy that I didn't share mine with hers, which given the situation almost made me smile at our politeness, but I didn't, of course. Our distress was apparent. The pitch of her voice was a few notches higher than usual and she clasped and unclasped her hands anxiously. Sweat seeped from my brow, my armpits, my hands, and my right arm trembled.

We debated what to do for what seemed like forever, but it was still daylight. The sky was an unnatural blue, as if it knew something unseemly was happening. Suddenly we saw a white station wagon pull into the National Snack parking lot from which we had fled.

"Mennonites," I said. Just as there were numerous groups of missionaries in Haiti, there were also a fair number of Mennonites. They were easy to identify by their clothing—plain, white, long-sleeved. Two women sat in the backseat, their hair pulled tight into buns covered by a white cotton cloth at the base of their necks. A young child sat between them; the two men in front both had long beards.

"Let's go then," Shari said, and shouted for Pierre to let us out. We tripped down the stairs three at a time, tumbling along the way. From out of the dark Pierre appeared, fumbling with the keys to raise the gate high enough for us to crawl under. We were so anxious to get to the car before it drove away that we didn't stop to consider Pierre's fate, leaving him alone as we dashed toward the car. We knocked on the window of the driver's side, startling the Mennonites, who were deep in conversation. They had just come from the countryside and were as surprised to find National Snack closed as they were to learn why. I was so grateful for their presence and generous offer to give us a lift to Shari's car that I felt my legs go weak with gratitude and held onto their open window for support. They nervously waited for us to get securely inside Shari's green Toyota before waving and driving off in the direction from which they'd come.

The motel that I was temporarily staying in while I looked for an apartment during my three-month stay was on the other side of town, so Shari suggested we return to her apartment, just a mile east of the palace. I'd never seen the area around the palace so empty, and for a brief second I was able to soak in the contrast between the whiteness of the palace and the dirty, worn buildings around it. Dusk was finally setting in, casting a pale glow over the bleached streets. But we didn't linger; the drive was mercifully quick. Shari drove in fourth gear and didn't pass a single vehicle on the way. I let out an involuntary shudder of relief once we passed through the gate that separated Shari's compound from the street. Immediately inside we met a small group of her neighbors, all foreigners, who were gathered by the pool. Two were in their swimsuits. Surreal. There were soldiers shooting up the town, and these people were sunbathing.

"What have you heard?" Shari asked.

"Nothing," said a Frenchman, "only that a friend of mine who lives close to the palace called to say there had been a lot of shooting, and all the streets are empty."

"Right," I said. I went inside to peel off my sweat-soaked clothes. I felt deflated, like a tire gone flat. Shari offered to make some pasta but I had no appetite. I took a cold shower but couldn't get rid of the nervous sweat. I didn't realize how tired I was until I put my head on the pillow, falling asleep to the banal music on the radio. Not one of Haiti's radio stations was broadcasting news.

The next morning I awoke to the sound of General Prosper Avril making a speech on *Télévision Nationale d'Haiti*, the National Television Station, TNH. The camera was fixed directly on his pale caramel face. The skin around his eyes strained in an effort to project the seriousness at hand. Still, he wasn't very convincing when he called himself President Avril and announced there had been a change in government. He never called it a coup d'état, though everyone else did.

The term "coup d'état" wasn't new to me, but it didn't have much meaning. I was the first to admit I was politically naïve. From the time I was old enough to read I was interested in world events, but I never thought I'd be in the middle of one. I'd done some reading about Haiti before I arrived, and I knew that Henri Namphy, the president who had just been ousted, had himself taken power in a coup earlier that year, but I didn't know a whole lot more than that. I had brushed up on international prices for handicrafts to know the fair market value when negotiating for purchases for my store, but I hadn't thought to brush up on survival manuals or seek out information on what to do during a shoot-out. "I brought the wrong books," I joked to Shari. "Should have been Che Guevara's *Guerrilla Warfare*, not Tom Wolfe's *Bonfire of the Vanities*."

Shari and I spent a restless morning at her apartment before she suggested we walk over to Tom's house, her boss who lived just a few blocks away. He was a Midwesterner who'd moved to Haiti a few years earlier to become the director of Catholic Relief Services. I considered him a veteran of Haitian politics because he had been in Haiti in February 1986, when a popular revolt forced then–dictator-for-life Jean-Claude Duvalier to flee the country.

Tom lived on a corner lot in a home surrounded by a high wall. We picked up a stone and rapped loudly on the gate to get the attention of the houseboy, whose job it was to unlock the chain wrapped around the handles of the big metal gate, and push it open. Tom, a strapping guy with a broad middle and big smile, shouted from the side porch for us to join him. He was sipping coffee with his wife, also a Midwesterner; their three daughters sat at a nearby table playing Scrabble. Pictures of the family displayed in little Haitian handicraft frames were scattered around the living room. That this family was carrying on with what seemed to be normal activities following a coup seemed bizarre. The girls stopped their game and asked us if we would like to have grilled-cheese sandwiches with them, and then perhaps play a game of Monopoly. A bowl of popcorn sat between them.

The game distracted me but I was still unsettled. I could have been in any home anywhere in the United States. But I wasn't. I was thousands of miles away in a place that made no sense. I couldn't get my bearing and just followed Shari's lead. Tom and his family seemed blasé about it all—would I feel the same way if I stayed as long as they had?

Later, Tom offered to take me home on his way to get groceries. "Busier than usual," he commented, maneuvering his way through the streets. "People are taking advantage of the calm and stocking up on provisions in case things explode again."

He said it as casually as if he were referring to a cold front coming through. Was I supposed to be reassured? What did he mean by that remark? More shooting? Another coup? A rebel attack? I didn't think he was being indifferent to the situation at hand, but I wasn't calmed by the possibilities he seemed to accept so easily. Maybe he's thinking like a Haitian, I said to myself as I made my way across the cement courtyard of the Magic Bud Inn, the quirky motel where I was staying. If I stuck around long enough, would I be just as relaxed? Unlikely, but extraordinary was the *mot du jour* in Haiti, so anything was possible.

I hoped to see a friendly face at the motel but it was deserted. The idea of being alone in my dark, unpleasant room depressed me even further. What I really wanted to do was plop down on my black leather couch in my San Francisco living room, wrap myself in my favorite red plaid blanket, and call my best friend to tell her about this bizarre weekend.

I consoled myself with the thought of how I would retell this story—surely it would become one of my standard classic "when I was in Haiti" stories. Impatiently, I tried to get an international line to the States, so I could start the first version even while I was living it, but I wasn't able to get a free line, let alone an operator. I played solitaire to pass the time.

Late in the afternoon, my mother got through to me. Her concern was palpable even across the phone lines, so I deliberately downplayed my own anxiety, but it seeped through anyway. She knew all about the coup because the networks were leading with the story and newspapers were running it on the front page, above the fold. She was reassuring but matter-of-fact—one of her best strengths—and her advice was straightforward. What's happening is political: "Get involved or get out."

"But how?" I asked. "What can I do?"

"What do you want to do?" she asked.

Going home—back to San Francisco—wasn't something I wanted to consider. If I packed up now it would mean that "they" were "right" and I was "wrong." The humiliation of hearing the "uh-huh" remarks, coupled with the smug satisfaction on the faces of my dubious friends and family members if I came back home steeled my determination to stay.

I knew that I had one friend who was going to be green with envy at my predicament. I'd become close to Medea, senior policy analyst at the Institute for Food and Development Policy, two years earlier. When she finally got through to me shortly after I'd hung up with my mother, she was laughing. "You can't believe what I went through to get your number," she said. "I spent hours looking for it, then finally reached your mom. Boy, is she upset."

"That must have been quite a conversation," I said. "I'm sure my mom tried to play it cool by not showing how worried she was while you downplayed your enthusiasm for my good fortune at being here in the middle of the coup."

"Something like that. So what's it like?"

"Thrilling and terrifying. I have no idea what I should be doing, Med. It's like history is being played out all around me, and I don't know what my role is."

"Try reporting," she suggested.

"Reporting? I'm not a reporter. Don't know the first thing about it."

"You can do it, Kath. You know how to write. It's no more complicated than that. I can call a friend at KPFA and see if he can give me a contact name for someone at Pacifica Radio. And I know the foreign editor at the *San Francisco Chronicle*. I'll give them both a call," she offered. "Haiti's a hot topic, Kathie. Take advantage of being in the right place at the right time."

The foreign editor at the *San Francisco Chronicle* called a short while later, asking for a firsthand account on my experience. I agonized over the 800 words, trying to come up with a sequential piece that was both exciting and factual. I wrote it longhand—I had no computer, not even a typewriter, and even if I had one, there would have been no way to send the article. Modems weren't part of my vocabulary in 1988 and there were no public places that had fax machines that were open at that hour. Internet and cybercafes were yet to be created. When I finished the article, I laboriously dictated it over a crackling phone line. Because the newspaper went to press on the West Coast, I had the advantage of the three-hour time difference, but still the extra time didn't help my writing. The editor rejected the piece—no explanation—and I was devastated. Never should have listened to Medea, I said to myself since there was no one else around who cared. What the hell was I thinking, that I could get published? I fell asleep lonely, depressed, and full of self-doubt.

But the foreign editor called unexpectedly early the next morning and asked for another piece, and that evening I dictated another article, this on the role of Haitian radio. It ran the next day on the front page. The printed version was so edited and reworked that I barely recognized the text, but it had my byline and I was proud—my name was in print in the *San Francisco Chronicle*, just like a real journalist. I ran up to the receptionist at the Magic Bud Inn and planted a huge kiss on his cheek. Drunk, he smiled with delight. Aha, I gloated—all you naysayers now take note that maybe my coming to Haiti wasn't so stupid after all. That night I fell asleep with a mantra of confidence that backed off some of my demons.

The editor from Pacifica Radio also called. I tried to relax my voice and mask my nervousness so that he wouldn't reject me before I had a chance to prove myself. He explained the basics of preparing a radio spot, and with a bit of massaging, my first sixty-second spot aired on their daily afternoon-news show the next day. I giggled in the same way I had when in first grade I won a swing set in a coloring contest. I'd gone from being a nobody to a somebody whose voice was being heard across America. Even though the Magic Bud Inn receptionist spoke no English, he continued to smile in a drunken stupor as I boasted of my success.

But I also felt like a sham. I had so much to learn. I was all too aware of how vulnerable I was as a stranger living in a very strange land. In addition to coping with the day-to-day chaos and uncertainty, I had just upped my own ante by tackling reporting. Gathering information with no contacts or language skills was just part of the challenge; the other half was putting the information together in a cohesive matter. Sixty seconds, including a lead, wasn't very long, but it felt endless for someone with no experience and very little confidence. I hadn't yet perfected the art of taking a lot of information and squeezing it into a limited amount of airtime or square inches. But with a byline and a radio spot under my belt, my journalism career was launched.

I came up with a plan to make myself a better reporter. I listened to the one radio station in Haiti that gave a nightly synopsis of the day's events in English, taking notes of names and places I should be familiar with. I visited other local radio stations and met with the news directors, the reporters, whoever agreed to speak with me. I called everyone I knew in Haiti who spoke English who might be "in the know" and grilled them on what they thought, and then placed them in categories: good quotes, good background source, someone who talks a lot but doesn't seem to know very much, Duvalier supporter, opposition leader. I knew I should be going directly to the source, but I was just beginning to understand what a source was. And without the language it was hard to get a direct quote. I forced myself to listen to Haitian radio, hoping that eventually Creole would start to make sense. It was slow going but I was more energized than I'd been in years.

I contacted other newspapers, including the *Christian Science Monitor,* which had published an op-ed piece I'd submitted on Haiti a few months earlier. Both the *Christian Science Monitor* and Monitor Radio, which then broadcast worldwide, showed interest in my story ideas. I was fortunate enough to be assigned to Faye Bowers, the *Monitor's* Latin American foreign editor, who had a rare blend of compassion and sharp journalistic instincts. She guided me gently in my reporting and helped hone my writing skills as I went along.

As I began to learn about the world of reporting, my attention shifted away from the variety of handicrafts I'd come in search of and refocused on the particulars of Haiti's current transition. History was happening, and I wanted to be a part of it—not just live it, but record it. That I now had the ability to be the eyes and ears for those who weren't there was more exciting than anything I'd ever done. I found it thrilling and intoxicating to be a witness, terrifying and strange as it was. And I was thirsty for information, not just on the political front, but to learn about how the country functioned, what motivated and inspired the population, what angered people, what tools they used to cope with their harsh conditions, what made them laugh.

I learned quickly that most of the news reported in and about Haiti stemmed from the capital, although 80 percent of the population lived in the countryside. Communication to and from Port-au-Prince was slow at best. Sometimes it took days for those in the remote areas to hear news from the capital and vice versa. Peasants in the countryside had scant access to such basic services as running water, electricity, and telephones, even transportation. Despite having traveled a lot, I still had taken most of these things for granted, and recognizing this startled me. It was finally hitting home how privileged I was. I'd never been truly hungry a day in my life, didn't know what it was to worry about having a roof over my head or clothes on my back. Those were always academic questions, never ones I needed to worry about for my own survival. Haiti was providing me a chance to reexamine myself and my place in the world. I'd never really desired to be anything more than a tourist when I'd traveled, but something about Haiti touched me. I wanted to build a connection to the country, to speak Creole, live in a neighborhood, cook Haitian food, and integrate myself as much as possible. This personal challenge excited, rather than discouraged me. Aside from the obvious dangers that made me uncomfortable, I wanted to figure out what, in me, I needed to understand in order to accept this country that at times seemed totally incomprehensible.

Although it was difficult to find both time and transportation to get out of the capital, when I did, my breathing returned to normal. It wasn't as though I could relate any better to the harsh and primitive conditions in the countryside, but life there was gentler. It provided relief from the disturbing urban images that haunted me: children in the capital bathing in the same water from which the pigs drank; little kids who should have been in elementary school scooping up runoff in dirty plastic juice cartons, salvaging what they could to wet their lips, bathe, and wash their clothes; open fields used as toilets by urban dwellers. And the sewage that bubbled up after a heavy rain, spewing rotten food that had been so trampled on it became one with the underlying footpath.

Too quickly I became accustomed to the site of nursing mothers offering shriveled breasts to starving infants, toddlers with bloated bellies at their side too weak to beg, just as I learned to fall asleep to the nightly serenade of roosters and feral dogs. I thought it might be quieter in another section of town, and was relieved when after several weeks I was able to trade my dimly lit, impersonal room at the Magic Bud Inn for a small one-bedroom, sparsely furnished apartment in the leafy section of Pacot, one building over from where Shari lived. My apartment complex had two front windows with permanent four-inch concrete shutters stacked like dominoes, one on top of the other. They were ugly, and I hated how they blocked the natural light rather than the mosquitoes and neighborhood noise, but I liked everything else about the place. The sublet came equipped with a one-burner Coleman stove to cook on and a phone line for three apartments—not ideal, but it was better than where I'd been. Once I moved in, I began to feel less like a tourist and more like a resident because I now had a neighborhood with real people, people who I saw in the supermarket, on the street and in passing during the day.

Plus there were trees on my street. Walking home I shrugged off the dust, dirt, and garbage-lined streets of the capital. Rounding the curve to my home, the atmosphere was more serene, almost too composed. There were no street merchants, barely any cars. It was passive and peaceful, a bit provincial, and reminded me of more settled neighborhoods in the wealthier suburbs of my hometown, Cleveland. Only here the trees weren't deciduous maples and oaks but exotic tropical varieties with flowers and berries and fruits and names I couldn't translate. My building was near the top of a small incline off one of the main roads that cut through the middle of the leafy section, just around the corner from several older, quaint gingerbreads with their balusters and spacious wooden porches lined with purple, red, and rose-colored bougainvillea. The brightly colored vines were so plentiful that I quickly got in the habit of clipping a few branches to liven my dank room.

The American embassy rented the house catty-corner from mine. The spokesperson for the ambassador was living there when I moved in. The headmaster of an English-speaking private school lived down the street and a retired general, Claude Raymond, was around the corner. My landlord said that General Raymond was associated with the Tonton Macoutes, a private militia François Duvalier created shortly after he came to power in 1957. Taken from the mythological figure "Uncle Knapsack," who kidnapped wicked children and put them in his straw bag, the Tonton Macoutes carried out the Duvaliers' maniacal dictums of rape, torture, and murder during their twenty-nine-year father-son dictatorship. No one was spared—not schoolchildren, teachers, or members of the Catholic hierarchy. Although they were often referred to as the secret police, there was nothing secret about what they did—their dirty work was evident everywhere and left the population terrorized.

One October afternoon as I was walking home, I passed a small group of people gathered on the side of the road, not far from Raymond's house. They looked as though they were trying to hide a *tap-tap* that they'd pulled off a small side street. *Tap-taps* are converted pickup trucks with slabs of wood for seats and brightly colored designs painted on the makeshift tops and sides. They were the most common means of transportation in the cities; but, like the bus systems I was used to in the States, they had specific routes they traveled and my neighborhood wasn't one of them.

"Why is this *tap-tap* here?" I asked.

"To hide the refrigerator," a guy in the crowd told me.

"Refrigerator?" I repeated, thinking I hadn't heard right. I was still very insecure with my Creole and my vocabulary was limited. I'd been taking lessons and trying to learn on my own, but it was slow going.

"Refrigerator," he confirmed, then turned away. I waited a few minutes to see if there was anyone else with whom I might speak, but I felt uncomfortable when people started looking at me so I continued on. The sun was hot and the heat from the road rose like steam in a Turkish bath. I slowed down as I turned the corner to allow a group of people to pass. They were carrying armloads of things—bulky parcels of clothes, shoes, food, lamps, rugs. I looked again—this was the kind of parleying that was common downtown, but unusual in my new neighborhood. The crowd was coming from Raymond's house, but the family cars weren't in the driveway. I knew it was dicey to be standing around watching, but my curiosity glued me to the spot. I stood like a lamppost amidst the steady stream of foot traffic moving up and down the driveway, in and out of the house. Emboldened by the fact that no one took special notice of me, I walked up the driveway as if I had the same right that everyone else did. I hesitated at the entrance, but when no one said a word, I stepped more confidently into the foyer.

"*Sak pase?*" I asked, using the customary greeting: What's happening?

"*Déchoukaj,*" said a guy balancing two chairs on his head.

This word had become popular in 1986, after the overthrow of Duvalier. Translated literally as "uprooting," *déchoukaj* was synonymous with popular justice—masses of people dismantling homes, offices, government buildings—anything they associated with those who had abused and/or exploited them. It was no surprise they went after Raymond. He was the alleged mastermind of an election-day massacre the year before, when armed gunmen shot voters as they stood in line to cast their ballots. I didn't understand why they'd chosen this day to *déchouke* his house any more than I understood the logic of the destruction, but this was Haiti and not second-guessing was one lesson I needed to learn. The court system being what it was, popular justice in Haiti was sometimes the only justice, even when the punishment itself seemed extreme.

Seeing the inside of Raymond's home helped me better understand the disparity between the rich and poor. Those who lived as Raymond did were motivated to maintain the status quo. The floors were tile, maybe marble, the ceilings high and the yard, which was visible through the picture windows, beautifully landscaped. Why would the wealthy want to pay taxes, educate the poor, or share power if it could contribute to the decline of their self-appointed entitlement? Seeing how Raymond lived explained why there was so much resentment and hostility in the country, when so few had so much and so many had so little.

Potted plants inside had already been turned upside down, the dirt ground into the floor by the swelling amount of foot traffic. A few Haitian paintings still hung on the walls but the rectangular pale patches showed where others had already been lifted. The heavier furniture was still there, too, but as I turned into the living room, a group of men struggling to remove a seven-foot orange couch pushed me aside. The love seat, along with some chairs, remained, but there were empty spots where end tables and other smaller, lighter pieces of furniture must have been. The dining-room table was thrown on its side, its chairs missing, and the spot where the rug had been had left a circular outline on the floor.

The kitchen floor was damaged by something that had recently been dragged across it. Aha, I thought, the refrigerator. In the spot where it used to stand were its contents: heads of cabbage, bunches of carrots, a spilled carton of milk, cracked eggs, peanut butter. Oil had leaked from its container and left a sleek film across one of the counters, along with condiments and cans that had been swept aside as someone searched the cupboards above. "Would you hold this for me until I get back?" one woman asked, pushing a pile of plates into my hand as she disappeared out the door with another. As soon as she was out of sight, I put the dishes down, and instantly someone else came along and grabbed them up.

The second floor was just as chaotic. Already the beds had been stripped, the television removed, pillows gone. Two guys struggled with the mattresses in one room while four women fought with another group of men over the remaining mattresses and bed frames. Photos of the family were scattered along with personal papers, books, clothes, shoes, and underwear. In what was probably a daughter's room, intimate objects littered the floor: a jewelry box with a twirling ballerina, a bronzed pair of baby shoes, a class photo still on the wall. A ceramic Mickey Mouse lay in pieces amidst a collection of trampled letters on the floor.

A photo of Raymond and what I presumed to be his daughters stopped me cold. I picked up a wallet-sized picture and studied the family. They looked as familiar as people I'd known growing up. My stomach lurched. Inherently I knew that being there was wrong, that I was as guilty as the rest of them—not for stealing, perhaps, but at the very least for being a voyeur. Disgusted and at the same time paralyzed by my fascination, I slipped the photo into my pocket. I passed the bathroom on my way back downstairs—a toothbrush and uncapped tube of toothpaste were still on the counter.

I felt nauseous, but still I stayed. I kept one hand in my pocket, coveting the photo, feeling the corners, outlining the shape with my fingers. My heart fluttered when a few policemen came but they appeared to be friends with the group controlling the chaos of the *déchoukaj*. They kept their eye on me with the same vigilance as they guarded the stash they'd set aside next to the back door, but they never said a word to me, nor I to them.

I found it odd that the policemen, who were part of the military, were stealing from a superior officer. I thought the military and police took care of their own. So what kind of training did these guys receive? Where was their sense of loyalty? Why were they not protecting him, instead of robbing him? I made a mental note to not assume I understood anything about how things worked here. Again, the difference between my norm and the one I was witnessing was greater than I imagined.

By the time the last person left, the house was absolutely, totally, and completely bare. There was not a single thing left to take. Even

the plastic plates covering the electrical sockets were removed. Outside, it was opaque black and there was nothing to light my way down
the driveway, the street, or the path to my house. In the dark I
clutched the photo of Raymond and his daughters, wondering what
had come over me. Back home, I took out my wallet, slipped the photo
of Raymond and his girls between the photo of my dad and my sisters, heated up a can of soup, and went to bed.

A few nights later, I received a call from Thomas, a Haitian photographer who had befriended me. His face was naturally droopy, making it
hard to read his expressions, which were already hidden behind a full
beard and mustache. He spoke English well, but had a peculiar habit of
phrasing questions in the negative or ending his sentences with an inter-
rogative "no?" I appreciated him; he was fun and easygoing but I worried that he was a bit too friendly—he had a widespread reputation as
a womanizer, much to his wife's chagrin. I had no interest in complicating my life with a married man, though he told me more than once
that it was common for a man to have at least one mistress.

"You can come to Carmen Christophe's house with me tonight,
no?" he invited.

Christophe was the mayor of Port-au-Prince. I'd seen Christophe
on television; she reminded me of an out-of-date movie star who
refused to accept that she was aging, an Elizabeth Taylor wannabe
who wore clothes two sizes smaller than she should have.

"I'm in your neighborhood and I could come by for you, no?"
Thomas said. "Could we not share a taxi?"

Wanting to make sure we understood each other, I said I would go
as long as I came home alone at the end of the night. He said of
course, but I didn't believe him. Still, I changed quickly from my
shorts to a skirt and waited for him outside.

Christophe lived in Péguyville, a wealthy suburb next to Pétionville, just up the hill from the capital. The temperature dropped as we rose in altitude and I was sorry I hadn't worn long sleeves—my first chill since arriving in Haiti nearly two months earlier. The incessant whirl of the generators provided electricity for the town's bars and restaurants, where the wealthy and internationalists spent most of their evenings. Pétionville was really the only place in the country that had this kind of nightlife. Or these oversized chalets. The homes in the hills made Raymond's house seem middle class.

Thomas knew Christophe from photographing her so often. She'd extended a standing invitation for an evening nightcap—her home was rumored to be a hub of activity. When we arrived, a long line of people hugged the wall that surrounded her property; we bypassed them because Thomas knew the security guard. "They are here every night waiting to get in to see what the rich mayor will give them, no?" he said.

The inside of the mansion was surprisingly bland, a sharp contrast to the beauty of the grounds. The large, cold rooms were sparsely furnished—straight-back wicker chairs, an odd table here and there, a foam sofa in the living room. There was no suggestion of Haitian culture, no Haitian paintings, no Haitian handicraft, nothing at all that reflected the beauty and charm of the country. I should not have been surprised. Handicrafts are traditionally made by "common folk," not the class of people that Christophe was interested in promoting.

Like Raymond, Christophe was a leading member of the Tonton Macoutes, and even though the government outlawed the Tonton Macoutes after Duvalier fell from power, members continued to function with the same political ideology.

Christophe boasted about her "showroom," decorated with exotic Taiwanese art: carved statues, jade tables, wall hangings, mirrored panels, hand-painted tiles laid in a meticulous pattern. Haiti and Taiwan had a strange relationship, one that leaders like Christophe and Avril took advantage of. Taiwan cultivated partners in the international community to gain recognition as a legitimate country. In exchange, this breakaway Chinese island offered broad financial assistance to supportive governments and to a poor country like Haiti it was a gold mine of resources. Christophe had acquired much of her furnishings on a trip there. In another setting the beauty of the pieces might have been more appealing, but in her house they seemed tacky, even tasteless.

On television Christophe appeared flashy, stylish, and charismatic. Inside the confines of her home, despite the nonstop parade of people, she shuffled around in a housecoat, torn slippers, and a wig. I assumed she had many wigs because her hair was a different color and style each time she appeared in public. This particular night she wore a bronze pageboy askew on her head. It was hard to guess her age—she could have been anywhere from thirty-five to fifty-five, with premature hair loss. She was a short woman with a stocky build; loose-fitting pajamas flattered her more than the too-tight suits she wore in public—suits that revealed the rolls around her middle and tugged at her pudgy wrists. Rings swelled her fleshy fingers. In broken English, she boasted about her contacts abroad, her popularity, and her big heart. I'd heard that that she was corrupt and that her fortune came through illegal lottery gains, often at the expense of the poor.

She received people all night long: poor people wanting a handout, shady politicians wanting favors, friends wanting a laugh. The hired help passed trays of fried spicy dough known as *marinad*, olives, and glasses of warm soda. I lost all track of time until I realized it was too late to find a taxi to take me home. Christophe insisted that Thomas and I spend the night and not having much of a choice I accepted but made it clear we needed separate rooms. She led me through a closed door into the actual living part of her house, as opposed to the public part, and took me into one of her spare bedrooms. It was sparse and tiny but neat and clean, and I was extremely grateful for her hospitality.

"Take anything that you need from the closet," she said in her heavy accent. "There are plenty of nightgowns and slippers. You'll find drinking water in a bottle by the bed." What she neglected to tell me was that the closet was also home to her wig collection, equaled only by her shoes. Shades of Imelda Marcos. I also wondered why she had such a collection of nightgowns and slippers—were they for her own use or did this kind of thing with tardy guests happen frequently? Regardless, I slept in my own clothes.

Christophe promised to give us a lift down the hill before sunrise so we could catch a bus back home; when she knocked on my door the next morning she was wearing the same flimsy housecoat and didn't appear to have washed her face. Or put on a wig. Her sparse, cropped hair lay matted against her scalp like a tight bathing cap. She called for the houseboy to bring her car around front, but it wouldn't start, so Thomas and I got behind it and gave a running push-start. With that, we jumped in, and Christophe drove us down the hill, back to a reality that was barely more familiar than the one I had just left.

It seemed to me that loyalists tied to certain political parties changed as frequently as the weather in Haiti. There were no structural changes, just a merry-go-round of power-hungry leaders. Allegiances were bought and sold all the time. And everyone, no matter what class they came from, was after money.

Most of this bartering was invisible to me—I never learned how payments were transferred from the one pulling the strings to those executing the orders, who was responsible for rounding up supporters or adversaries or who was at the head of the money trail. This chain of distribution was as much an enigma as was the way the poor survived, but the more time I spent in Haiti, the more I realized that there were many clever ways to get something for nothing, and as a newcomer I was an easy target. There was the time I bought bags full of kitchen supplies from a group of market women only to discover, once I was back home, that they had put in a strainer with a hole and a juicer with no spout. It took me weeks to discover that the houseboy charged me $4 for candles that cost 20 cents.

And then there was the solicitor who came to my door asking for money for a literacy program. I wanted to embrace the project but was unable to put aside my suspicions. I couldn't imagine door-to-door solicitations were very successful in Haiti.

"Explain to me how this works," I asked the soft-spoken but articulate young man who was nicely dressed and smelled of too much aftershave.

"We have classes for people in the neighborhood," he said proudly, "and all this is possible because of people like you—all your neighbors support me." He showed me the list of names and addresses of neighbors I recognized. Next to each name he'd scribbled an amount that varied from just a few dollars up to $50. I gave him 50 gourdes, the equivalent of about $10. He was back a few weeks later, this time with another request and a similar list of supporters. As my Creole improved, we had longer talks and I asked more probing questions, none of which were answered thoroughly.

"When can I visit one of your classes?" I said.

"I'll bring you a schedule next week," he smiled, and never did.

"Where's the closest school you offer your classes?" I asked the next time.

"We're on a two-week break, but as soon as we resume, I'll come and get you. We can go together." He did not return again for another month. When he did, I told him I didn't have any cash.

When he came the following month I was on the phone—I motioned for him to come inside while I finished the call in the back room. When I returned, he was gone, as was the money in my wallet. The names on the list, I learned later, were really those of my neighbors, but he had invented the contributions.

One day a young man collapsed on the street outside my house. I quickly brought him some water. He seemed weak and disoriented, so I called a doctor friend of mine who lived nearby.

"*Li pa gen anyen:* There's nothing wrong with him," my Haitian friend said, annoyed that I had disturbed him.

"Of course there is," I said in disgust, thinking my friend was just too lazy to drive over and find out. "He collapsed, didn't he?" I called the Red Cross; the dispatcher said they would be there shortly, and then I offered the young man something to eat. He inhaled the food as if he hadn't eaten in days, and color came back to his face. When he stood up he didn't appear to be dizzy anymore, and the Red Cross found nothing wrong with him.

The following week I was driving in another part of town and saw this same young man walking down the street. As I turned the corner, he looked carefully in all directions and, seeing no one, scattered his books around him, then let out a loud yell and feigned another collapse. I drove off in the opposite direction.

The spell that Haiti spread over me was not easy to define. It produced a physical and mental metamorphosis. My body hardened, as if it was fortifying itself to fend off foreign elements. I looked at the world differently, too. I was still the same Kathie, born to privilege, but for the first time in my life I was confronting the elements. Haiti didn't have a comfort zone I was familiar with and challenged me in a language I didn't understand. Gracious as the country was, there were no footholds for me to latch on to. I had to be more confident in my instincts, which were initially what allowed me to see, in the height of my fear during the coup just a few months earlier, that there was an opportunity for me to grow if I stuck it out in Haiti rather than go back to San Francisco. I needed to rely on my powers of observation, which were being sharpened as I became more skilled at reporting. Haiti also required a soul-searching trust, the ability to navigate in conditions that were far more dicey than any I'd encountered before.

And yet, just being in Haiti was liberating. While the lack of rules and social norms that I had grown up with transformed routine tasks into tremendous challenges, there was a freeness about Haiti that I adored. I didn't have to respond to labels that nurtured but also encumbered me as I was growing up: daughter of City Councilman Harold Klarreich, and Susan Klarreich, Ph.D., sister of Karin, Betsy, and Beth. Although I was proud of those associations I also wanted to be known for myself. As a foreigner in Haiti, particularly an American, there were some "given" assumptions about me—that I was either a diplomat or a missionary, presumably wealthy, and a potential meal ticket. But no one really knew if I was rich or poor, Catholic or Jewish, Republican or Democrat. They didn't know if I was an only child or one of twelve, and because asking direct questions isn't part of Haiti's culture, I was free to decide what and how much information I wanted to divulge. I had the option of creating my own persona or remaining as obscure as I wanted.

It also provided me a chance to figure out whom, exactly, I wanted to be. It wasn't a second birth, really, but an opportunity to pare down the clutter—just making do with two suitcases for three months already showed me how little I needed to get by. It beckoned me to shed an armor I didn't even know I wore in the States and define my new self with a thoughtfulness I'd never considered.

I liked my new anonymity, as it was, although I knew I was not really anonymous. In Haiti, everyone eventually knows everything, or at least think they do, and as a foreigner I stood out. I was referred to as a *blan*—a word literally translated as "white," but commonly used to identify any foreigner in Haiti. Still, I wore several hats—I was the reporter, the shopkeeper, the cheap American to some, the generous American to others. Every day brought new surprises and revealed parts of my personality I didn't know were there.

Days were easy to fill, but at night, in the quiet of my apartment, I felt alone. I bought a journal, a plain, unlined black book and a special blue pen. I waited to write in it for the first time under the veil of darkness. I sat in the hard, unforgiving chair of my sublet, close to the window, and lit a candle. In the shadow of the evening I sat, alone with my thoughts, pen, and paper. The candle's light cast a single glow on the empty white page, a blank reflection of myself. The balmy air caressed my face as I creased the pages of the journal with quiet deliberation, one after the other, the crispness of the paper folding gently backward with the pressure from my fingertips. Inside these blank pages I hoped to find the answers to the questions I couldn't stop asking myself. Why had Haiti embraced me where it repelled others? How was it that the things that scared off others charmed and attracted me? What exactly was I doing in Haiti, and for how long would I be doing it? This idea that we all have a purpose in life haunted me, because I couldn't figure out what mine was.

I imagined what I might be doing in a few weeks' time back in San Francisco, among family and friends. It was a scene that held no surprises. Everything there was familiar, and although not predictable it was all within parameters I was comfortable with. I didn't have any complaints about my life in the States, really, but it lacked something I couldn't identify. Maybe it was that it was too comfortable. Haiti was anything but. My thoughts drifted to what it would be like to stay in Haiti longer, to actually identify myself as living there rather than just visiting for a finite period. I had just spent three tough months adjusting to a country I had barely known, learning a new language, adapting to the cultural differences and trying not to be swallowed in the political upheaval. Somehow I'd jumped the hurdles and was still standing. That was a good feeling, one I was proud of. It made me realize that I had skills and talent and even ambition and curiosity I hadn't explored, and I wanted more.

On more than one occasion, when faced with a difficult decision, my dad, who had died just after I graduated college, had often encouraged me to make a list of pros and cons. I uncapped my pen. Go, I wrote on one side, and drew a line down the middle of the sheet. Stay, I wrote on the other. But that was all I wrote. I knew that the list wasn't going to matter. Despite the logic, it was my heart that prevailed. San Francisco was a known quantity. But Haiti, an open-ended book of experiences and emotions so unfamiliar I couldn't even identify them, offered me something singularly unique. I wasn't making a rash decision—I was a responsible thirty-three-year-old, *laj de kris*: Christ's age, as the Haitians frequently told me. Being Jewish, I always laughed off that reference, but maybe I had heard it so frequently in Haiti that I had begun to internalize the idea that this was, after all, the year to make a bold, unconventional move, bolder and more unconventional than any obscure thing I'd done in the past. I always knew I had an innate curiosity about things, that I liked adventure and wanted to explore, but I didn't know the degree of that drive until Haiti. I hadn't thought of myself as complacent, but I was beginning to think otherwise. With this thought in mind, I put away my journal, lay down on my bed, and blew out the candle, ruminating in the dark about what to do.

When I woke up the next day, I knew I was going to come back. It wasn't that I had an epiphany in my sleep, it was just a feeling of peace I had that being in Haiti felt right. So I returned to San Francisco as scheduled for the end-of-the-year holidays, but gave notice to the company that owned the store I was managing. I explained my decision to my friends and family, who knew better than to try to talk me out of it. Then I told Medea, which was tough, because although she supported the move as a friend, she wanted me to work together on a project we'd cofounded earlier that year, Caribbean Exchange, a nonprofit organization we'd created to promote cultural exchange between Haiti and the United States. It put a strain on our relationship that made my departure that much more emotional. My sister Karin, with whom I had become close over the years, felt I was deserting her and abandoning my nieces and nephew. While that clearly wasn't my intention, there was truth to what she said—I had been an important part of their young lives and I was leaving that for an unknown, a place where I not only had no family but barely had friends. My mother was sad and worried. But I was determined. When I found someone to sublet my house for an indefinite period of time, I packed a few more clothes, photos, and books, and bought an open-ended ticket to Haiti.

On the return flight, as the coast of Florida disappeared and the vast expanse of the crystal blue waters of the Atlantic appeared below, I felt a sudden tightening in my belly. The blood rushed from my face as I began to second-guess myself, doubting the wisdom of leaving behind a secure job, friends, and family. I heard Medea's voice in my head and wanted to turn the plane around by sheer will. I stewed in my panic even as I tried to slow down my breathing and remember what had led me to this decision. I pulled out my journal and reread what I'd written days before; the clarity of the words about why I'd decided to return calmed me. Nothing was forever. If I didn't want to stay, I could return to San Francisco, reclaim my home, and find work. With a new sense of tranquility, I closed my eyes and drew images of the things that I looked forward to returning to in Haiti: the people, the new apartment I was going to sublet, the story ideas I wanted to pursue. I'd gone to Haiti initially with some idea of what the country was like but the three months I'd spent there internalized it. It was more vibrant than I could have imagined, and more fascinating. It allowed me to feel basic instincts, base emotions. I started to feel the heat on my face, smell the aroma of the cooked food, hear the sounds of the music on the streets, in the *tap-taps*, on the radio.

And as I imagined these things the thought of the face of a Haitian musician I'd met kept flashing before me. I'd dated a few Haitian men during that initial three-month period, but always my thoughts went back to the musician, and I wondered if something further would develop with him now that I was going to be a quasi-permanent resident. With such thoughts, I drifted off; before I knew it, the flight attendant announced we were landing, and there, below me, was Port-au-Prince, with its tin-roofed slums, vast pockets of deforestation, and bustling activity. Along with the others in the cabin, I applauded in appreciation when the wheels touched down, grateful for the safe landing, and smiled knowingly when the woman next to me said, "*Mwen kontan, kontan anpil, toune lakay mwen:* I'm happy, so very happy, to be home again."

Chapter II

Madame Dread

Lamou vire tèt.
Love turns your head around.

The first time I set eyes on Jean Raymond, it was as though someone sliced a vein from my heart into the center of his. I was as unprepared for those palpitations as I had been for the coup just a few weeks earlier. But that experience had been a political adjustment and I found my footing without great anguish. Instinctually I knew this man would require a lifetime of emotional and physical energy.

I had been invited by Thomas, my Haitian photographer friend, to the National Theater to see a traditional music group perform. It was on a Saturday night, about halfway through my initial three-month stay. "You have to see this group, Foula," Thomas said. "You'll love them, no? I'll pick you up at 7:00."

My eyes were drawn to the drummer as soon as he walked onstage.

He had a gait that was both confident and yet reserved, a contradiction that drew me to him. His body was slight but muscular, and his arms rippled as he set down his big wooden drum. His skin was like toffee, rich and creamy. Even from twenty rows back, I imagined how soft and sensuous it would feel. He rolled up his sleeves, his hands unusually small for a drummer. His brown dreadlocks were short, just a few inches, and as he moved onstage they flopped gently across his smooth, oval forehead. His thick beard and mustache shadowed his full upper lip as it curled and tightened in rhythm with the music.

Most of the time his eyes were closed, his head back, spine arched as his hands, like paddles, flew across two drums simultaneously. He didn't just use his hands, he played with his whole body. His arms moved with the fluidity of warm maple syrup, working in perfect harmony to produce a deep, rhythmic sound. He didn't need to see—he and his instrument were one. That's confidence, I thought. This he knows how to do, better than anyone.

When he did open his eyes, his face took on new light. I couldn't see the color of his eyes, but I imagined them to be an intimate deer brown. I followed them as they looked into the cheering, raucous crowd, then felt a warm tingle when our eyes locked. He never stopped playing but it seemed at that instant that we were the only ones in the universe, that no one else on the stage or in the crowded auditorium moved or even existed. He held my gaze intensely and I found myself short of breath. Then he tipped his head ever so slightly, smiled, and accelerated the pace of his drumming.

The rest of the concert was a blur. I was unconscious of and unconcerned with any of the other band members onstage—the tall saxophone player, the thin, spindly guitar player, the round bass player, or the dark second drummer. I moved in tune with the dancing crowd—on top of, in between, and over the stiff wooden seats, carefully positioning myself so that I wouldn't lose sight of this man. My Creole was too rudimentary to understand the group's lyrics, but I wasn't paying attention to them; my mind was racing as I calculated how I would make contact with the drummer.

First, I had to say something to Thomas. I knew he had every intention of getting into my bed that night, but that wasn't part of my plan. I had been thrilled when he invited me to the concert because I thought Foula might be a good match for Caribbean Exchange, the group I'd helped cofound with Medea back in San Francisco. As part of the organization's mission, which was to support cultural activities in Haiti while raising awareness about Haiti's social, political, and cultural conditions in the United States, we could raise money to buy better instruments for the band, or upgrade their sound equipment, or help them with a tour. It was exactly the kind of project Caribbean Exchange embraced, and finding such a project was one of my goals during my initial three-month stay. Foula band members were serious musicians who had spent years attending Vodou (voodoo) ceremonies, studying syncopated African rhythms, and developing a unique sound by combining those with jazz melodies.

Caribbean Exchange was the perfect reason to go backstage, and since Thomas was familiar with Caribbean Exchange, I knew he'd understand. Why wouldn't Foula want to collaborate with my organization, especially since it wasn't going to cost them a thing? It was clearly a win-win situation all around, except, perhaps, for Thomas.

I knew I was rationalizing my infatuation, but I didn't care. When the concert was over, I told Thomas I'd meet him out front in a few minutes. Then I took a few deep breaths, began my mantra of "*eskize*" as I jostled my way through the crowd and walked across the stage as if I had a right to, following the groupies toward the band.

It took me a few seconds before I spotted him by the back wall. His bronze arms hung casually by his side, his faded jeans fit loosely around his slender hips. But his dark, deep eyes were already burning a hole in my heart. Of course he spotted me sooner than I did him— I was the white one in an otherwise-black crowd. As I worked my way over to him, I heard someone speaking English. I turned to see the bass player speaking to a tall, sandy-haired man. The musician's English was singsongy and punctuated by a deep, sonorous laugh that fit his broad face, full cheeks, and full belly. I waited for the bass player to finish before introducing myself.

"I'm Chico," he said in reply, a smile on his face. "Wow, to make a connection with Caribbean Exchange. That's so nice."

"For both of us," I said.

"Come to our rehearsal," Chico offered. "You can meet the other band members."

"Great," I said, and really meant it, but I was having trouble concentrating because I felt the drummer's eyes burning a laser precision hole in my back. Shamefully I prayed that when I turned around he would be standing next to me. But he was in the same spot, alone, back to the wall, his deep eyes staring not unkindly but not invitingly, either.

Flustered, I didn't know what to do next. Suddenly I felt vulnerable, out of place, and insecure. I turned away awkwardly. Despite my longing to stand face-to-face, I just couldn't bring myself to walk over and meet him, and I flashed on my first impression of him as he had walked onstage—confident but timid. This is the timid part, I consoled myself as I turned the corner of the building to find Thomas, who, as I suspected, began his sweet talk to persuade me to let him go home with me. Just at that moment, I saw my neighbor Shari and making a hasty excuse, I jumped in her green Toyota and made a quick exit back to my apartment.

It was several weeks before I saw the drummer again—not because

I wasn't interested but, like everything in Haiti, things just took a long time. I learned his name was Jean Raymond, and he hung out in Bas Peu de Chose, a popular neighborhood by the cemetery. I couldn't get any real information about him because as a *blan* who didn't speak Creole well, it was impossible to be subtle about my interest without announcing myself, and I was far too self-conscious to have that happen.

I arranged to go to a rehearsal with Ritva, an artsy Finnish woman who for years had been coming to Haiti to escape the cold winters, but also because she'd fallen in love with the country, and a Haitian man. By the time I met her, she had left the first man for another, a musician who frequently played the flute with Foula. She knew Jean Raymond but didn't have much information about his personal life, and since our friendship was new, I restrained from hounding her to ask her boyfriend Ti Frank for more details about this mysterious drummer.

Ritva was an anomaly in Haiti, with her long blond hair and Nordic features, but almost everything else about her mirrored Haiti. She wore flip-flops and flowing skirts and spoke Creole as if she owned it. She was muscular, yet sensual, danced traditional Haitian dances and spent hours on the streets sketching people, the market women, the street kids. Their teasing didn't bother her—she dished it right back, and had a way of blending in where other foreigners stood out. Because we lived in adjoining buildings and neither of us had a car, we often ran into each other as we meandered our way up the hill to our apartment complex. Slowly a friendship formed. It was a significant one for me not only because Ritva knew Haiti, and I trusted her as a guide and sounding board, but also because we shared similar lifestyles and a love of Haiti. We were not in Haiti as diplomats or missionaries or consultants, we just loved the country and its culture.

The morning of the rehearsal I obsessed about what to wear,

turning back and forth in front of the mirror trying to decide which of the two skirts I had brought with me was the most flattering. In the States I rarely wore anything but pants, but here women wore skirts and dresses because slacks and shorts, as in many countries in Africa, were considered risqué because they showed the shape of your ass. Eventually I decided on the simple red cotton one that showed off my waist without accentuating my thighs, a plain white blouse and a pair of dangling copper and red earrings.

Ritva and I worked our way down the hills that led us from the rare leafy section of Pacot to the dusty streets of Bas Peu de Chose, with their honking horns, foot traffic, and the smell of sizzling oil from the cooked-food vendors. Foula was practicing in a deserted house just up from the cemetery on a street called Monsignor Guilloux, about a thirty-minute walk from my house.

The rehearsal was well under way by the time we arrived. There were the regular band members, Ti Frank, a lean, attractive woman who was dancing, and a group of *blan* speaking French. They had a tape recorder that was recording as the band practiced—the French-women seemed to be taking notes, too. I wondered if they were doing research or were journalists or musicians themselves.

When I made eye contact with Jean Raymond, my stomach muscles fluttered; I also saw something in his expression that hadn't been there the night of the concert. His face was tight, his mouth pulled back in agitation. I didn't know what to make of it, or of the energy in the room. In addition to the group of French speakers, there was a constant stream of people wandering in and out, people who didn't seem to have any connection to the band but acted as if they had a territorial right to enter. That happened a lot in Haiti, I noticed, that everyone thought everything was their business, even if it wasn't.

On either side of the room were large windows with wooden shutters held in place by large metal hooks. Outside, the neighborhood kids crawled on top of each other to get a better view of the rehearsal inside. I moved to the side and sat on the floor, my back against the wall, mesmerized by the dancer, who in her tight, fashionably ripped jeans floated across the cement floor with the fluidity of a gentle stream. Her untamed hair, tied back with a bandana, fell unnoticed when Jean Raymond's solo roused her to gyrate in strange, sensual movements. His drumming coaxed her body to life with exotic motion, and just as quickly willed it to a catatonic state when he stopped. Without the music, this graceful sphinxlike creature looked like any one of the skinny girls going in and out of the room.

I hoped to approach Jean Raymond when they stopped playing but his body language stopped me. He was fixated on the group of *blan* who had turned off their tape recorder and were now speaking French to two of the musicians. One of the two, the sax player, noticed Jean Raymond's posturing and said: "*Li pa anyen*: It's nothing."

"*Kite sa, monchè,*" Chico the bassist chimed in, seeing the scowl on Jean Raymond's face. "Let it go, man."

"*Poukisa? Pou yo ka pwofite sou travay nou an?*" Jean Raymond responded: "Why, so they can take advantage of our work?"

The French girls were oblivious to the musicians' conversation and Jean Raymond's hostility. But the more they chattered, the more disturbed Jean Raymond became. His body was stiff as he clenched his teeth and clasped and unclasped his hands. When the girls eventually wandered into the other room Jean Raymond got up from his drum, walked over to the tape recorder, calmly took out the tape they had been using to record the rehearsal, and smashed it to pieces. When he was done, he left it in a heap on the floor. Then he packed up his drumsticks and left without saying a word. I sat stunned, unsure what had happened and what I was supposed to do next.

A short while later, Chico offered to walk down the hill with me. "What happened in there?" I asked.

"That's how he is," Chico said with a shrug, understanding my question but not answering it. "We just accept it."

"Accept what?" I said, confused.

"His anger," Chico said.

"But what's he so angry about?" I asked, pushing further.

"This guy's had it rough," Chico explained. "Was raised by his grandmother until she moved to the States, then at fourteen he was out on the streets taking care of himself. Never even lived with his mom. No one has ever given him anything and he's not about to hand out the one thing he has—his talent—for free. Foreigners who come here treat Haiti like a term paper or a charity case—you know, help the poor; wow your friends with this weird Vodou stuff. He's a singular kind of guy, doesn't take that kind of shit."

This piqued my curiosity and made me more determined to get to know Jean Raymond, to show him all *blan* weren't alike. There was something about him that I couldn't let go of—I thought about him more often than I wanted to admit. His face haunted me throughout the day for weeks after that, and often appeared in my dreams. It was his image that was in my mind as I returned to Haiti after the holiday period, when I said good-bye to San Francisco and resettled in Port-au-Prince. I moved out of the small apartment I had sublet and into a cottage just around the corner from Ritva. It was a one-bedroom tucked behind the building where Shari used to live, but Shari was gone. Haiti had proved to be too much for her. When she left for her end-of-the-year vacation, she never returned. I missed her, but missed Ritva even more when she returned to Finland shortly after the beginning of the year; we'd become close friends and her companionship had eased the loneliness I often felt. I missed her company at Foula's rehearsals, too.

So it was with some trepidation but excited anticipation that I decided to go to one of Foula's rehearsals by myself shortly after my return from San Francisco. I couldn't help thinking about the drummer and wondered if seeing him again would evoke the same feelings I had when thinking about him on the plane ride back to Haiti. I called Chico to find out if Foula had the same rehearsal schedule they'd been on before my brief month away, but he wasn't home. Figuring I'd find him practicing, I walked over to Monsignor Guilloux by myself, only to find the building shut tight, the wooden shutters drawn closed. "They haven't been here in a few days," one of the neighbors said. I turned back down the hill dejected. It was late afternoon and the sun dispensed a sallow hue over the cemetery. I walked with my head down, shuffling my feet through the shadows and debris that lined the streets.

At the bottom of the hill, someone called my name. I turned my head. Jean Raymond was standing in a back alley, or *koridò*—a small strip of cement leading to a maze of tightly constructed tin shacks on what had been someone's long front yard. He flashed a wide, welcoming smile that made me miss a step. I smiled back as he cocked his head toward the alley, signaling me toward him. I took a few deep breaths as I crossed the street, hoping he wouldn't notice my tremor as he reached out his arm to draw me around the street traffic, closer to the alley, closer to him.

"*Bonswa,*" I said, the customary greeting.

"*Bonswa,*" he said, still holding on to my arm.

"You didn't have rehearsal," was all I managed to say.

"You went away," he said.

"You noticed," I answered, and then we fell silent. All I could think of was finally, after months of intense scrutiny by Jean Raymond—obsessive, relentless observation on his part—I had somehow managed to pass some test because here he was, holding my arm. And all my fantasizing about being this close to him was as real as the pores on his face. I felt the smoothness of his skin, smelled the scent that was particular to him, and the world around us seemed to come to a complete stop.

My elementary Creole embarrassed me, but Jean Raymond was sympathetic and patient. He repeated words, pantomimed and gestured until I got the meaning. I knew from the beginning that he held an intensity I had never experienced before—he was like a bell, emanating rich, hearty tones. But the sounds were heard only after resonating against the hard, metal shell, and they weren't always warm or welcoming. I'd seen him angry, bitter, and full of resentment and frustration, but this day he exposed his warm, gentle, compassionate side. He was tender and kind, a respite from the confusion and chaos of daily life in Haiti. I felt a connection with him that was electric—it scared and attracted me at the same time.

"Would you like to come to rehearsal tomorrow?" he asked. "I can come by and pick you up."

"Yes." I smiled widely. "Tomorrow, the day after, the day after that . . ."

"I wondered how long you'd be gone and if you were coming back, but I had no one to ask."

"I wish you'd asked me."

"I couldn't, but I can now. Now I can ask you lots of things."

"Do you want me to write down my address and phone number?"

"I know where you live," he said. "I go by there all the time."

I was incredulous, even though I shouldn't have been. "But you've never stopped in?"

"No," he said, and squeezed my arm a little tighter. "But I will now."

It wasn't long before I was a regular groupie, attending as many practices a week as my schedule allowed. When the band lost their lease on the Monsignor Guilloux building, they moved to *Laplèn,* a rural area immediately north of Port-au-Prince. Travel was an hour and a half each way; we changed *tap-taps* twice and then, beyond the bridge that crosses the dry river Gri, took a twisted path through farms and residential homes. But it never seemed long because Jean Raymond and I were like young lovers, content just to be together. Foula rehearsed under an arboretum of locust trees and the open sky, rigging up an electrical system by plugging their amp and a lightbulb into the city line. This common—though illegal—practice was called Cumberland, named after the American who first brought electricity to Haiti.

I sprawled out in a hammock and closed my eyes while they sang about the poor people's sun, *Solèy Malere:* "We have respect, we have love, on every street, in every house, holding hands, heads together, we want to rebuild our country." Or Market Day, *Jou Maché*: "Four o'clock in the morning, everyone up before daybreak, today is market day, everyone comes down." They sang about *Afrika,* the home of their ancestors, and *Zonbi Nan Bwa,* what it was like to be poor. Jean Raymond's playing seduced me as I watched his hands fly over the drums. I felt proud of him even then, as though I had a right to.

Although the group had previously participated in numerous international festivals, in the United States, Mexico, and the Caribbean, things slowed down for them in 1988, straining even further their meager financial resources. Talent wasn't the problem, it was lack of management, a common challenge for artists everywhere. But Foula had a particular set of problems unique to Haiti, with limited venues and rampant insecurity in the country. Even when Foula played to sell-out crowds, like the one in the National Theater the first time I saw the band play, they never came out ahead financially. They had rent to pay, food to buy, household expenses and transportation fees to cover. Like so many Haitians, Jean Raymond lived by debt—to his landlord, the market women, and whomever else he could persuade to let him buy on credit. His home-away-from-home was the *bric-a-brac*, or pawnshop, where quick cash was an immediate solution to a long-term financial problem that never seemed to disappear.

I was sensitive to our economic differences and struggled to find a comfort level with which we both could live. It was awkward when I bought my first car—even though it was a beat-up jalopy—because it was a tangible demonstration that I had more than he did. Not that that was ever a question. Still the car increased our flexibility—instead of the restriction of taxis or walking or relying on friends to loan us a car, we drove places after dark. Our favorite spot was the greenest area of the city, a run-down square facing the National Palace, the *Champs de Mars*, the area where I'd experienced my first coup d'état. We nibbled on pizza, shared ice-cream cones, and dipped tiny pieces of conch in hot sauce that we purchased from a street vendor.

The street kids were never far. "Jean Raymond, Jean Raymond," they shouted as we shared a plate of fried food—plantains or sweet potatoes: *fritay*. "*Bay nou, bay nou:* Give us some."

Jean Raymond didn't mind their crowding, just like he didn't mind the groupies when his band rehearsed or the crowds that gathered when he and his friends jammed, but having people so close to me all the time made me uncomfortable. Our personal boundaries were different, and to give myself some breathing space I handed Jean Raymond our plate of food, went off and bought another, and handed it to the kids.

"*Mèsi, Madame Dread,*" they shouted gleefully. "*Wo, wo, wo, bél ti Madame Dread.*" The nickname stuck. In Haitian tradition, women are referred to as Madame So-and-so, based on the first name of their husband; in my case I was named after Jean Raymond's dreadlocks.

No longer were the nights lonely. If I wasn't with Jean Raymond, I sprawled out on my bed, my cheek pressed firmly against the telephone, unconcerned with the interminable power shortages. I barely knew how to say what I wanted to—my vocabulary was still limited, and even if it hadn't been I was still struggling to define my feelings, about Haiti, my life there, him. Instead of trying to figure it out, I just smiled into the phone, content to hear his voice.

I knew early on, from that very first experience watching him destroy the tape during rehearsal, however, that trouble lurked in every corner. I didn't delude myself that the differences in our backgrounds, education, culture, and economics were going to disappear magically as we fell deeper in love. It was inevitable that each of those factors was going to present its own set of problems, but I was unable to see just how difficult a road it would be to find the right balance between our worlds. That I had fallen in love with Jean Raymond in a way that I had never experienced with any other man was already a result, I knew, of Haiti, but I couldn't articulate just what had caused it or why. I just knew the change was there and I was a happier person for it.

It wasn't that I was ignorant or blind to the variables, but rather I seemed to be constantly surprised by the way they manifest themselves. My challenge was to step over or around them, not be stuck smack in the middle of them. The trick was identifying the differences and the trouble they could cause before they hit me squarely in the jaw. But in the beginning, I rarely saw the punches coming. Several months after I bought my jalopy, it began to fall apart. It soon became apparent that I was just throwing good money after bad, so Jean Raymond introduced me to his best friend, Sergo, a mechanic who bought and sold cars for extra money. Sergo had a round baby-face with the most infectious grin I'd ever seen. His skin gleamed and his white teeth shone. His laugh was loud and hearty, and people were pulled to him like a road show, forever stopping on the street to exchange pleasantries, jokes, and the latest gossip. His open-air garage was like the neighborhood barbershop, a place to gather, a comfort zone in the midst of sometimes over-whelming commotion. I explained what kind of car I wanted to buy and how much I was willing to spend. After we agreed on the terms, I gave him my phone number and told him to call me when he found something suitable.

Jean Raymond jumped on me with rage when we left. "What do you think he's thinking now?" he asked, teeth clenched, hands flying in anger. "He's my friend. I introduced you, and now you give him your phone number?"

"And?" I said, still not understanding what I'd done wrong.

"And so he will think that I'm a nobody. I was the one who intro-duced you. When he's found a buyer, he's supposed to tell *me*. That's the way things work here."

I didn't understand Jean Raymond's territorial feelings for me, and his feeling of responsibility toward my car, but I said nothing, not sure if this was machismo or a cultural thing or something else entirely, but it bothered me. I didn't mind admitting when I made a mistake, and took pains not to make cultural gaffes, but that was not the case in this exchange. In defiance I stayed away from rehearsal for the next two days until he came over with flowers and apologized for losing his temper. I accepted because I was in love but the warning flag had been raised.

Several weeks later, I went to the countryside to watch a Vodou ceremony where Jean Raymond was drumming. The trip took several hours on bumpy, unpaved roads, and I was exhausted even before it started. By 2:00 A.M. I couldn't keep my eyes open, and not wanting to disturb Jean Raymond while he was playing, I asked the host if there was a place to lie down. When Jean Raymond saw me walk away with the host, backpack in hand, he stopped drumming and grabbed me away, furious.

"What are you thinking," he sputtered, "walking off with the host at this hour of the morning?"

My droopy eyes opened wide as I recoiled from his reaction. I'd been looking out for myself for so many years that it almost seemed intrusive to have someone else reprimand me for doing so. My instinct was to fight him on points such as these, to prove my independence, but I was not yet on solid ground. Haiti itself was, after all, a serious challenge and navigating a relationship with a Haitian man, and this one in particular, was more complicated than any other relationship I'd ever been involved in. Wanting to remain sensitive to our cultural differences and feeling protective of our relationship because of its newness, I held my tongue, but didn't let go of the feeling. There was still a lot to learn and I wanted to choose my battles wisely.

Eight months into the relationship, I invited Jean Raymond to meet my family in San Francisco. I told my sister and mother that I was bringing home my boyfriend, but I didn't say much more. Because my own home was being sublet, my sister graciously invited us to stay with her. "She's not like me, exactly," I said to him.

"Meaning?"

"Well, she leads a more traditional life," I soft-pedaled. "I'm not saying she is prejudiced, or anything like that. It's just that she lives in the suburbs, and she hangs out with other people who live in the suburbs—it's a rather homogeneous community."

"So what's the problem?"

"It's not that there's a problem," I tried again. "I just want you to understand that they think it's weird that I left my life there to come here."

"I see," he said, but I knew he didn't.

My family didn't know Jean Raymond and I knew they couldn't harbor any feelings against him personally but I suspected they had some resentment nevertheless because they thought he was the reason I stayed in Haiti. There was some truth to that. But it was not the only reason. I didn't explain to them how connected I was to Haiti because I didn't yet have enough of an understanding of the pull myself. I kept searching for but couldn't find the words to explain what kept me, what Haiti offered that was more powerful than the country's poverty, violence, and political instability. What I could convey—and they did understand—was how seriously I took my journalism career. Even if my sisters didn't read the newspaper, they respected what I was doing, and stayed abreast because my mother sent them copies of my articles. And if she knew beforehand about a radio report, she'd alert them to those, too. I missed them a lot and knew they missed me, just as I knew that my mother worried endlessly about me, but still I wanted them to just accept my decision to live in Haiti. And I desperately wanted them to embrace Jean Raymond as the important person he was in my life.

I was not in the habit of introducing boyfriends to my family. There had been few men of any consequence in my life, so it was significant that I invited Jean Raymond to join me on this trip. I gave them a little background about Jean Raymond so that they wouldn't be shocked when they met him. Still, there was an awkward moment when my sister opened the door and eyed the dreadlocks dangling below Jean Raymond's straw hat, saw the straw bag he carried over his shoulder and the leather necklace around his chocolate-colored skin. These were things that I had grown accustomed to and which I naturally accepted because they were part of the man I loved. It was a quick reality check to see my sister's reaction; I had changed more than I realized in integrating and accepting Haitian culture, as was evident by my lack of anticipating certain reactions.

Brushing aside my concerns, I reached to give her a hug and she stiffened, not because she wasn't happy to see me but she was unused to such an intimate greeting, one that now seemed as natural as the two-cheek kiss. "Come in, come in," she said as she moved through the hall to the family room off to the left. My nieces and nephew trailed behind Jean Raymond, curious but unsure how to react to him. My brother-in-law extended his hand and towered over Jean Raymond, who suddenly seemed a dwarf in size. And I knew by the way he scrunched his shoulders that he was uncomfortable. His eyes darted around nervously and he reached for my hand.

"*Konbyen tan nou beʒwen rete la?*" Jean Raymond asked: How much time do we have to spend here? We'd barely walked in the door and he wanted to leave.

"We just got here," I answered in Creole, and turned to accept a daiquiri my brother-in-law offered. "Relax."

He never did. In part it was the language—I translated as best I could, but often there were numerous conversations going on at once, and I couldn't keep up.

"What's happening with the handicraft business?" my mother asked, while Jean Raymond pulled at my sleeve to translate the lyrics of one of his songs so he could explain his music to my brother-in-law.

Or when I was just sitting in the kitchen just hanging out with my nieces, he asked me to go in the other room so he could explain a card game to my nephew.

It was my first experience with the language issue, and I had unrealistic expectations of Jean Raymond, which caused some friction. It was a new role for me to be the go-between, and brought out just how much I was still an American girl. I had the pull from my family to be completely available to them while wanting to be loyal to Jean Raymond. It was confusing because there were some conversations

I just wanted to have with my family, and when I did that, he felt left out. That first night, my nieces broke the ice by pulling him upstairs to participate in their pillow fight. They thought him exotic and unusual—they didn't know other musicians, let alone a black one with dreadlocks who wore jewelry. My nephew loved Jean Raymond's habit of eating fried spaghetti for breakfast. "Way better than Cheerios, Mom," he said, and begged my sister to make it for him before school each morning. My mom wanted to know if Jean Raymond braided his dreadlocks every morning. She was pleasant, but reserved.

During that trip we were real tourists. On the ferry to Alcatraz, he held me tight, uncomfortable being so far from dry land. He didn't swim and boats frightened him. His favorite store was Sharper Image—the gadgets fascinated him, as did the street bands at Union Square. In Monterey we rolled around in the sand dunes and chased each other until we couldn't breathe. We drank a bottle of wine when the sun set and fell asleep under the stars.

But we had our share of rough moments. Jean Raymond had refused to believe that a direct flight from Miami to San Francisco was six hours, and pouted the entire length of the trip, declining both meal and beverage. "*Ou fè ekspre,*" he said. "You did it on purpose." Distances in Haiti were long, but only because of the roads. A flight from one end of the country to the other was under ninety minutes, so a six-hour flight across the United States seemed incomprehensible.

The hotel we stayed at in Monterey served a Continental breakfast, which he scoffed at. "This is for poor people," he said, sneering at the bagels and cream cheese. "Don't they have something hot, like cornmeal or millet? Spaghetti?"

My choices for lunch and dinner met with a similar response. "There's no place to eat in the United States," he complained. "We're always in a restaurant where someone I can't see cooks my food. How sanitary is that?"

"No less than buying food from communal, uncovered pots on the polluted streets of Port-au-Prince," I replied indignantly.

He refused to try sushi, mocking the tiny portions of rice and skimpy pieces of fish. "*Pwason gwo sèl*," he said, referring to the traditional Haitian dish that includes an entire fish, head intact, along with a mound of well-salted rice, without which no Haitian meal is complete. It was a relief when Jean Raymond discovered Chinese and Thai food and mastered enough English to buy takeout without me being there with him. But he was less successful buying beverages. One day he complained about the awful taste of a beer he'd bought. He pulled the empty can from his brown bag. Root beer.

Back in Haiti, Jean Raymond smiled wide when he was able to get a plate of good, home-cooked cornmeal. Watching him circulate in the environment that he knew and loved, it was clear that he was a man who was unquestionably at home no other place in the world. There wasn't much Jean Raymond touched that he didn't add flair to, no music he played that didn't make a room come alive. I fell in love with him because his instincts were honest and sincere, and they kept me honest, too.

Dealing with his temperamental side was by far my greatest concern. He threw a tantrum with the same passion that he played his music, studied a rhythm, or made love. It took me a while to understand this level of his intensity, which he applied indiscriminately. When he learned a new rhythm, he played it for hours or days until he mastered it, unconcerned with food or sleep. Some mornings I woke up only to find he'd never gone to bed. When something upset him, he talked about it endlessly until I thought I would drown in his words. His ability to go on and on and on seemed superhuman.

One afternoon we were in the living room when he started on a tirade about something so trivial that it wasn't even worth remembering. The conversation was one-sided—whatever he imagined I had done or said started him on a roll that was so great there was no turning back. He paced up and down the room, gesticulating wildly with his hands. His voice was loud and I prayed that the neighbors weren't home; already I could imagine what kind of gossip they would spread if they were. Jean Raymond's serene, gentle face snarled, one lip curving up, the other down. I'd seen this before and knew that once he reached this state, it was impossible to reason with him. The best thing to do was to ignore him and wait for him to exhaust himself. This warlike attitude attacked me like a swarm of bees and I shut down, trying hard to keep my breathing focused and my energy directed anywhere but toward him. I walked over to my desk and began filing the loose papers. But this increased his fury; his voice rose louder and his arms waved back and forth like a windup toy. I wanted to poke and jab at him but instead just glared in silence, concentrating on the inhales and exhales. He shouted louder, and finally, unable to resist, I shouted back, demanding that he leave me alone. "*Kitem!*" I screamed. "Leave me alone. Just leave me the hell alone." I walked toward the door but he was one step ahead of me and stood firmly in front of it, his arms crossed.

Not wishing to engage in a shoving match, I turned my attention to the kitchen, furiously piling the dirty dishes in the sink. I poured half a bottle of dishwashing detergent in the sink and grabbed dish after dish, rubbing each one with increasing intensity as if it would make Jean Raymond's hysteria dissolve. As I began to rinse them, Jean Raymond came closer. His voice rang like a shotgun in my ear. In a rage, I picked up a glass of sudsy water and threw it at him.

"Not one more word, not one more fucking syllable," I yelled.

"One goddamn sound out of your mouth and we're through. Do you understand? I don't want to hear one more thing, or I'm out of here, and you won't see me again."

The silence was as deafening as his tirade had been. He took the back of his hand and wiped the suds from his face. I stood perfectly still, breathless and shocked at my own behavior, unsure of his next move, unsettled by mine. He shook his head back and forth, still reeling from my uncharacteristic reaction. Then he began to pace again, but this time it was deliberate, controlled, and calculated rather than manic. I turned back to the dishes robotically, then passed a dry mop on the floor to wipe up the water that had pooled. Without a word, Jean Raymond took the mop from me to finish the job, then drew me into his arms, snuggled his itchy beard in my neck and rubbed his dreadlocks across my face.

"*Eskize*," he said: Excuse me.

I said nothing. I didn't go to rehearsal with him that afternoon but instead went to a dance class, came home, and went to sleep early. I had no idea what time he came in, but the next day he awoke in a foul mood, complaining about our next-door neighbor who irritated him by making too much noise. I wanted to point out the irony, but said nothing. He invited me to go with him to rehearsal but I declined, opting again for a dance class. When I returned later that evening I found love poems tacked around the house. The following week he took my collection of papier-mâché animals and decorated the living room, strategically placing the paper tiger in front of a bowl of water, hanging the parrot from the door. He had his sister make *tchaka*, a traditional food of whole corn and vegetables that I loved and left it under the proverbial plastic container on the kitchen table. He sent friends round to pick me up and bring me to wherever he was playing.

But he'd also leave the house without telling me where he was going, spending hours perfecting a rhythm and neglecting to call. He'd forget a date, a meeting time, a significant anniversary. I took it all in stride, making minor adjustments to my expectations so that everything wasn't a crisis. Like the country I'd chosen to live in, Jean Raymond was never dull. I followed my heart and hoped for the best.

Chapter III

Vodou Jew

Vérité se je.
The truth is what you see with your own eyes.

It was late afternoon one fall Saturday early on in my initial three-month stay when my friend Maggie called and suggested a trip to the cemetery. Light masked the filth of Port-au-Prince. As the sun set on the bay, it cast pink, purple, and orange shadows over musty browns and grays. Instead of bouncing off the city's harsh metal roofs, its deflected rays diffused the layers of perennial dust and dissolved the images of pollution that floated on the water's surface.

"Great light, a great time to take pictures," she said. The cemetery was a sprawling maze of oversized tombs and unkempt tombstones covering several downtown blocks. In 1986, when dictator Jean-Claude Duvalier fled Haiti after a popular uprising, people flocked to the cemetery to ravage the Duvalier family tomb. Corn was now growing on top of what once was the burial place of Jean-Claude's father, dictator François Duvalier, known as "Papa Doc."

"Okay, " I said. I was raised Jewish, but was neither religious nor irreverent about the dead. And I was always up for an adventure with Maggie. She'd ~~bad~~ been covering Haiti as a photojournalist for more than a decade, photographing people I'd only read about: Jean-Claude "Baby Doc" Duvalier and his she-devil wife Michèle Bennett, military dictator Henri Namphy, and ousted President Leslie Manigat.

As we parked on rue Monsignor Guilloux, she uncurled her long legs from the white Charade rental, tied her waist-length hair in a knot, and grabbed her cumbersome camera bag. She flashed me one of her wide, warm grins. "It's okay," she said in her Texan drawl. "They won't mind."

"They?" I asked.

"The spirits," she said.

I rolled my eyes, wondering what I was getting into as we parked the car outside the west gate. "I'll watch it," said Djonni. There was a "Djonni" on every street corner, and the only thing these young boys watched for was to see if someone made a mistake that they could benefit from, be it money or goods inadvertently left behind.

We passed an old man curled up in a ball on one of the labyrinthine cement paths that weaved through the disorderly cemetery. His thin body was covered with scraps of cloth he was using as a sheet, hardly distinguishable from his threadbare clothes.

We turned the corner and faced the cross of *Bawon Samdi* (Baron Samedi) standing tall and prominent, a weathered cement structure more than five feet tall. Its presence was as much a part of the Haitian cemetery as the *poto mitan* (center pole) was to Vodou (Voodoo) temples. *Bawon Samdi* consoled the living and ferried messages to the spirits above—no respectable Haitian cemetery was complete without it.

On this day, believers had blessed *Bawon* with cassava, plastic jugs of water, piles of twigs and charcoal arranged in a mound, green peppers, a live chicken tied to a frayed rope, a bottle of rum, pieces of broken glass known as *ʒenglen* and a large, hollow gourd filled with a mixture of leaves, lemons, and water.

We walked slowly down the narrow aisle by the *Bawon* and stopped. A man sat silently by the cross, his eyes closed. A thin soldier in full uniform approached him. The soldier's right pinky had an extra piece of skin, almost like a sixth finger, which flapped against the side of his front pocket as he reached in for a pack of *Comme Il Faut*, the locally manufactured cigarettes. The two men smoked in silence. Maggie and I watched in silence. When the soldier left, an older man whose belly hung low over his baggy pants replaced him. He had a wild look in his cream-colored eyes. As he approached the silent, seated man, Maggie leaned over and whispered that the first guy must be the keeper of *Samdi*'s cross. When the elderly man began to chant, removing his shirt to reveal rolls of fat around his middle, Maggie added: "*Oungan*. He's the Vodou priest." I nodded as if this was to be expected, but my heart was palpitating so furiously I wondered if she heard it.

The keeper stood, raised the large, blackened gourd, and began to rub its contents on the *oungan*'s back, making the shape of the cross.

The *oungan* chanted loud, indistinguishable words, knocking his fist on the front of the cross, then slapping it on the sides. He lifted the chicken and swung it around and around in an offering to the *Bawon*. I moved to the side in silence. Maggie loaded her film.

From the side of a tomb appeared a thin man smoking a *Comme Il Faut*. He was wearing khaki pants and a striped tan shirt. If it weren't for his extra pinky, I wouldn't have known he was the soldier who had just left. In his loose-fitting cotton shirt and nonregulation shoes, he appeared younger, more innocent. He handed the keeper a small brown paper bag, then turned to face the *oungan*. The ritual began.

For the next thirty minutes, the young soldier stood silent, submissive, attentive, entranced. The *oungan*, with the help of the keeper, removed all of the soldier's clothing except his underwear. The two men handed the blackened gourd back and forth, taking turns bathing the soldier's entire body with its contents. They passed the chicken over his head, under his arms, between his legs, rubbing, stroking, massaging, and pressing it into the pockets of his bare brown body. They plucked the feathers off the distraught chicken and mashed them up with the leafy mixture in the gourd. They opened the mouth of the chicken and the soldier spat in it, eight times.

At times the soldier's knees buckled, unable to withstand the weight of the two men pressed against him in this ceremonial bath. Even as a spectator, I felt the force of his experience, uncomfortable yet mesmerized, unable to look away. Maggie kept her lens focused on the action.

When the men finished applying the mixture, they rinsed the soldier with a jug of water. The keeper handed the young man his brown paper bag. He opened it, pulling out new underwear. He removed the pair from its plastic wrapping and replaced his old ones.

Then the *oungan* lit the peppered charcoal and stoked it to create a small flame. The dazed soldier stepped over it three times. The *oungan*, still chanting, removed some powder from a glass jar with one hand and with some clear liquid in the other, poured them both over the fire to spark the flame. The soldier's expression remained stoical and impassive as he responded to commands to move this way and that. The *oungan* picked up the cassava, broke it in to small pieces, then fed it to the soldier.

While the soldier chewed, the procession from a traditional

Catholic funeral marched by. The wails were loud, louder than the music coming from the tubas and drums in the funeral band. Dozens of men in long-sleeved white shirts and women in black marched by, smartly dressed despite the heat. The keeper moved closer to the side of the cross to let them pass. The *oungan* and soldier didn't notice. And no one noticed me, nor did they care about Maggie's snapping shutter.

The *oungan* removed blue powder from a folded piece of newsprint and made the sign of the cross in front of the altar. Maggie leaned over and whispered that he was drawing a *vèvè*, a ritual design used to invoke the spirits. He drew the same image on the remaining three sides of the cross, then turned the empty gourd upside down. The soldier jumped on it, smashing it into dozens of pieces. Slowly the *oungan* spun to a halt like a windup toy that had run out of steam.

The ceremony ended as abruptly as it had begun. As casually as if he was offering a cigarette, the soldier pulled money from his front pocket and gave it to the *oungan*. The keeper turned the soldier around as he would an obedient child and led him quietly down the alley, past the tombs, and out of the cemetery.

Only then was I aware that I had been holding my breath. I was only peripherally aware that other people had come and gone during the ceremony, offering their own contributions to the *Bawon*. They seemed as unaffected and uninterested in the event as the *oungan* and soldier seemed in them, or us. I, on the other hand, couldn't take it all in fast enough, but part of me was shocked. I didn't know that this was a common way for a lovesick man to purify himself. I'd known men to numb themselves with alcohol, or get high to relax, or go for the proverbial one-night affair to forget a bad relationship—but this? There was nothing in my past that I could relate this to, no other experience I could draw on to help me assimilate. That others here didn't think this bizarre, even unnerving, made me realize the extreme gap in my frame of reference. I stored this thought, knowing that it would serve me well in the future as a reminder that there was a good chance I might not perceive things the same way that others here did.

The *oungan* released a loud belch and, for the first time, looked up and noticed Maggie and me, two *blan* in the crowd. He lunged toward me, grabbed my hand, and twirled me around wildly. Caught up in the moment, I swung around twice before passing him off to Maggie, who gaily circled a few turns, her smile as generous as her charm. The *oungan* smiled back, happy and satisfied. As he turned to leave, he tripped on the old man who was still asleep on the ground in the same position he was when we first entered the cemetery.

"Satan worship," some Haitians said, when I spoke to them of my cemetery experience.

"If you're not careful, those people will put a curse on you," said others.

"Those people? Nonsense," I replied, and began earnest research to educate myself about Vodou. I went first to the library, but quickly realized that the Haitian library system had little in common with the one I was familiar with in the States. Stocking and maintaining literary resources for a country nearly 80 percent illiterate had never been a government priority. There was only one public library in the entire country, just down the street from a row of government ministries, but it was rarely used. Long tables and chairs filled the room—but there were no bookshelves. All the materials found in libraries that I was familiar with—literature, magazines, books, references—were behind closed doors in an effort to control their disappearance. Nothing about their system encouraged or nurtured the use of books. First I searched through the title catalog that gave only the title, no description of the book or its contents. Then I filled out a card, and had to wait for the attendant to come back with the material. That often took a half hour. If the book wasn't what I wanted, I had to start the whole laborious process over again. After several afternoons like this, I decided there had to be a better way to get information.

So I perused the two bookstores in Port-au-Prince that had a decent selection from which to choose, even though their stock was in French. I found a few books that familiarized me with the language, terms, and symbols used in Vodou. Like any religion, there is a hierarchical system. Those who wish to be initiated into the religion are called *ounsis*—male or female. They study with a Vodou priest or priestess—*oungan* or *mambo*, respectively—to learn the various disciplines involved. If they don't study formally, they become an *oungan* Ginen, Ginen being the word Haitians use to refer to the dwelling place of the Vodou spirits, their ancestral homeland of Africa. If they get traditional training, they go through specific initiations, including *kanzo*, which involves fire, and a ceremony called *sevis tèt*, which translates literally as a service for your head. That training prepares them for the responsibilities of a Vodou priest or priestess.

I studied the designs of the sequined banners used in the opening of Vodou ceremonies and that adorn Vodou temples. I asked friends what they thought of Vodou—the worst critics were those who had never gone to a ceremony, but felt qualified to speak because they were Haitian, or because they knew So-and-so who had been to such-and-such a ceremony and witnessed evil sorcery. Their secondhand information made me more determined than ever to learn about Vodou firsthand.

The following spring, I attended one of the country's most traditional and popular Vodou ceremonies in Souvenance, a village in the

Artibonite Valley outside Gonaives, several hours north of Port-au-Prince.

Souvenance typified the Haitian countryside with its pink-orange and aqua-blue houses adorned with multicolored curtains lining dusty dirt paths. Apart from the few *boutiks* that sold everything from matches to eggs to bread, and spots where market women sold *fritay* (fried vegetables or meat) there was little variation in daily life: Women tended to the children, the food, the laundry; men to the fields and, far too often, other men's women.

On this Easter Sunday thousands of peasants, city people, the Diaspora, and curious *blan* were there. At the entrance of the courtyard the cross of the Haitian spirit, *Bawon Samdi,* keeper of the cemetery, was lost in what had become the food court—dozens of people preparing and eating steamy bowls of rice, beans, pork, cornmeal, and vegetable stew from an eclectic assortment of plastic bowls. Panning the group of people gathered behind them, I spotted my journalist friend Mike, a tall, balding Brit with a loud voice and quick mind. Mike had moved to Haiti the year before, after freelancing elsewhere in Latin America. "Just in time to watch the sacrifice of the steer," he said, as he squeezed over to make room for me. Riveted, I timed my breaths with that of the steer's as its life seeped away slowly, almost sensually, drop after drop, until the blood came gushing out and he was no more.

Although I had planned to return to Port-au-Prince that evening, the atmosphere was so seductive, exotic, and intriguing that when my friend who had given me a lift said it was time to go, I made a split-second decision to stay for the entire week's celebration. He looked at what I had brought with me—a sweater, water bottle, some bug spray, and money—and asked me if I knew what I was doing. He shook his head in disbelief but promised to come back for me the following Friday.

It took a little bit of maneuvering to get myself situated for the night, but with Mike's help, I rented a straw mat, borrowed a sheet, and bargained for the privilege of sleeping on the floor of a grass-covered hut with three other people for $3 a night. It was customary for villagers to rent out their homes during the holiday week—for them it was a bankroll for the next few months, if not the entire year.

For the next five days, I lived like a Haitian peasant, rising with the sun and partaking in normal daily rituals. Before greeting anyone, I brushed my teeth with my finger (it was better than nothing, and there wasn't a toothbrush to be found)—Haitian culture is such that it would have been rude to greet anyone without doing so first. Then I headed for the water pump, where I filled a water bottle, or bucket if one was available, and bathed with Mike's soap, stripping down to my underwear. Haitian women let their breasts show, but never removed their underwear—I was too prudish to show my white breasts so I kept on my T-shirt and let the heat of the sun dry it as the day wore on. Some days I went with a group down to the river, where we washed in the same water women used to wash their clothes. I never got clean, but I removed the surface layer of the dust that continually seeped into my skin and hair.

During the rest of the year, cooked food was available only at certain times during the day because of the long preparation time, but during the annual weeklong celebration, the women woke up extra early to make sure there were pots of sweet syrupy coffee and bread available before sunrise. By midmorning the hot food was ready—bubbly cornmeal, rich rice and beans, fried goat, plantains and sweet potatoes. When available, I bought a hard-boiled egg, bananas, and avocados to supplement what turned out to be a diet heavy on carbs. Then there were the trays of chewing gum, hard candies, and cigarettes, along with local sweets made from peanuts and syrup that young village girls sold for extra money. Bottled water was hard to come by—I begged off of other *blan* who had driven from town and, when all else failed, I supplemented with Juna, Haiti's version of Kool-Aid. Terrible tasting, but wet. At night I tried *kleren*—raw rum, preferring the drier varieties infused with herbs, twigs, and grasses, to those sweetened with fruit, called *kleren tranpe*.

The crowd thinned out Monday afternoon, after the ceremony under the sacred *Mapou* (silk-cotton) tree. Mike was still there—he had come to Souvenance the year before and knew what to expect. I was grateful for his company, not just because he was a nice guy but also because he spoke Creole and willingly acted as an interpreter and a guide, taking me on some early-morning hikes in the hills surrounding the town, and explaining local customs. Except for a few filmmakers and journalists, the rest of the people who stayed were Haitian. I was worried that I would feel self-conscious—particularly because I was struggling with the language and confounded by the ceremonies, but everyone was generous and tolerant. In part they appreciated that I wasn't looking at Souvenance as a field course or potential moneymaking venture, but rather an opportunity to learn more about their culture, and they were willing to be my guides.

I spent my days watching and listening, learning about the sounds, rhythms, and history. A compulsive reader, I was surprised that it didn't bother me that I didn't have a book—or paper or pencil. I just observed, recording images and events in my mind. All day long there was music; some of it organized, much of it spontaneous. When there was no ceremony, young men gathered around a drum or a guitar. Sometimes women joined in and danced. Sometimes the musicians fell asleep from exhaustion or too much to drink. Children roamed freely, half-naked, while women gathered wood to cook. Stars lit the way as the sun set, only to get lost in a layer of clouds. The air cooled, ever so slightly, before the heat from the morning sun rose again.

I watched as women danced, in white or in colored clothing, indoors and outside under the elegance of the magnificent *Mapou* tree. They bathed in mud and water and had a ritual cleansing with a specially prepared *ben-yen* (bath). They danced in a ceremony honoring the large *Asòtò* drum and in another just for children. There were all-night dances and equally long discussions, under the shade of the locust and macajou trees, on music, politics, and Vodou.

On the third night the air was heavy with music as hundreds of people danced to the drums in the Vodou temple known as the *peristil*—a large covered area partially open at the sides. The *ounsis* (Vodou initiates) tolerated me as I imitated the dance steps, our sweat dripping in unison despite the balmy breeze. I was in the rhythm. I felt the beat of the drum enter me. I danced as though there was an energy driving me—it was no longer my body swaying to the music, but someone else's. Go outside and get some fresh air, I told myself, but I couldn't travel the distance, even though it was a matter of yards. I sat down, disoriented and disturbed. I couldn't focus; I could barely speak. I was in an altered state, but not from alcohol or drugs—whatever it was that had gotten into me was stronger, more powerful, and definitely more frightening than anything I'd ever experienced.

Mike came over and said something to me, but I couldn't make out the words. When I opened my mouth to respond, I saw my own words escape, floating into space. Discouraged, Mike tried again, then shrugged and walked away. "Come back!" I screamed, but the words evaporated. I wanted desperately to grab hold of Mike's hand, force him to make me myself again, but my arm wouldn't move.

Eventually I went back to the dance, standing in the middle of the dance floor looking not like a novice American, but an experienced *ounsi*. I have no recollection of that, though I remember trying to shake off this thing that was overpowering me. It was no longer me inside my own body; I couldn't find myself. I struggled to make my legs respond to my command to go outside, to get fresh air into my collapsing lungs, but I couldn't be sure what was real and what was in my mind. I eventually left the *peristil*, the dancers, and the music, swerving as if I was drunk. Instead of gaining control by increasing the distance between the drum and me once I made it outside, this other power gained strength. I leaned against a wall in the courtyard, unable to stand without its support.

Suddenly, without warning, I leapt up in the air like a bolt of lightning, then hit the ground and rolled over and over. I believe I heard voices—people shouting at me—but I can't be sure. I wanted to shout back, but still I had no voice. There was a thick layer of fog between the rest of the world and me, and not even my flailing body could break through it.

I felt hands on me, as though people were trying to move me somewhere. I fought them off and if it weren't for the protection of the *lwas,* I would have broken some bones in my struggle. I rolled in the dirt as though I was free falling down a hill. I catapulted, arching my back, swaying side to side, alternating between euphoria and depression. I laughed, and then fell into violent sobs.

I wanted to melt into the brown earth, humiliated and embarrassed because I could feel the commotion around me. I had remained so anonymous as an observer the last few days, and now this. Desperate to get away from the crowd, I put my hands on the ground to push myself up, but fell back—my legs were crossed in the classic position of *sèp,* a punishment executed by the *lwas* for anything from adultery to theft. Neither of these two things applied to me, but I was sure somewhere in my recent past I was being punished for something I'd done wrong, only I was in no state to figure it out. I was as clueless about why the *lwas* were shaming me publicly as I was about what was happening to me.

Sometime later, Pascal, the son of the senior *oungan*, lifted me up. My legs unfolded as easily as a jack-in-the-box. Pascal had the strength for both of us and I meekly accompanied him through the *peristil* into the *ounfò*, a special room in the back that contained an altar. I knelt and kissed the ground three times without knowing why before Pascal released me and Mike led me back to my hut.

I have recollections of a fitful sleep, wanting to be comforted in someone's arms but I was alone in the room—the others had returned to the dance. I didn't understand that the *lwas* were protecting me. It was foreign enough to accept the idea of spirits before I could accept their strength. I was not a nonbeliever, but at each foreign juncture with the spiritual, I had only my Jewish upbringing as a frame of reference. This didn't fit in that box. It didn't fit anywhere. No feelings any rabbi evoked through any sermon I'd ever heard came close to reaching this kind of religious experience.

When I awoke early the next morning, I felt almost radiant, a bit embarrassed, and entirely confused. Mike gently explained to me what had happened. He said it was the most fantastic thing he'd ever seen. I didn't want to believe him, but his explanation was the only thing that justified my appearance. My hair was hopelessly matted, caked with crusty dried dirt, my clothes were layered with mud, the toepiece was ripped from my blue plastic flip-flop; I had a large scrape across my forehead, and bruises over my body the way a child does after rough play. Even my bones ached.

I wanted to deny that such a thing happened to me, a nice Jewish girl from Ohio, but images flashed before me that while dreamlike in appearance felt, in my gut, too real to ignore. I walked over to the *Mapou* tree and lay under the security of its majestic branches to ask for guidance. I didn't want to have a responsibility to a *lwa* that I neither accepted nor understood. It was unnerving to remember parts of the experience but there were whole episodes Mike recounted that I had no recollection of at all.

Pascal, the *oungan*, mentioned me in his closing remarks after Friday's ritual *ben-yen* (bath). He said that never before had a foreigner experienced *sèp* at Souvenance. For him, it was proof that the *lwas* were everywhere. For Mike, the fact that a foreigner with little experience of Haiti could be possessed disproved the academic explanation of possession as just another form of socially acquired, learned behavior. Others suggested that I wasn't possessed because with a true possession there is no recollection of the incident. I accepted all of these explanations. Nothing about Haiti was clear to me, so I didn't expect this to be, either.

My experience at Souvenance forced me to evaluate my relationship to the spiritual world—something I had never done, other than to say an occasional prayer or curse this greater being I sometimes called God. And what was God to me, really, other than a name I repeated out of habit from my Jewish upbringing. I wasn't ready to reject the notion of a higher spirit, but neither was I willing to embrace one just because something unusual had happened to me. I needed to explore further. Not understanding Vodou while living in Haiti seemed as senseless as not speaking Creole.

But I was stuck in a Western way of thinking. I wanted a tangible explanation of the spirits, something I could wrap my arms around, some proof that Vodou could fix a broken arm or heal a distraught love affair by setting a bone or reuniting a couple. I wanted to know about each spirit—what foods and colors they preferred, what kind of ceremonies they liked to have performed for them. I wanted to understand why one person chose to become a *bòkò,* a Vodou priest who deals in both good and bad magic, or a *ganga,* who is like a leaf doctor, or *laplas,* the chief assistant to the Vodou priest.

With enough time and patience, I was certain I would find answers to those questions. But there were other questions whose answers escaped me. I wanted to know what good or bad came from the small, wrapped packages of carefully predetermined contents I saw tucked away in the corners of buildings and streets, cemeteries and other obscure places, these objects called *wangas* that people placed in specific spots to work their magic. What was in them and how was it decided where they were placed? Who decided that and how would one know if they worked? What was this thing referred to as *espedisyon,* the sending of evil spirits against an enemy. What was the difference between that and to *djòke* someone—put an evil spell on someone?

Over time, though, I realized that Vodou wasn't about explanations. It wasn't about getting from one to ten by passing through two to nine. It was about a belief, one whose logic made sense only to the believer. And that because of my experiences in Haiti, through Jean Raymond and other people I met, I was more open to the possibility of allowing things to happen to me. I was, in general, less repressed. Like a therapist trying to understand the psyches of her clients, I could have persisted in my efforts to make sense of my reaction to and embracing of Vodou, but I decided instead to let go and give myself up to whatever lessons there were to be learned from it.

A friend of mine, Azo, betrayed by one of his girlfriends, sought counsel from a local *oungan.* A swaggering, muscular guy with a reputation for boasting about the different women in love with him, Azo didn't see the hypocrisy of his mission, but I wasn't going to point that out. Haitian men think it is their right to have as many mistresses as they want, but they will not tolerate such behavior from their women—wife, girlfriend, or mistress. The conversation had already come up between Jean Raymond and me several times. I questioned him specifically about what kind of relationship he had with the mother of his two-year-old, whom he claimed he was no longer with when I met him. And then more generally, because of the sheer number of lithe, nubile groupies who loved the band and followed the guys around like tire treads on a jeep. Of course Jean Raymond denied any interest, but I knew that as long as I was with him, it would be an issue. With Azo, I was intently curious to see how the *oungan* was going to treat such a case and I asked if I could tag along, promising not to say a word. Azo told the *oungan* I didn't speak Creole, so although it was highly irregular for me to be there, the *oungan* agreed.

My friend's consultation was in a crowded area just west of the capital. The *oungan*, an elderly man with creases of experience shadowing his eyes, led us down a well-swept path sandwiched between two hollowed drains that channeled wastewater to the street. At the end of the corridor, we slipped through a narrow door into a room containing a special altar for the spirits; a table adorned with figurines, candles, plastic icons, mirrors, bottles, and magazine pictures.

"We'll light a candle first," the *oungan* said, and Azo nodded as he knelt next to the altar. I stood off to the side, my back against the only window, a shuttered wooden opening covered with a thin light green cloth through which the smell of sewage seeped in. The *oungan* wore a brown shirt and a tattered pair of blue cotton pants. The light inside the room was dim; the candle's shadows dancing over the cement floor, walls, and tin roof. Outside, stalls of used clothes hung from hangers over baskets of sundries for sale.

"There's a problem with a girl," the *oungan* said, and Azo nodded.

He hadn't explained the reason for his visit, but seemed to accept as natural that the *oungan* knew this already. The *oungan* took a bottle from the altar, and in an offering to the spirits sprinkled several drops on the ground. Then he threw back his head and took a long swig himself. He did not offer any to my friend and ignored me, placing the bottle on the opposite side of the table from where he'd picked it up. I had no idea what was in it, but when he picked up a second bottle, took a swig and then sprayed the mouthful on the ground the smell of *kleren*, the popular raw distilled rum, permeated the room.

"*Chita*," he said, and Azo sat on a wooden crate next to a small card table. The *oungan* bent down and folded back the floral curtain, revealing a shelf beneath the altar. He withdrew a deck of cards. Pulling up his own wooden crate, he sat on the opposite side of the table and slowly dealt the cards, studying them for several minutes. Then he said, "You are angry with her, but you are angrier with the man she was with."

Azo nodded, as if this was what he expected. I was skeptical—how could he know this just from lighting a candle? Or from the cards? I wanted to ask him, but I squeezed my lips together tightly to avoid opening my mouth since I'd promised to be invisible. I silently wondered if he hadn't been forewarned of the situation by someone else or if he was guessing and just plain lucky. It just didn't seem possible that he could intuit this so quickly.

"What is it that you want?" the *oungan* asked. "Revenge? Get your woman back?" He lit another candle, while I waited, a queasy feeling forming in my stomach. This was unknown territory for me, and I wasn't sure I liked it. The old man opened his mouth as if he were going to say something, then shut it quickly and peered deeply into the light of the candle as though something had just caught his attention. Suddenly he put up his hand to block Azo's answer and with the other motioned in my direction. "She has to leave," he said, his voice pitched deeper and louder. "The spirits don't want her here."

Azo turned to me and silently motioned me toward the door. I left quietly, not at all unsure that this wasn't a good thing, but unnerved at the possibility that the spirits had noticed my resistance. Still, if there was going to be some shady deal of revenge, I wanted no part of it.

When Azo came out twenty minutes later, he was somber. "*Pa mandem anyen,*" he said. "Don't ask me anything." I had no intention of doing so. We walked back to our neighborhood in silence. Days later, the man with whom Azo's girlfriend had cheated took his son to the doctor because the boy had a fever that wouldn't break. The doctors didn't know what was wrong and, despite medication, the boy's condition got worse. When I learned of this, I felt a cold chill run through my veins, a chill that the Caribbean heat couldn't dispel. It was one that Azo must have felt, too, because he stopped coming to my house; I avoided his regular hangouts. A few weeks later, the young boy died.

Azo and I never did anything together again. When our paths crossed, we went through the customary greetings, then quickly continued on our separate ways.

I don't really believe that Azo had anything to do with the young child's death, but the timing gave me serious pause, particularly since the word on the street was that Azo was responsible. It was the first time I understood how profound, widespread, and serious was this belief in Vodou.

A few weeks later I was sitting on the steps outside the home of Gerald, an accomplished soccer player I had met originally through Azo. Gerald cut hair when he wasn't kicking a ball around. His regular clients were members of the infamous Leopard Corps, an elite group of black-booted soldiers equipped and trained in counterinsurgency by a Miami-based company, Aerotrade, under contract to the CIA. When their skull-crushing tactics were aired on CBS in April 1986, the Black Caucus raised hell and forced Congress to cut U.S. military aid to the post-Duvalier regime. Every Friday night, three Leopard soldiers on weekend leave came directly to Gerald's for a haircut, then played or watched a soccer match on Saturday and returned to their post on Sunday.

This particular evening we were watching a game between two teams from the densely populated area known as Mache Salomon, just blocks from the stadium. The most popular field in Haiti, at least in the cities, is the street, and this Friday night there were dozens of people outside enjoying the breeze and the game. When it was over, the players began to discuss the upcoming military championship where the different branches of the army were scheduled to play against the Haitian marines.

"Watch out," Gerald said to the Leopard soldiers who were waiting for their weekly buzz. "Those marines are tough—you guys could easily get your asses kicked."

Gerald didn't realize his faux pas until the words were out of his mouth, but it was too late to swallow them. He'd insulted the soldiers, and that he'd done it in front of others exaggerated the offense. Two of the Leopards grimaced, but the third, standing closest to Gerald, puffed up like a bloated bull, lowering his head and raising his eyes in such a way that it sent an involuntary shiver down my spine. Scrambling to neutralize the situation and put motion back into stagnant air, Gerald added, "But I'll be there rooting for you." But it was too late. The soldier raised his thick arm as if to hit Gerald who, smaller and quicker, instinctively made a tight fist with his right hand and in one smooth motion, socked the soldier squarely in the jaw. Without a moment's hesitation, Gerald turned and bolted down the street out of view. The sequence of events passed so quickly that by the time the soldiers realized what had happened Gerald was gone.

It was nearly three weeks before Gerald reappeared. I was at the stadium just a few blocks from Gerald's house watching a Friday-night soccer game when he sauntered up. He said he'd gone to the countryside so that things could cool off. While there he sought help from an *oungan*, who lit candles and read his cards. Then, Gerald explained, he gave the *oungan* the name of the three Leopards who were there that evening. The *oungan* asked him to write each name seven times, then took that piece of paper, wrapped it in leaves with some large rocks of salt, and tied the whole thing tightly to Gerald's right foot.

Gerald said the *oungan* performed a number of rituals, including chanting, *kleren* offerings, and the sprinkling of rosewater around his feet. After a while, the *oungan* removed the leaf from his foot but tied it up again, as if he were tying up a mean spirit. He led Gerald to the cemetery and there, in front of the cross of *Bawon*, he placed three pennies. He told *Bawon* not to kill the men, but make sure that the next time Gerald ran into them they would be respectful, not hostile. He pulled a special candle from his pocket, lit it, sang a few songs, and then told Gerald he could go back home.

"No matter where you are the next time you encounter these Leopards, you will be safe," the *oungan* said, and Gerald, who had been a Vodou practitioner all his life, had no reason to doubt him. "So here I am," he said happily.

When the match finished, we left the stadium together. We had just turned the corner of his street when we saw the three Leopard soldiers walking toward us. It was the kind of encounter that felt scripted. I tightened immediately, fearing the worst, but there was no hesitation in Gerald's gait, or that of the three men. They flung their arms wide and with big, welcoming smiles gave Gerald a huge bear hug. "Where ya been, man?" they asked. "Ain't nobody can cut our hair the way you do." They surrounded him with playful ribbing, laughing and joking as they turned and walked with him back to his home.

I left as the first of the clippings fell, wondering what it was about Vodou that could make such things happen. And why it was that I believed that an *oungan* could produce this result, and not that which had happened to the poor little boy who died.

The spirits are generous, but demand respect in return. This respect comes in different forms, depending on the spirit's personality and the kind of ceremony performed. Each spirit has specific likes and dislikes, colors and rhythms it prefers, so each ceremony has its own specific rituals. That May I went to a ceremony for *Kouzen*, the agricultural spirit. May is *Kouzen*'s month, and Saturday is the day he likes to be honored.

I wasn't nervous about going to this ceremony because it was a morning celebration for a specific *lwa*, not an evening dance where my possession had taken place. And even more importantly I trusted the *oungan*—he was a friend of Maggie's and someone I had met many times before. I was there at his special invitation, and I was sure he was going to watch out for me. I still didn't understand that mine was a unique Western way of thinking, that getting possessed wasn't—in a Vodouisan's mind—a thing that I needed protection from. For believers of Vodou, looking out for me meant that the spirit could mount me. The expression "mount" was generic—not meant in a sexual way, but one used to describe what happens to the person the spirit is visiting.

The morning was still cool from the previous night's dramatic rainstorm, with its bold bursts of lightning and explosive thunder. Inside the temple, the air was just starting to warm. The altar was on the far side of the light blue room, past the red *poto mitan*, the center post. Most *poto mitan* have the symbol for *Danbala*, an important serpent spirit of fertility from the *Rada* category of spirits, which are believed to have originated in Africa and are generally benevolent. Without this symbol, the *ounfò* may belong to a *bòkò*, a Vodou priest who practices both good and evil.

Kouzen should have been pleased with the offerings; piles of mangoes, bananas, and pineapples sat alongside brimming baskets of grains, carrots, plantains, and squash. Branches adorned the cloth-covered tables; machetes and sickles were displayed neatly. The arrangement was so picture-perfect, it could have been a photo shoot for a Hallmark Thanksgiving card if it weren't for the straw hats and *Kouzen*'s blue denim clothing hanging on a hook nearby. Worn *makouts*, traditional straw bags embroidered with pink and green tassels, dangled by their tattered straps on hooks nearby.

At the base of the altar, the carefully drawn *vèvè*, a ritual design used to call up a specific Vodou spirit—in this case, *Kouzen*—was already in place. Large tin drums of food, one of which was cooling in an enormous bucket of water, surrounded it. A tiny woman in a pink-checked dress picked up a vat that weighed more than she did and, with small Olive Oyl muscles, she heaved the pot upside down in one swift motion. She then took a large wooden spoon and scraped onto a large platter the beans and rice that had stuck to the bottom. Her sleeveless T-strapped dress revealed the delineation of her muscular back as she lifted the domed platter onto her head and walked elegantly to the altar, where she placed it to the side as another offering for *Kouzen*.

Other women arrived with hollowed gourds and dished out the

food. Several bowls were offered to *Kouzen*. The rest was set aside for those participating in the ceremony.

A stream of scruffy young boys carrying large plastic gallon containers emerged from the back room. A middle-aged woman began pouring a transparent liquid into the containers that were already partially filled with leaves, herbs, and bark—each jug a special type of *kleren*. *Kouzen* liked all the variations of the distilled rum—sweet, sour, tart, tangy, and he liked to be toasted many times during the ceremony.

As I sat down, Edgar, the pencil-thin *oungan* whose bony wrists protruded from the base of his long-sleeved white shirt, came to survey the altar. He looked disgruntled. *"Li toufe,"* he muttered, displeased with the arrangement. "It's choking, it's choking."

He ordered two young boys to the back room and they returned with a rickety wooden table. *"Li two ba;* It's too low," Edgar barked, and the table was immediately raised with some worn cement blocks. A Christmas-patterned tablecloth was placed over the new altar extension, and Edgar rearranged the fruits and vegetables, plucking and placing things until he was absolutely sure that *Kouzen* would be satisfied. Once the altar was complete, Edgar took a straw broom and swept the dirt floor, removing plucked chicken feathers, food crumbs, and general debris. He sprinkled oil from the *tètgridap*—oil lamp—as an offering and lit the lamps before they were returned to the altar. He exhibited the same kind of loving detail my mother did for our birthday parties, graduations, and religious confirmations. I found it comforting and endearing, but I was impatient for the ceremony to start.

The *ounsis*, Vodou initiates, and *sèvitè*, Vodou disciples, veered toward the top of the four-tiered cement-block platform that had been constructed just for the ceremony. Seated together, they looked like a mass of blue denim. Spectators like myself were seated on the opposite side. I was distracted, however, by a large-boned woman in tight-fitting, unflattering biker shorts who came into the temple leading an older woman in a striped tan dress. It was odd to see a Haitian woman dressed like that. The older woman, whose cotton dress matched the color of her skin, seemed disoriented. She allowed the younger girl to seat her in a chair, where she remained motionless, a blank expression on her face held impassively while her eyes wandered aimlessly. It wasn't long before the young woman began to complain loudly and angrily to anyone that might listen that regular doctors couldn't solve her mother's problem, only an *oungan* could. I wondered if she was ill, possibly mentally challenged.

"My mother has been like this since Monday," the daughter complained in a loud, whiny voice that had a Creole accent resembling mine. Diaspora, I thought, which explained the biker shorts. "We've taken her to specialists, but no one has been able to do anything for her. She won't eat, she won't talk. She's driving us nuts. We don't know what's wrong with her or what we should do with her. *Li pa nòmal*—it's not normal."

The young girl was clearly disgusted. "I brought her here because I didn't know what else to do. I think she's possessed."

Disturbed by the commotion, the *oungan* walked over to the older woman. He bent down and held her face gently in his hands while he peered into her vacant eyes. She neither looked back nor away. Edgar said, "Just let her sit," and returned to the altar.

The oldest drummer, a weathered, toothless man, came in quietly. He searched for three sturdy chairs and placed them across from the risers. A second drummer, wearing dark sunglasses, went to the *poto mitan* and removed a wooden drum that had been suspended by a frayed cord. He placed it sideways on a chair across from the *ounsis*, then he, too, sat down, waiting patiently for his cue. The youngest of the three drummers, ashes dropping from his cigarette, was either still drunk from the night before or had started drinking early—his walk was unsteady, stumbling, and he had trouble sitting straight. But as soon as he started to drum, his attention was focused, and with that, Edgar picked up the rattles and the ceremony began.

At no point during the ceremony did I have even the slightest hint of feeling anything other than myself. I had no inclination to get up and dance and had no response to the drumming. I felt pleasantly calm and relieved to think that I could resume going to ceremonies. I'd missed that. I loved the action, rhythm, movement of the ceremony, the dancing, and mounting. I didn't realize then that the Vodou spirits that were being called that day by the drummers and dancers and *ounsis* weren't spirits that had an influence on me. I couldn't have known that then because I was only beginning to differentiate one *lwa* from another.

The older woman remained motionless the entire time, while everyone around her participated in the ceremony in some way. Early on in the ceremony, Edgar had become possessed by *Kouzen*, and was now, hours later, ambling around in the blue denim shirt and *makout* bag that had been hanging by the *poto mitan*. Sauntering with a swagger he didn't have before he became *Kouzen*, he deliberately approached the older woman, and in a new, affected tenor tone, said to her: "Aha, you've come back."

She appeared not to hear him.

"You were here for this ceremony last year, weren't you? Don't you remember?"

No response.

"You borrowed twenty dollars from me and you've never paid me back."

The woman gave no sign that she understood, but her daughter, who wandered over when she saw *Kouzen* speaking to her mother, suddenly nodded as if it was all becoming clear to her.

"Ahhh," she said to *Kouzen*. "I had no idea that she'd been here last year. But of course this all makes sense. She never repays her debts."

The daughter reached under her T-shirt to the right side of her black sports bra and pulled out a 100-gourde note, the equivalent of the money borrowed. *Kouzen* laughed.

"*San goud?*" Kouzen mocked, his voice rising a notch. "One hundred gourdes? *Ebyen, kote enterè a?* Where is the interest? You're a year behind on your payment. I'll take nothing less than thirty dollars."

Resigned, the daughter reached into the left side of her bra, pulled out a wrinkled 50-gourde note and handed the two bills to *Kouzen*. With the transaction complete, *Kouzen* bowed and retreated back to the altar. The possessed woman's eyes followed, gaining light as they focused. Her face lost its trancelike mask and her cheeks relaxed, taking on color, moving in and out as her breathing returned to normal, too. Without as much as a glance at her daughter or *Kouzen*, she lifted herself off the cement risers, arms outstretched, and joined the other *ounsis* in front of the altar.

Regardless of one's wealth or social class, almost everyone participates in the annual celebration of All Saints' Day, or *Gede*, in Haitian culture. Every year on November 1 and 2, rich and poor alike make offerings to their loved ones via *Bawon Samdi*, the keeper of the spirit. Outside the cemetery dozens of *machann* sell small yellow wax candles, single cigarettes, and shots of *kleren* or *kleren tranpe*.

I arrived at the cemetery just as the sun was breaking through the clouds. I'd been told that the early morning was the most interesting time to visit, and since it was my first *Gede*, I didn't want to miss a thing. Hundreds of people milled about in the streets. The cement corridors between the tombs were already stained with coffee and rum from offerings to the spirits. *Bawon*'s cross itself was buried in a sea of candles, surrounded by hollow gourds of green goo, plates of food, and enamel cups of clear liquid. I watched the offerings to *Bawon* in honor of the dead; there was no division of classes when ancestors were involved. What the living offered, and how much they offered, varied according to one's social and economic class, but honoring the dead was a universal ritual.

The next day I attended a Vodou ceremony in honor of *Gede* south of the capital. I brought, as an offering for the *oungan*, a bottle of five-star rum and a carton of cigarettes; invaluable advice from Maggie, who also warned me that *Gede*, the mischievous Vodou spirit of death, was fresh and presumptuous. As soon as I approached the entrance to the *peristil*, someone who had already been possessed by *Gede* and was in full costume with a purple and black jacket and black pants, cane in hand, approached me, bowed graciously and snatched my goods. Not a good omen, I thought, as I cautiously proceeded inside.

The musicians playing at the ceremony lulled me into a stupor with their drumming, building emotion, speeding up and slowing down in a rhythm that seemed both familiar and foreign, but I didn't feel as though I was going to lose control. Rather, I was fixated on the *ounsis* as they prepared a goat for slaughter. Several of the women were about my age—I wondered how wide the gap was between our two worlds. They were as comfortable preparing the goat for slaughter as I was unnerved by it. They led the animal from behind the temple out to the courtyard, bound it with a tight rope and took turns with their long, sharp machetes. Their white dresses slowly became red as they picked it up and passed its dying body from shoulder to shoulder. An animal offering to a *lwa* was as natural for Vodou practitioners as priests offering communion for Catholics. The drums sang, coaxed, and guided the *ounsis* through their ritual, beating a rhythm that stayed with me all night long. The image of the undulating women dancing with the goat's lifeless body on their shoulders left a permanent imprint.

Emboldened by my success at having gone to several ceremonies without being mounted by a spirit, I accepted an invitation to go with my journalist friend Mike to a December ceremony held annually in one of Haiti's rare, densely wooded areas in the hills above Port-au-Prince. We headed out at night. It was dark and I couldn't see the path, but I could hear the drums in the distance. There was only a partial moon that night—the shadows it cast played tricks on my eyes as the branches bounced back and forth with the wind.

I didn't see the lanterns in the *lakou* (courtyard) until I was right on top of them. Just outside the temple area, a crowd had gathered around one of the trees. At the very top, wobbling on a thin branch some thirty feet above the ground, was what appeared to be the body of a young man. As we got closer, we heard the excited chatter of the group. "*Danbala*," they laughed with glee. "He's been possessed by *Danbala*."

"The snake," Mike explained. "*Danbala* is one of the most powerful *lwas* in Vodou. When he mounts you, he usually takes the form of a snake."

"But how did that guy get up there?" I asked.

"How do you think?" Mike replied. "When you are possessed, you aren't thinking about practical things, like how you will get down. He probably just shimmied on up there and is going to spend the night, unless he falls down first." I knew that *Danbala* was associated with rain, fertility, and wisdom, but climbing a tree—and so high—didn't seem very smart. As we headed toward the temple, we could hear the chanting for *Danbala: "Pa prese, Bondye devan, lwa yo dèyè. Badin anwo, Badin anba:* Don't worry about God; He is everywhere, but the spirits are right behind."

Inside, I greeted the manbo, as is customary, then sat by myself as Mike went off to talk to people he knew. I watched the *ounsis* and felt intoxicated by the music almost immediately. Within a short period of time, the noise, energy, and an insupportable weight overcame me. I don't remember shutting my eyes, but the next thing I remember is waking up on a straw mat not knowing where I was. I had on a gold scarf; underneath, my hair was a tangled clump, and again my clothes were caked with a layer of brown dirt. I cringed, sure that I'd been possessed again, and panicked until I saw Mike snoring on a blanket nearby. Comforted by his presence and too freaked out to think about what it was that had happened, I moved my mat next to Mike's and fell back asleep, exhausted.

In the morning, over a much-needed cup of potent coffee, Mike described what had happened. Shortly after I sat down, I leapt into the air as suddenly as I had done in Souvenance, and tumbled to the ground, where I rolled for a few seconds. Then I got up and began dancing in rhythm amidst the other *ounsis*. From time to time, I flung myself on another *ounsis* or hurled myself on the ground until the *ounsis* took hold of me and tied a scarf around my head. That seemed to contain the *lwa*, and my pace slowed down. I wandered outside to the tree where *Danbala* was and Mike followed me, trying to find out who had possessed me. He said only when he asked me if I was *Danbala* did I appear to hear him, and despite his efforts to get me to come back inside, I planted myself firmly under the tree where the other snake had climbed, refusing to move. Hours later I wandered back into the *ounfò* and danced; then I eventually tired, curled up on a straw mat in the back of the *peristil* and went to sleep.

On the walk home, I held on tightly to Mike, wanting to stay grounded to something real while I mulled over the events of the night before. Walking with us was a Haitian drummer.

"This is too weird," I said. "I can't make sense of any of it."

"Why?" he asked.

"Because possessions don't make any sense."

He crinkled his eyes. "Possession, not make sense? That's as much a part of a ceremony as the singing and dancing." He was making me feel stupid. My "possession" was so normal for him that seeing it as abnormal confused him. Believers didn't question the decisions the *lwas* made when they mounted someone any more than they would the natural cycle of birth and death, so he didn't know how to respond to me. The more I went on about it, the more I alienated myself from him. Mike, a pragmatist, just thought that I should accept my relationship to *Danbala* and stop fussing about it. Finally realizing that I couldn't find the comfort or explanation I needed, I fell silent.

To someone like Mike, who was happy to accept Vodou on its own terms, my experience was exceptional, whereas my Haitian friends thought it unremarkable. To anyone involved in Vodou, it was normal. To anyone unfamiliar with Vodou, it was just bizarre. I didn't know what to think. It had happened to me, but I didn't know why. Was I just more open and receptive? Was I susceptible? Was I flawed or special? I had no answers but the questions kept coming.

Ultimately, I resigned myself to the fact that Vodou was more powerful a force than I wanted to tackle. My persistent efforts to rationalize my own experience in a Western sense, to integrate it with my past, were futile. I couldn't reconcile the differences, and I couldn't accept that I couldn't make sense of it. In the end, I just stopped going to ceremonies.

Jean Raymond never identified himself as a member of any religion; when asked, particularly by foreigners, he identified himself as a Vodouisan. Sometimes, Jean Raymond drove to Souvenance to consult with a Vodou priest, returning with certain items that he placed strategically around the house. I never asked what they were, nor did I disturb them; but I found them in my drawer, under the bathroom sink, in a kitchen corner. Jean Raymond carried his special "lightning" rock to protect him, one that I found in the most unlikely places—behind my desk, under the bed, in a file cabinet, but I always left it alone. I honored it as I did heirlooms I kept from my father, because I believed in the sacred energy stored in them.

Jean Raymond's father, who moved to New York shortly after his birth, held contempt for Vodou. His mother Agnes, a peasant woman who lived in the small southern town of Paillant, was a Catholic and attended mass regularly but it wasn't until I confided to her that Jean Raymond and I were experiencing problems did I learn that she was also an avid believer in Vodou. After complaining to her about how unreasonable Jean Raymond could be, she drew me closer and whispered, "Don't worry, I know some things from Africa that I can do to help you." Even Agnes, tucked in a remote hillside town without good reception for either radio or television, was aware of Hollywood's stigma of Vodou, and not wanting to alienate me she preferred to use an expression that she thought would be more palatable rather than risk using the word Vodou and alienating me.

One afternoon I spontaneously made the three-hour drive to Paillant to visit Agnes and happened on an annual ceremony she held to honor her family ancestors and protect the living. The front gate was decorated with branches, and a white *vèvè* was visible on the ruby red earth below. Agnes had several large aluminum pots of mixed grain cooking in her outdoor kitchen. She had a few neighbors helping her, but everyone else was at the dance, two hillsides over. I knew what I would find if I went—dozens of people in an outdoor ring, drinking libations, making offerings, and becoming possessed. I chose to stay behind and help out with the food, unwilling to risk another encounter with the *lwa* and all the emotions that would evoke.

Jean Raymond's family had Haitian-style family reunions, complete with their own religious and cultural idiosyncrasies. My Jewish family get-togethers had their own traditions, with Sabbath candle lighting, challah, gefilte fish, and chopped liver, dances like the hora for the proper occasion. Jean Raymond and I joked that we practiced VodJew. Vodou sequined banners and paintings decorated our walls; drums and bamboo instruments adorned our living room as well as the menorah and we placed a proverbial tribute to the *lwa Legba* by the front door to welcome people alongside our Jewish mezuzah. I offered drops of rum to the spirits when I took a drink as routinely as I said Sabbath prayer on Friday nights, lit the Hanukkah candles, and fasted for the Jewish Day of Atonement on Yom Kippur.

I am no closer to understanding my relationship to the spiritual world now than I was when I first went to Haiti, but I have accepted the idea that I have one, even if I can't define it. Based on my experience with Vodou and my loyalty to my ancestors, I know firsthand that such energy exists. It's just that I've been slow to embrace it. Or explore it fully. Still, I haven't closed the door completely. I think that some day I may return to Souvenance, not as a journalist, or as the naïve *blan* that I was when I first went, but as a soul seeker who finally understands that the *lwas* can teach me things I can't learn anywhere else.

Chapter IV

Reporting Live

Lanp pa limen san mèch.
The lamp won't light without a wick.

I was in a deep sleep when the sound of machine-gun fire woke me up. Unfortunately, I was now all too familiar with the sound; I was seven months into my stay, and I'd heard it more often than I cared to remember. I opened my eyes to a penetrating black, so deep and bottomless that it was impossible to see the trees through my window, let alone the wall clock above my feet. I fumbled around the side of my bed for my flashlight and shone it straight ahead: 3:20. No dogs were howling, no roosters crowing. The shots were coming from the west, in the direction of the palace. I knew that whatever was going on must be serious because the gunfire didn't stop. Another coup d'état, I said to myself, and rolled over to go back to sleep.

Greg's phone call finally cajoled me awake hours later. Greg was one of the few foreign journalists frequenting Haiti whom I genuinely liked. Maybe it was because I didn't feel threatened by him as I did by other "parachute journalists" who flew in and out of countries on an hour's notice, flaunting their expense accounts and experience. Around them, I felt like an amateur, but with Greg I felt like myself. Even though he technically fit the category of being "one of them," he defied them by his idiosyncrasies, which I adored. Instead of being competitive and promoting rivalry, Greg was anything but that. I found it endearing that he carried his personal belongings in a plastic bag, and often went out on the beat without paper, jotting cryptic notes on his hand instead. When his shirt buttons popped off, he used paper clips or staples. His shirttail was usually tucked in unevenly, if at all, and his shoelaces frequently trailed. His hair was always a bit rowdy, but underneath he had a mind as organized as an encyclopedia; he could recite data about Haiti with more precision than anyone I knew. He began covering Haiti in the 1970s, out of Paris, and was working as a freelancer for *The Guardian* when I first met him in 1988.

He frequented the Oloffson Hotel, a charming, dilapidated gingerbread just minutes from my home. "Come immediately," he said. "I want your company this morning." I took a quick cold shower, turning on the news as I dried off only to find music across the dials. The government had been censoring the news for the past few days now. In fact, things had not been going well for the military dictator for months; warring factions of President Avril's government started sparring shortly after he took office in September 1988, seven months earlier. Now daily rumors fueled the panic; school directors sent students home, merchants secured their iron gates, *machann* packed up their goods and stayed off the streets.

When I arrived at the Oloffson, Greg had an iced tea waiting for me on one of the white wicker tables that lined the verandah. The hotel used to be a military hospital during the nineteen-year U.S. occupation (1915–1934)—since its recent renovation it attracted off-beat journalists and adventurous tourists, several of whom were milling around the large open bar area on the other side of the porch that morning. "Let's take a drive," Greg said.

"Do you think that's a good idea?" I asked, "with all that shooting last night?"

"Oh, come on," Greg said. "It'll be fine—a lot more interesting than sitting around looking at other journalists who aren't ballsy enough to go out."

We reasoned that if we drove slowly, displayed our press badges prominently on the dashboard of the car, and stopped for all road-blocks, we would be fine. We weren't after anything in particular. We just wanted to see for ourselves what was going on because the cen-sored radio reports said nothing of significance, a sign that important things might be happening. Taxis weren't running and gas stations were closed, but with half a tank of fuel in my newly purchased jeep, we set off.

The rainy season was still a month away but the air was heavy with humidity. The streets were empty. It was only then, without the mer-chants, the crush of foot and vehicular traffic, that I could conjure up images of how charming and fresh Port-au-Prince must have been a half-century ago. The wobbly wooden buildings were remnants of once-elegant ancestors. The decorative porches, shingles, and Victo-rian turrets were today brown, beaten, and weathered. Wooden panels were rotted, roofs gutted. Garbage lined the street.

I suggested we go down rue Pavée—Cobblestone Road—then cut over to the military quarters on rue de Caserne, Barracks Road. Just after making the first turn, a soldier flagged me to stop. He was not smiling, and he was fully armed. Greg and I calculated our options and decided we best do as he said. "Bollocks!" Greg said under his breath as we cursed ourselves for not having a wad of gourdes to buy our way out of what we feared could be an unpleasant situation.

The soldier was wearing a dull olive-green shirt and slacks, one of the two standard uniforms from the branch of the military known as the Caserne Dessalines, a unit whose loyalty was bought by its drug-running colonel, Jean-Claude Paul, until he was poisoned in 1988. The soldier's baseball cap sat low on his forehead, his cannonball eyes were angry. He ordered us out of the car. My legs shook. Greg, normally pompous and cheeky in a British sort of way, turned docile, apologizing profusely as we gingerly descended from the car, hands in the air. The soldier pushed us up against the jeep and frisked us. As he did I could see, from the corner of my eye, more olive green and khaki uniforms peering at us from above, the rooftop patrol. They were on top of every building in sight, and their weapons were fixed on us. I made eye contact with Greg, indicating the armed rooftop soldiers, and tilted my head for him to follow my lead.

"*Mwen pa gen anyen avek mwen koulye a,*" I said to the soldier: I don't have anything with me now.

The soldier stared, waiting for the pitch.

"If you want, I can come back later and make it up to you," I offered. Twice that month I'd been able to bribe myself out of bogus traffic violations with the police, but those were on days far more normal than this, and guns hadn't been pointing at me. Greg nodded in support of my offer.

The soldier ruffled through my purse to see if I was lying. Coming up empty-handed, he paused, then ordered us back in the car. I was unsure if it was an order to leave or if he was going to get in with us so that I could make good on my bribe. As I caught Greg's eye, I stuck out my chin in the direction of the door and signaled that we should get in. As we turned to our respective sides of the jeep, another car from the opposite direction that we'd come from sped past us. The soldier who was harassing us motioned for the car to stop, but the driver paid no attention. That was all the trigger-happy rooftop patrol needed. In a single, terrifying instant, they simultaneously opened fire, letting out one rapid round after another. I don't remember diving into the jeep, but when I opened my eyes, Greg's head was flat on the floor next to mine. Bullets whizzed over us. I couldn't identify the noise I heard until I realized it came from me—a nervous vocal explosion that boiled up from profound fear, a cross between a laugh and a cry that cut into the ripple of gunfire.

We were quite a sight, our heads together, butts in the air, bullets flying from all directions. Even the soldier ducked for cover behind our jeep. Only when the rebel car peeled around the corner did the foot soldier who had been pressuring us for money straighten himself upright and tug at his uniform to regain what little dignity he had left. "*Ale*," he shouted at me in disgust: Go. Before he could change his mind, I closed my door and crouched as low as I possibly could but still high enough to be able to see over the dash. Greg did the same. Then I backed up the length of the street, heading east on rue Pavée, and screeched out of target range. After a block, I slowed down, managed to sit upright, and tried to regain my breath, which was coming in short, tight gasps. Greg stared straight ahead, beads of sweat dripping steadily onto his already-damp shirt.

"Keep going?" I asked as we came to a stop at an empty street corner.

"Keep going," he said.

That I was even asking the question gave me pause, if just for a second. I was no longer that inexperienced, overwhelmed woman who'd fallen into reporting when I first arrived in Haiti seven months earlier. I was now a reporter, doing what a reporter does. The moment's hesitation about the sanity of it all flew by as quickly as the whizzing bullets had, and with focused determination I put the jeep into first gear.

Backtracking toward the National Palace, we passed the body of a young boy—not yet a teenager—at the foot of a Texaco service station. A small group of people around him said he had been there all night but no one could identify him. He was propped up on the front flap of a *tap-tap* that had *Jesus Renmen Nou* (Jesus Loves Us) painted on the front. His thin bones thrust through his threadbare clothing. Flies swarmed around the gaping wound in the back of his head where the bullet had entered. I found it hard to look at him, but even harder to turn away. Greg didn't share my fascination and tugged on my sleeve to get me back in the car. As I drove away, I continued to glance over my shoulder until the *tap-tap* was no longer in view.

On the sidewalk of rue St. Honoré, sandwiched between two funeral parlors, the body of a young man lay under graffiti that said: "American solutions cause death." A woman at a nearby street corner told us that she had warned the young man to stay away from the neighboring Dessalines barracks because, she said, you know how things are in the country these days, but he had insisted he was hungry. "He just wanted to buy a loaf a bread," she mourned. "Just a twenty-five-cent loaf of bread. How do I tell that to his family?"

The soldiers had shot him through the side. The hole where the bullet entered was now covered with small insects. *Konpa dirèk* (a Haitian cross between merengue and salsa) filled the air from neighborhood radios. Occasionally a cyclist or pedestrian passed by, stared first at the body, then us, then moved on. Someone had already stolen the victim's shoes. A hole in his left sock exposed his brown toes. No bread was in sight.

I felt disconnected to my body as I got back in the car and started the engine, only too happy to leave behind the grotesque remains of violence. Still, I was quite aware than in a short period of time, I would probably drop Greg at the hotel and go back to my nice safe house in my nice safe neighborhood. Would I think about the horror I'd just witnessed? There was a part of me that wanted to forget, to ignore a world where such killings were nothing more than a statistic in a human-rights report or a story to repeat among friends. But I knew those images were as much a part of my life as the Haitian music that played in my mind as if it were on a continual reel, indelible and impossible to erase. I felt fearful, intrigued, and disgusted, all the while aware that these experiences that so acutely defined my life were as much a part of my daily vocabulary as *bonjou* and *mèsi*.

My thighs trembled as we drove to the State Hospital to see if we could get an accurate death count. I wanted to talk to the living, to have someone make sense of this macabre afternoon. I wanted to understand the way Haitians accepted death in contrast to my fascination and repulsion of it. But I realized, as we entered the main door and passed by the body of a man on a stretcher, that the hospital was the last place to provide that sort of comfort or answers. We approached a patient on a table who appeared to have just received treatment for knife wounds; his bandages were fresh and clean. His IV was attached to a full bag of fluid, but his lips were stiff and blue. He was no longer breathing.

At first glance, the men's wing seemed like a typical hospital ward, filled with long rows of sick people. But there were no facilities, no doctors, no nurses, not even a nurses' station. There was just the wrenching sight of dozens of unattended patients surrounded by a smattering of family members, many of whom looked malnourished. It was the first time I had been in the State Hospital and the inefficiency, neglect, smell, and pathetic state of health care overwhelmed me. Patients were responsible for their own sheets, syringes, medication, and food, and by the looks of the records, that, too. When the hospital ran out of beds, some patients shared, head to toe; or a second mattress, if one was available, was placed on the floor under someone else's bed.

The only other person in the room who wasn't a patient or family member was a neatly dressed young man standing off to the side. He had a pad of paper in his hand and when he came over to speak with us he identified himself as a local newspaper reporter. He led us down a hall and showed us three bodies, each with bullet wounds, and another victim whose oxygen tank, left unattended, ran out during the night. None of the corpses were covered with a sheet; they were left alone among the living.

The morgue was hidden behind the maternity wing at the back of the hospital complex, an irony not lost on me despite all that was happening. The attendant said the only body that had been brought in since he came on duty the night before was the one we had just seen on St. Honoré. He showed us the spot where last night's firing had left shell damage on the cement wall encircling the hospital grounds. He pointed out the sixteen-inch shell; it was too heavy for me to lift. Then he showed us where a grenade had exploded, shattering the windows of cars parked nearby.

The sound of mortar fire and automatic rounds surrounded us. It was so loud it was difficult to hear. I was gripped by fear, not just for my safety, but for the future of Haiti. I couldn't fathom how, yards from the National Palace, such gross medical conditions existed. If this was the best the State had to offer, it was hard to see how anyone would survive. Even Greg, who always had something to say, remained silent.

A group of street kids appeared out of nowhere and recognized me. "Madame Dread!" they shouted, tugging at our sleeves to follow them. They dragged us around the corner and shouted gleefully as they pointed to a bloodied jeep of the Presidential Guard. "*Yo tire yo net, net, net ale,*" they yelled: "They've killed them—killed them completely." They described the event so quickly that I had difficulty understanding what had happened. A patrol of Dessalines soldiers had opened fire without provocation on the Presidential Guard, another unit of the military, killing all four men from the other camp. Two of the victims had been thrown face forward through the shattered windshield. Their eyes were still open, their crisp uniforms soiled with spots of fresh blood. The Dessalines soldiers confiscated their weapons but left their shoes. While a crowd gathered to gape at the horror, a jeep from the Dessalines Barracks arrived and removed three of the bodies. I pulled back instinctively, letting the curiosity of the crowd shield me. It was too much—too much violence, too much blood, too much death. For a brief second I wondered if Haiti wasn't too much for me, if it wasn't time to retreat back into myself before I drowned in the country's tumultuous sorrow. But there was the pull of the unknown, the possibility of pushing myself further than I'd ever been, that kept me moving forward. I didn't think of it as brave or stupid, heroic or reckless. It was just my life; it was what I wanted to be doing, and knew I would continue to do until it didn't seem right anymore. That trust in myself, to know when it was time to move on, was one of the many gifts that Haiti had already given me.

The corpse of the fourth soldier was too mutilated to lift up in one piece. I stood across the street like a zombie, staring at the contorted remains of the young man who just minutes before had been cruising the street with his compatriots. The crowd had parted, and I couldn't take my eyes off the exposed buttocks, the torn flesh and drying blood, the fragments of fabric and car parts and splintered glass. The jeep's rearview mirror reflected a pack of menthol *Comme Il Faut* cigarettes sticking out of the dead soldier's front shirt pocket.

The crowd that had gathered around the remaining body dispersed with the approach of the French ambassador's car; a long, sleek black vehicle with bulletproof windows drawn up tight and the French flag flying on the antenna. The car stopped parallel to the jeep and one of the automatic windows opened noiselessly. A man with a bulletproof vest took out a camera and snapped a picture. The window glided back up and the car drove off.

Minutes later, the Haitian Red Cross came and took away the body. Greg and I walked to my car and once inside locked our doors, rolled up the windows, and drove back to the Oloffson through the deserted silence of the capital's streets.

Christian Science Monitor Radio
Two-and-a-half-minute piece, aired 4.11.89

For the first time in over thirty years, Haiti's military battled against itself. But for seventeen of the last twenty-two hours, they used only blanks, while the paralyzed city listened to the explosion of grenades and automatics. This extraordinary event culminated with real bullets and the surrendering of the dissident soldiers. Kathie Klarreich reports from Port au Prince.

In a press conference yesterday, Haitian President Prosper Avril reconfirmed his position as Chief of State after eight days of political turmoil. President Avril attributed the unrest to his recent firing of four military officers for their involvement in drug trafficking, a response to pressure from the United States. The accused mastermind of the coup attempt, Duvalierist Roger Lafontant, had his visa revoked from the United States and was deported to the Dominican Republic. The commanding officer of the rebel battalion the Leopards is under arrest in New York. And commander of the dissident Dessalines Barracks has sought refuge in the Papal Nunciature.

To control unrest, President Avril declared a state of emergency and placed a curfew on Port-au-Prince. Meanwhile, four major radio stations had their transmissions sabotaged. Damage at one station is an estimated $25,000. Currently only the National and Catholic radio stations are broadcasting news. This has made reporting difficult in a country where literacy is a mere 20 percent.

Events heated up Friday evening when shooting broke out between Dessalines soldiers, who were calling for Avril's ouster, and the loyal Presidential Guard. Blanks were used to intimidate the rebels, but when several Presidential Guard were killed Saturday, the Presidential Guard responded in kind. The Dessalines soldiers surrendered about 4:00 P.M.

President Avril quoted six military soldiers dead, while other sources quote thirty. President Avril cited the death of only one civilian, while this reporter personally saw three who had died as a result of the weekend fighting. President Avril reported a total of seventy-five wounded.

In response to a request for medical assistance, the US provided $25,000. Throughout the entire course of events, the US has given its support to General Avril.

Today civilians are cautious about resuming daily activities. They want to know if the army is really united. Where are the Dessalines troops who did not surrender? Will the Leopards join in unity with the other battalions? And will there be reprisals against

the dissident soldiers? Peace seems unlikely until these questions
are resolved.

For Monitor Radio, I'm Kathie Klarreich in Port-au-Prince.

Nine months later, in January 1990, just after Jean Raymond and I returned from our first trip to the States together, President Avril imposed martial law, empowering the government to approve any news that was broadcast. The government also imposed the right to deport people and required visas for Haitian citizens who wanted to return home. In a separate note it warned that it would be watching journalists and political activity.

This was my first experience with martial law, and it made me anxious. I conjured up images of armed militia patrolling the streets and selectively forcing citizens into their homes or dragging them off in trucks never to be heard from again. I had already seen how cruel the military could be to the average Haitian citizen when martial law wasn't in effect, so the thought of the military having more power terrified me on their behalf. I wasn't particularly worried about my safety—the enemy was not the *blan*, and particularly not the *blan* journalist.

But Jean Raymond saw things differently. *"Pa sòti,"* he said when he heard the announcement about martial law: Don't go out.

"What do you mean, don't go out? Of course I'm going out. It's what I do. It's my job," I said. With each passing day I was becoming a more confident, engaged journalist, and I wanted to prove myself. That I was based in Haiti was a tremendous advantage, and if something happened, I was poised to get a real scoop. It wasn't that I was ignorant of the risks involved in the reporting, but the thought of staying home when something was unfolding out on the streets was unimaginable. My own evolution into being a journalist had seemed so natural and instinctual that it didn't occur to me that I hadn't given

Jean Raymond a chance to catch up. I couldn't help but bristle when he tried to reason with me.

"Do you have to be in their face about it?" Jean Raymond argued. "If the government is telling you to back off, back off."

"They're not telling me any such thing, they're telling that to the local journalists. I work for the foreign press," I said indignantly. Despite martial law, I was still reading articles in American newspapers, and handed Jean Raymond a stack of clips from the *Miami Herald,* the *New York Times,* the *Washington Post,* and the *Los Angeles Times* on recent events. "See, other foreign press is still writing."

"So? Who knows them here? They fly in and out, rent cars, and stay at hotels that are well protected. And their families, their husbands and wives and mothers and fathers are safe in another country. They are anonymous, Kathie. You aren't. Neither am I."

When I realized where he was coming from, I fell silent. I couldn't tell him that I was a nobody out there because the truth was there were very few foreign journalists living in Haiti full-time, and we were visible. But I hardly thought I was significant enough to have to worry about him or his family, let alone myself.

"But I'm not important," I argued feebly. "There would be no reason to want to shut me up—or anyone close to me."

"You think the military thinks like that? Come on, chérie, you've seen what they've done to other people. If something happened to you, do you think anybody at your newspaper would care? They'd feel bad for about five seconds, then send someone else to take your place. Think about that. Think about me," said Jean Raymond before grabbing his keys.

He left without saying good-bye.

His storming off was unsettling. We seemed to be haggling about every little thing recently. Our cultural backgrounds shaped our differences of opinion, and over time it was becoming increasingly more apparent how delicately we needed to walk the line of compromise if we wanted our relationship to work. There were days when my frustration level was so high I thought I would explode—it just didn't make sense to me that he had all the liberties in the world, but wanted to curb mine. His stalking off was the perfect example, but I had to wait until he came back and calmed down before pointing that out to him. I promised to be judicious in my reporting, and told him I'd make a concerted effort to let him know where I was going to be at all times, in case something happened. It was, I thought, an easy promise to keep. Until I met Jean-Marie Montes.

"You've got to meet this guy," my friend in the States wrote. "You'll love him. I've known him for years and am selfishly sorry he's moved back to Haiti to live. He's been talking about it for so long, and now he's actually done it. He's complaining about the same sort of cultural transition you had when you first got there. Even though he's Haitian, he's been out of Haiti for so many years, I think he feels more American than anything else. I gave him your number, but try giving him a call. You two have a lot in common."

Erratic, unreliable phone lines were the bane of my existence, and trying to reach Jean-Marie was nearly impossible. When I was able to get through, a different person answered each time, and they were all evasive about whether or not Jean-Marie was even reachable at that number. I left messages with little hope he would receive them. After several attempts, I gave up.

He called a few days later.

"Would you like to have a cup of coffee at *Tableau Ronde?*" I asked, suggesting a popular restaurant near the palace where I liked to people watch while sipping coffee.

"No, I don't think so." He didn't offer a reason why.

I hesitated, not knowing if he didn't want to meet me or if he didn't want to go to *Tableau Ronde*.

"*Au Bec Fin?*" I asked, guessing by his telephone number that that snack bar was in his general vicinity.

"No, not there, either," he said. "Do you know where the TeleCo is in Pétionville—not the main one, but the one a block away from the main market?"

"Sure," I answered.

"Okay, how about if you meet me on the corner across the street from it, say 4:00 tomorrow afternoon?"

"How will I recognize you?" I asked.

"Don't worry, I'll recognize you," he laughed and hung up.

Still operating on American time, I was there a few minutes early, and expected him to be late, figuring if he was anything like Jean Raymond, time didn't mean much. But his years of living in the States had him well trained, and at 4:00 on the dot he walked up to me with a knowing smile. Again, being the foreigner—the *blan*—I was easy to pick out. There was an instant feeling of comfort and familiarity as we exchanged the perfunctory two-cheek kiss. I knew I was headed for trouble because I felt lighthearted before we even exchanged a word.

I was caught completely off guard. It wasn't that he was extraordinary looking, though he was classically handsome, with a solid face and a toned, muscular body with broad shoulders, the kind of guy I'd always been attracted to. But it was more than his looks. It was the way he looked at me, a penetrating inquisitiveness, as if he saw something I didn't know was there. It was intimate, but respectful. It was the opposite of the leering looks women learn to ignore from lusting men, or the playful ones they responded to in kind. It was even different than the looks I had come to know intimately from being with Jean Raymond. This one bore into my soul as though he were looking for a truth I wasn't even sure was there. I responded with a shy smile as he took my arm and led me down a side street to a tiny restaurant where I'd never been.

"Why did you move back?" I asked.

"The one-line answer? It's time to see a change in Haiti," he said with a lighthearted laugh. Then he turned serious. "It's so hard, watching the government rape the coffers, treat the country like a fiefdom, sanction impunity. How can you stand it, Kathie, when you walk down the street and have to smell the sewage, step over piles of uncollected garbage? It makes me crazy to see these kids on the street with distended bellies, illiterate, hungry. When are we going to have a government that cares about that?"

"But what can you really do about it," I asked. "I don't mean that facetiously, but look, it's been four years since Duvalier left and things are no better off. Well, maybe a little—but poverty, illiteracy, corruption, those things are so institutionalized that I don't see how they are going to disappear quickly, if at all." It didn't take long to see Jean-Marie's political orientation was driven by a strong passion for his country. We spent most of that first visit talking about Haiti. "Be careful when you report," he said after I recounted the conversation I'd recently had with Jean Raymond about martial law. "These guys don't fool around."

"Which guys?" I asked.

"Let's just say, for the time being, the ones with the power," he said, adding quietly, not as an afterthought but a vote of confidence despite our new acquaintance, that he was in a loose sort of "underground" movement that was working to install a true democratic system.

"I live in a 'safe house,'" he confided. "I'll take you to it next time we meet. That's why the people who answer the phone always seem so vague—they may be different people passing through, and no one wants to leave names with messages." Then he gave me a set of pre-arranged code words to use when we spoke on the phone just in case the line was tapped. My initial reaction was to laugh—it seemed so pretentious, like something from a spy novel—but Jean-Marie didn't strike me as the kind of guy to do something without reason, and so I nodded and agreed to use them when we talked again. I was flattered, too, that he was trusting me with this information after only just meeting me. Part of it was the reference of our mutual friend, but I suspected that whatever energy I felt toward him, he felt toward me, too.

Jean-Marie intrigued me—I found him genuine, earnest, not too moralistic but driven by morals. And I couldn't ignore the physical attraction. It took me by surprise because it was the last thing I was looking for. I knew that he had recently split with his wife but I didn't know any of the details and it wasn't my place to ask. When we said good-bye that afternoon, I instinctually knew that it was just the beginning of a long hello.

When martial law was lifted, I resumed reporting with less precaution. There was no good news. The state-owned flour mill laid off 147 workers without providing any explanation. The Haitian military arrested five people in an antigovernment protest. Blackouts persisted. The government fired 312 workers at the State Cement Factory. More antigovernment protests.

Greg, back in town, called. I wondered if he wanted to see me or if he wanted to take advantage of my newly purchased car, then caught myself. I would not have had that thought a few months ago. Slowly Haitian suspicion was slipping into my subconscious. How many other ways had it affected me that I wasn't even aware of?

I picked up Greg at the Oloffson Hotel and we headed toward the palace. We came up on the Champs de Mars Square just as a motorcade of fifteen official government cars, lights flashing, sirens blaring, whizzed past us, inches away from taking off the side of my car. We did a sharp 180-degree turn and followed the frosted-paned vehicles that moved at a fast clip.

We placed bets whether or not President Avril was on his way home for good. The military dictator lived in a modern gingerbread house in Juvenat, at the crest of the steep Canapé Vert Road before Pétionville. My Honda held its own as we started the climb but puttered to a chug at the top of the hill. We lost site of the motorcade until we came around the first curve, when I was forced to slam on my brakes to avoid knocking over a group of soldiers hastily constructing barricades. Another dozen had the barrels of their guns directed at eye level, aimed straight at us. A young man with green eyes fluttered his gun up and down our noses. "*Fè bak. Fè vit,*" he said: "Move back. Do it quickly." Having learned my lesson once already, I put the car in reverse. Within minutes we were effectively sealed off from Avril's house.

Later in the day, the government announced that after seventeen months in office and a "week of mounting protest," President Avril had resigned. Army Chief of Staff General Hérard Abraham agreed to take over as interim president for seventy-two hours. No presidential successor was announced, but according to the 1987 constitution, the next in line of succession was the president of the Supreme Court.

There was talk of a Council of State—eight representatives from the provinces, and eleven professionals—who would form a coalition government. At the not-so-subtle nudging of the United States, Abraham announced there would be elections sometime in the near future. I scooped other foreign journalists on the story that day, and it felt great. My confidence in my reporting and in myself soared. I celebrated with Jean Raymond by going to a fancy restaurant for dinner, something we rarely did. In part, I wanted to prove a point that I could be a good journalist *and* a good girlfriend. My euphoria extended to

Haiti itself, and I actually felt hopeful that things in the country might get better.

Canadian Broadcasting Corporation
Aired 3.12.90

After resigning only two days ago, Haitian President Prosper Avril left the country early this morning, bound for the U.S. From Port-au-Prince, Kathie Klarreich has this report.

At 6:05 this morning, an entourage of American officials accompanied General Avril to Port-au-Prince's public airport. After a brief exchange with U.S. Ambassador Alvin Adams, Avril boarded a U.S. Army C141 with his wife, two teenage children, and one servant. Accompanying them was a U.S. consular official to help with immigration procedures in Florida. No other foreign officials were present.

A general strike was called nationwide today demanding Avril's departure. Although the streets were full of people, public transportation was not yet running. Observers had little reaction when the plane took off, other than smiling and saying he's gone. This response is quite different from the massive jubilant celebration four years ago when Jean-Claude Duvalier left the country in similar fashion.

A 112 party Assembly of Consensus demanding Avril's departure said that he was not being forced into exile, but transition to a civilian government was not possible as long as he remained in the country. There is no official word as to the condition of his parole to the United States.

Meanwhile interim President General Hérard Abraham has about twenty-four hours left before he's supposed to turn over the provisional leadership, but one private radio station is reporting that a young court judge, Ertha Pascal Trouillot will be sworn in later today. If so, she will be Haiti's first female president.

For CBC, this is Kathie Klarreich in Port-au-Prince.

I saw Jean-Marie frequently; each time I flushed with excitement. And guilt. There was the pleasure I got just from spending time with him, but there was also the titillation of taking our friendship to another level. I wasn't naïve. I knew that if I didn't think this through, one day I would walk in and the loose screws holding my world together would bust from their sockets and everything that I'd built with Jean Raymond and fantasized about with Jean-Marie would implode. I kept my attraction in check but still it was there every morning, accompanying me from my morning coffee through my cup of tea at night. It played the devil in my dreams, drawing electricity across the telephone wires and shadowing me like a ghost. It ate at me from the inside, like hunger pains, a raw feeling of neediness crawling unexpectedly out of the dark.

I wanted to talk about it, but didn't trust myself to express the words because then they would be real and I would have to own them. And I wasn't about to tell Jean Raymond, who was really the only other person who knew that Jean-Marie and I were friends.

It was at this point that I understood, again, the importance of close women friends, something I'd always had in my life but struggled with in Haiti. The few friends I had made were nothing like the community I'd developed during my college years in Ann Arbor or afterward in San Francisco, where the women in my life were as much a part of my family as my real family. Of the foreigners I'd met, many weren't interested in living the kind of life that I was living, which was the Haitian life, not a foreigner's life transposed to Haiti. I wasn't unique but finding like-minded women had proved to be more of a challenge than I expected. And developing real friendships with Haitian women took time. I adored many of the Haitian women I met, but I hadn't been able to move those casual friendships to another level. Part of that was the lack of context, and part of it was that intimacy as I thought of it was an American concept, a luxury afforded those who had time to think about it. Intimacy in a Haitian woman's life came from the everyday activities of survival. There were a few female reporters, but the majority of the people I met through work were men. And I knew from my experience with Jean Raymond that Haitians like to know someone thoroughly before they open up to them. Although it was hard for me, I had to be patient.

Fortunately, I had broken the barrier with one woman, who single-handedly filled the void that a community of women would otherwise have occupied. I first met Gisele in 1986, on my very first trip to Haiti before I ever considered living there. I walked into her handicrafts store on rue 3, just up the hill from the Oloffson Hotel and a few blocks from where I eventually settled. A hearty woman with a resounding smile, Gisele was speaking English with one customer, French with another, and Creole with her staff. All at the same time. She went from language to language, person to person with the same ease as if they were all of the same class, color, and importance. I loved her for that from the moment I saw her.

The following year, when I flew from San Francisco, where I was living, to Berlin to attend a handicrafts "fair-trade" conference, she was the first person I saw when I walked into the room. She gave me a warm hug. "So," she said to me with her bright smile, "you followed me all the way to Europe just to become friends with me? I see you are persistent. Is there anything else I should know about you?"

Whether or not she wanted to, she learned a lot—maybe more than she bargained for, as she was the first person I looked up when I eventually moved to Haiti. She was a patient guide as I grounded myself, and made the slow transition from handicrafts to reporting, from being single to my involvement with Jean Raymond. I shared a lot with her but my internal conflict about Jean-Marie was one of the few things I just couldn't bring myself to confide. Every time I went to her store to speak with her about it, I always backed off. I was sure she wouldn't judge me, but still I couldn't bring myself to admit my feelings because I was so confused. The secrecy was both a weight and a pocket of helium—it pulled me down, but also lifted me up.

I knew very little about Jean-Marie, in fact, but with each conversation I felt more drawn to him. One afternoon when we were having coffee at a small, obscure place downtown and joking about the luxuries of Miami, I finally asked why he left his wife.

Jean-Marie looked down at his coffee cup, and stirred it absent-mindedly. "I met her when I was young. She was even younger. Too young. Too young to get married, and certainly too young to have a baby."

"Do you still love her?" As soon as the words were out of my mouth, I wanted to grab them back, bunch them up in a fist and throw them away. Questions like that were only going to get me in trouble—it was like lighting matches next to kindling and not expecting to see flames.

"I think you always hold on to some part of the person you have a child with," he said. "At least I'd like that to be so. But with her, it's not going to work. She wanted to stay in the States and get an education, and that was the right decision for her. I need to be here."

"What about the baby?" I asked.

"I feel badly not being around him, or being around for him," he said. "That's the hardest part. But I don't see my separation with him as something permanent." He twiddled with his coffee cup. "Do you want kids?"

"I never used to, " I said. "But I've been thinking more and more about it. Sort of a delicate topic. I've always said that if I were going to have a child, I'd want to be stable enough to raise one on my own, because you never know what's going to happen in a relationship. Things start out good, all kinds of promises are made, you have a child, and then boom, you're on your own. I know Jean Raymond is interested, I'm just not sure I'm ready."

Jean-Marie smiled. "The beginning of a relationship is special, isn't it? So many plans and dreams about things you're going to do together. How come it doesn't stay that way?"

"Sometimes it does," I said.

"But not that often. I've had a few bad experiences."

"Is there someone else now?" I asked. My inner voice was screaming "shut up!" but on I went, wading into a riptide, waiting to be pulled under.

"Yea, I suppose." He reached for my hand. "But my timing's off, again."

I interlaced my fingers with his, aware that my cheeks were flushed and my heart racing faster than I wanted it to. I started to say something, then stopped. The silence might have been awkward, but it wrapped around us like a warm overcoat and we sat there, content, until the waitress collected our cups and handed us the check, signaling that it was time to go.

Part of my attraction to Jean-Marie was familiarity—we shared a culture, language, and similar level of education. I had gotten so comfortable with Creole that I could even understand jokes, but it was and always would be easiest in English. I was able to bounce ideas off Jean-Marie in the language I was reporting in, which added another dimension to our friendship that I didn't share with Jean Raymond. Jean-Marie and I also shared the commonality of growing up in the States, which meant he had rocked with the Rolling Stones, mellowed with James Taylor, indulged in shaving-cream fights on Halloween, and made prank telephone calls after school.

After that conversation about timing, I tried to circumvent the personal, but it inevitably popped up. When it did, we avoided looking directly into each other's eyes, the one spot that reflected what we were really feeling. As time went on and we became more comfortable with each other, our familiarity was like an old pair of shoes that fit snugly around the heel, but left wiggle room for the toes. I wanted desperately to ignore my attraction, and the interest he showed in me, but it wasn't something I controlled. All the time we spent together provoked feelings of disloyalty to Jean Raymond, and yet I hadn't done anything wrong. We'd never even kissed.

But Jean-Marie and I were flirting more boldly. What we didn't discuss was as significant as the things we did. It was all there—I could see it in the simple way his mouth turned only at the corners when I walked into a room, when his hand reached out to take hold of my arm, pull me in when we exchanged the two-cheek kiss, and then drop down to hold my hand just a minute longer than necessary. When he went away for a few days, the hours felt a little longer, the country lonelier. Conversation raged in my head about what to do, what to say or not to say, to Jean Raymond, to Jean-Marie, to myself. I couldn't leave one for the other, didn't want to leave either, but couldn't live with such strong feelings for both.

Shortly after Jean-Marie returned from a three-day trip to the countryside, he invited me to attend a meeting with some of the other people in his "underground group," an invitation that I took to mean I'd been initiated into a higher level of security and confidence. It was a particularly difficult time politically. The new government wasn't working well, and there were problems with the Council of State's ability to act as a check and balance. Jean-Marie was extremely concerned with the increasing amount of civil unrest and took an even more active role in advising the Council of State about what was going on at the grassroots level. The post office was threatening to strike and the National Television Station closed for restoration. The State Flour Mill and City Hall also closed. The international department of the State Telephone Company went on strike, as did the National Electric Company, which also threatened to cut power completely in Port-au-Prince.

The meeting was held at his "safe house." I got off the public bus a few blocks above the street where he lived, and turned down the alley next to the house with the red gate. I walked along the dirt road for a few hundred yards until I came to a black gate, then tapped out the code—knocking loudly twice, waiting, knocking three more times, then twice more. I heard the creak of a door opening from behind the gate, then saw an eye peer out from the small metal peephole in the center of the black gate.

"Hold on," Jean-Marie said, and fiddled with a padlock and chain that he had to remove in order to pull open the gate. He gave my hand a squeeze and kissed me on each cheek as we walked inside.

The meeting was short—everyone was on edge and seemed in a hurry to get home before dark. Jean-Marie asked me if I wanted to stick around and look at some recent articles on Haiti. I had never been in the back part of the house before, only the common meeting room. "The bedroom isn't really mine," he said sheepishly. "I mean, it wasn't supposed to be mine. It was supposed to be for whoever needed a place to sleep." He laughed. "I've needed a place to sleep since I landed in Haiti, and I've been here ever since."

It was small and impersonal: a mattress on the floor, a desk, chair, and lamp. His books were sprawled everywhere, but nothing was on the walls, only chipped paint. I sat on the stiff mattress and leaned my back against the wall for support. I stretched my legs out in front of me and reached out to take the folder of articles he offered as he propped himself next to me. Suddenly he was right there, his shoulder leaning on mine, his cropped hair grazing my cheek. I could smell his shampoo, the detergent from the shirt, the scent of his cologne as it mixed with his dark oak skin.

I couldn't concentrate on the articles. I couldn't concentrate on anything but his nearness. It was as much a struggle to stop myself from running out of the room as it was from folding myself into him. He ran his hand lightly up and down my thigh, looking straight ahead, not saying a word.

I don't know how long we sat like that. Somehow my heart continued to beat and my breaths came in and out as if everything was normal, but it seemed nothing short of a miracle that my body was functioning as it was supposed to. I felt my pulse in my cheeks, felt the weight of my eyelids, the blood running through my body as I stared down at our legs extended in front of us. Here he was, as easy to put on as a sweater, but images of Jean Raymond wouldn't go away. By giving into my desire, I would be risking my relationship with Jean Raymond—even if he never found out. I'd made a vow to myself, years earlier, that I would never be dishonest in a relationship. I'd seen too many people I love be hurt from infidelity. And of my partner, I expected monogamy. Or used to, until Haiti, where fidelity was as fickle as a sunny day. Not that it wasn't pervasive in other countries, too, but most Haitian men I knew cheated. While I had no proof, not even an inclination that Jean Raymond had cheated on me—he continued to deny that he ever even looked at another woman—I wasn't naïve. If almost every other Haitian man I knew had a mistress, I doubted that I was with the exception. Cheating was as pervasive in Haiti as Vodou was ingrained in the culture.

But it wasn't part of me. I didn't know enough about Jean-Marie to know how he felt about cheating, but I thought I knew how he felt about me. And that he hadn't pushed earlier made me care for him even more. I didn't dare look at his face, afraid of my own reaction.

Before I had a chance to play out any scenarios, Jean-Marie spoke. "It's up to you, you know."

I shook my head, not trusting myself to speak.

"It's okay, either way," he said, turning to look at me.

I nodded and took a few deep breaths. When I finally turned to face him, I saw in his eyes the desire I felt in mine. My hand trembled and he took hold of it, stroking it with a calm, deliberate motion.

"I don't know, I just don't know," I said and laid my head on his shoulders. The cotton shirt felt smooth on my cheek, and I took my other hand and placed it on top of his.

"I can't decide for you, Kathie," he said.

"I know, only everything's all mixed up for me. I've never been this confused."

"If I tried to persuade you now, it would come back to haunt us," he said. "You're smart, you'll figure out what to do."

"I need some time," I said, not knowing then that it was the one thing we didn't have. I wanted to say more but the emotion was like a cork in my throat and instead I lifted my head and turned to face him.

He saw my tears, confusion, and desire, just as I saw the longing and understanding in his. It was that same soul-searching gaze I felt the first time I met him. He turned back to look at the front of the room again, and continued to stroke my hand. I pressed my face against the side of his head, taking in the smell of his hair, feeling the weight of his body rise and fall with each breath. After a few minutes, I withdrew my hand, gathered up the articles in the folder, and placed them in his lap. I tucked my legs under me as I turned to give him a kiss on the cheek, gently passing my hand on his chin, and then I walked out without saying another word.

This double life I was leading left me restless. I used to sleep through the noises of the night, but now Jean Raymond found me by the window at all hours of darkness. "It's the roosters," I said. Or the gunshots. Or the heat.

Something fundamental was shifting, like tectonic plates before an earthquake, and I needed to know what direction I was headed, where I would land after all the dust had settled. If I split with Jean Raymond, I wanted to make sure it wasn't because of Jean-Marie. It would have to be because my relationship with Jean Raymond wasn't as intimate, satisfying, or fulfilling as I wanted it to be. The only way to have a complete relationship was to give completely, and I knew, guiltily, that my feelings for Jean-Marie were affecting everything, particularly the way I was behaving toward Jean Raymond.

I decided to go to Miami for a few days by myself, to think things through. Jean Raymond was in the countryside, and I wasn't expecting him back for a couple of days. I went over to Jean-Marie's to tell him that I was going away but he wasn't home, so I left him a note. "I'll be back in touch in a few days," I wrote on a small piece of paper that I shoved under the metal gate. Then I drove home, confused and depressed.

I tried to write in my journal but I didn't have the emotional energy. I needed something to distract me from my own thoughts, which were bouncing around like rubber balls. I'd recently splurged and bought a small generator, one that allowed me to plug in a few lights, use my computer and, on rare occasions, watch television. I turned on the 8:00 P.M. nightly rebroadcast of *All My Children*. It was a mindless treat I gave myself because it allowed me to make fun of my own moral dilemma as I watched Donna break off her engagement with Chuck while Erica was in the throes of deciding which of the two Montgomery brothers to marry. Just as Erica threw herself into Jackson's arms, the generator died. I searched for matches to light the lantern, then cuddled up with an old issue of *Vanity Fair* when I heard the familiar creak of the front door. The lantern flickered as Jean Raymond came in.

"I came back early," he said. I nodded silently, unsure whether I thought this was a good thing or not. He took a swig of water from the jug on the counter before walking over to give me a kiss. He saw the look of despair on my face and wrapped me in his arms. He didn't ask what was going on and I didn't offer an explanation. We were out of fuel for the oil lamp. We searched for some candles and lay on the bed, serenaded by rain and drifting wind. I gave into the night, which begged for intimacy. The patter on the roof cut through the silence of our thoughts as we drifted off to sleep.

It was sunny when we woke the next morning, and Jean Raymond and I took a walk in the neighborhood. After a quick shower, I put on a pot of coffee when I heard someone walk up the stairs and knock on the door. "Get that, will you?" I said to Jean Raymond, who was reading the paper on the couch. From where I was standing, I saw Jean Raymond's whole body stiffen when he opened the door. I didn't know who it was, but the tension blasted into the room like an arctic freeze. Jean-Marie extended his hand and Jean Raymond took it ungraciously.

"*Kouman ou ye?*" Jean-Marie asked: How are you.

"*Mwen la,*" Jean Raymond said and walked over to the couch without inviting Jean-Marie inside: I'm here. Although it was a typical response, the way he said it dripped with irony.

"Hey, what brings you here?" I said, coming over to greet him. I could feel Jean Raymond shoot darts at my back as I kissed Jean-Marie on both cheeks.

"I have this 11:00 A.M. meeting over at the Hotel Santos," he said, referring to a former hotel often used for meetings that was just minutes from my house. "A bunch of popular organizations are getting together with the Council of State to discuss the political situation. Things are really declining and we've got to do something about it fast."

"Do you have time for a cup of coffee?" I asked. "I just put some on."

Jean Raymond got up and threw the paper down on the couch. He walked into the bathroom and closed the door with just slightly more force than necessary.

"Don't mind him," I said in a hushed voice. "He came back unexpectedly last night."

"If I'd known he was here, I wouldn't have come," Jean-Marie said, looking troubled. "It's just that I got your note and wanted to talk to you before you left."

"I haven't said anything to him yet about leaving," I whispered, pouring a demitasse. I was so nervous I wanted to melt into the coffee like the sugar cube Jean-Marie had just added. He nodded in understanding as Jean Raymond came out of the bathroom. I motioned toward his cup of coffee; he picked it up and went back to the couch, deliberately snubbing the two of us.

Jean-Marie put down his coffee, having taken only a sip. "I've got to go," he said.

"Please, come back after the meeting and tell me what happened," I said. "I'll just be home working this morning."

"Will do," he said, and gave me a two-cheek kiss as he opened the door to leave. "*Pita*, Jean Raymond," he said: Later.

"I don't think so," Jean Raymond said after Jean-Marie closed the door. "*Koulangèt,* (damn it) Kathie, who does he think he is coming over like that?"

"He just told you, because he was on his way to a meeting at the Santos."

"Obviously he feels at home enough to come over unannounced."

"Come on, Jean Raymond, he's my friend. Leave it alone."

"No, I'll leave *you* alone." He grabbed the car keys and slammed the door on his way out.

I stuck out my tongue when he left but I felt guilty. This was painful for everyone. I felt that Jean Raymond was reading my thoughts, the ones I wanted to stop having but couldn't. I cleared the dishes before sitting down to work at the computer, recording relevant information from the morning-radio news report. Several minutes later, just before 11:00 A.M. I heard a round of gunfire that sounded close by. I wasn't indifferent, but it was a sound that was by now so familiar I did nothing more than mark the time.

About ten minutes later, the radio announcer reported that there had been a shooting at the Hotel Santos. The initial details of the shooting were fuzzy. The radio reported that four armed men, two in military uniform, shot at someone who had just entered the courtyard, at close range. The victim died instantly. The assassins then jumped into another vehicle and shot at a car pulling into the parking lot as they pulled out. They seriously injured a Council of State member and another person in the car.

I put a cassette in the tape player to record the news as I listened to it. Immediately I thought about Jean-Marie and knew when he stopped back on his way home he'd tell me what happened. I dialed Monitor Radio in Boston and NPR in Washington. They were both interested in a radio spot and said they would call back within an hour's time to give me a chance to get more details.

As more reports on the shooting came in, I jotted them down and added them to my text. I was on automatic pilot—I'd done this so many times before that it was just routine, and I wasn't processing, just reporting. It was only in the middle of typing his name that I realized the fatality was Jean-Marie.

I slumped over the computer as if I'd been knifed in the belly. I screamed "No!" so loudly that it rang through the living room and came back to hit me in the face. Ugly noises climbed up my throat and hurled themselves at the radio, through the open window, at the hysterical figure in the mirror. The sounds made no sense, but they tore out my insides and took with them the grief and anguish and love lost that would never be recaptured, could never be consummated, could only be remembered. Please, please, please I said over and over again to no one and everyone. Tell me you've got it wrong. I grabbed the tape from the cassette player and rewound it, playing it over and over again, each time waiting to hear a different name, to hear the announcer say anything but Jean-Marie Montes. Please, I sobbed. Not Jean-Marie. The tears gushed like a geyser, a river flowing down my cheek, dripping off my chin onto my desk, the radio, the cassette. I heaved sobs I didn't know I was capable of, making deep, grunting noises as I wheezed air in and out, unsure how my body could continue to function with all its normal acts when my heart had received such a definitive blow. In a final act of desperation, I turned back to the radio, flipping from one station to another in hopes of hearing a rectification that never came.

As I sobbed shamelessly, I replayed the morning's visit over and over in my mind. What if it hadn't been so awkward with Jean Raymond? Would Jean-Marie have stayed longer? If he'd known that Jean Raymond was going to be home, would he have stopped by? If not, would he have been safely inside the Santos at the time the assassins drove by? What if he'd finished his cup of coffee or had no coffee at all? What if I wasn't home when he came by? What if we'd never met and he'd gone directly to the meeting? Focusing on the what-ifs helped me avoid thinking about the what-would-be-no-longer. The thing I couldn't accept was that not only would Jean-Marie not be coming back on his way home, but that he wouldn't be coming back at all, ever. How ironic that the only man I knew who took the trouble to speak in code and live in a "safe house" would be the random victim of a drive-by. Was this how he was destined to die? No, I screamed in one final shout of defiance, one last effort to purge the injustice that would now rest in my soul forever.

The call from NPR jolted me to reality. My editor told me to forget filing after hearing the pain in my voice. But I couldn't. Not because I was an altruistic journalist. To say that Jean-Marie deserved at least that sounded trite even as I said it, but it was all I could offer. Though it took several tries, I was eventually able to hold my voice in check to record the report. In all my subsequent radio spots, that was by far the most difficult sixty-second spot I ever made.

The war against democratic elections in Haiti escalated this morning with an attack against members of the government, leaving two people wounded and one dead. Kathie Klarreich reports from Port-au-Prince.

At 10:45 this morning, four men, two in military uniform, appeared at the Hotel Santos in Haiti's capital, a meeting place for members of the Council of State, Haiti's electoral board, and popular organizations. They opened fire, killing one member of a popular organization, and wounding two—one still unidentified, the other a member of the Council of State, Serge Villard.

The shootings are reminiscent of attacks preceding Haiti's

1987 presidential elections, when dozens were killed. Antidemoc-ratic forces are again out to intimidate people, in spite of the pledge from president Ertha Pascal Trouillot and the army to sup-port elections and hold them as soon as possible. Earlier this week, more than eight people were killed in less than twenty-four hours. Elections are scheduled for the end of September.

For National Public Radio, I'm Kathie Klarreich in Port-au-Prince.

Chapter V

CIA

Bon tè bezwen bon kiltivatè.
A good farm needs a good farmer.

I first heard the rumor that I was a CIA agent from a musician outside Jean Raymond's inner circle. Ritva, my Finnish friend, had heard it from her boyfriend Ti Frank, who'd heard it from his brother, who'd heard it from someone else. *Teledyòl*, as the rumor mill is often referred to, is one of the fastest ways word gets around in Haiti.

"I don't know," Ritva said with her characteristic shrug. "You could take it seriously or not. Depends."

That Ritva was noncommittal didn't surprise me. She was very much a Haitian when it came to all things political—refusing to say what she really thought, even to me, one of her closest friends. I wasn't surprised to hear the rumor—at some point, if you're American and you stick around long enough, it's like the floods during the rainy season, bound to happen. But I was caught off guard. I'd heard rumors of this kind about other Americans, but in some naïve, sheltered way, I never imagined I would be targeted. I was still working on planting my feet on the ground and didn't think I'd caused enough of a stir for anyone to really notice me. But this was Haiti, where everyone is noticed and nothing is as it seems.

When, the following week, Ritva said she'd heard the rumor again, this time from someone in Jean Raymond's inner circle, I got nervous. "What have you heard about me?" I questioned him one afternoon as he arrived home sweaty from rehearsal. "What kinds of rumors are circulating?"

"*Anyen:* Nothing," he answered, turning on the fan as he pulled off his shirt.

"Don't be like that," I countered, and turned the fan to the swivel position so he wouldn't get sick from a sudden blast of cold air. I'd adopted the Haitian habit of avoiding standing in front of refrigerators when I opened them for the same reason. Jean Raymond was convinced that I'd contracted bronchitis earlier that month because I'd gone from hot to cold too quickly—that and lying on the tile floor to stretch out after a dance class. "Ritva told me that several different people are spreading rumors that I'm a CIA agent. What do you know about this? What aren't you telling me?"

"I didn't want to upset you," he said. "Forget it, it's nothing I can't handle."

That only made me worry about what damage control he might be up to, but I didn't push him further. It didn't seem important, particularly since there wasn't any truth to it. But truth had nothing to do with how events unfolded in Haiti any more than facts had to do with popular perception.

I confronted this when I started working on a piece for the United

Nations publication *Action for Children*, which had hired me to do an article on street children. There were several people with whom I wanted to speak, individuals who had set up homes for street children, but the most obvious person to interview was Jean-Bertrand Aristide, who had founded *Lafanmi Selavi*, the "Family Is Life" Center for boys, three years earlier.

Even more significant than his work with street children, however, was Aristide's role in bringing down the Duvalier dictatorship. His popularity stemmed from the fact that he was one of the first people to speak of topics that heretofore had been uttered only in the dark and private compounds of shantytowns: He denounced the evils of the Duvalier dictatorship, the imperialist United States, the corrupt Haitian military, the power-hungry manipulations of the bourgeoisie. Aristide was of the people and therefore he could speak for them. Born in the southern town of Port-Salut, his father, a small farmer, died when he was just three months old. His mother moved the family to Port-au-Prince and sent Jean-Bertrand to religious school; from there he went on to obtain a master's degree in psychology. The church provided him the opportunity to travel to Rome, Jerusalem, Great Britain, and Canada, where he perfected his English, Spanish, Italian, and Hebrew. But he needed only one language to get his message across to the Haitian people, and in Creole he shouted loud and clear and often that social change was possible and the Haitian people had the tools to do it. Like a rampant infection, youth groups took up his cry for liberation theology and social change, and the Aristide dynasty was launched.

But it was hard to track him down after the assassination attempt in September 1988 and only after persistent groveling with numerous people who built an iron wall around Aristide was I able to secure an interview. "Titid," as the young Catholic priest was called, had been virtually invisible in public for the last six months, but he appeared almost every day at *Lafanmi*. Even in obscurity, he was still the most important person on the Haitian political scene. His supporters were all the poor who never had a voice; his enemies, all those who wanted things to remain status quo—the government, the military, the corrupt businessmen and wealthy elite who profited from lack of regulation, rules, and taxes.

The center was on a shady street in a residential neighborhood just fifteen minutes downhill at a brisk pace. I dressed casually but professionally, and made sure I packed a pen, notebook, tape recorder, and extra batteries in my blue backpack. If someone hadn't described the center's location I would have missed it—all that was visible from the street was a large metal gate sandwiched between two nondescript houses. There was no one on the street. I knocked on the door and waited. Eventually someone opened the peephole and a pair of dark eyes stared out at me, direct and unfriendly.

"I'm here for an interview with Father Aristide," I said nervously.

"*Tann,*" the man said: Wait, as he closed the peephole and disappeared. So I did, in the hot sun, for ten minutes, until he returned and said it was okay for me to come in. He spent another minute fiddling with more locks before he opened the door just wide enough to let me through. Then with a quick flick he shut it again, replacing the chain and padlock.

Security was clearly tight, which was no surprise, given the prior attacks on Aristide and the amount of political tension still in the air. In Haiti, the church played a significant role in education, guidance, spiritual healing, social gathering, and politics. Aristide represented the voice of the layman, the popular voice—not the church hierarchy—so it wasn't completely unexpected that when St. Jean Bosco was attacked just days after my initial arrival in Haiti, Father Aristide received no support from his superiors. A month later, the Salesians expelled him from their order. But there had been intermittent, massive demonstrations in support of Titid from the people. While he stayed cloistered from the public eye, tens of thousands of people came out to protest the Church's action and show their support for the man they believed could finally make a substantial change in their lives. One such demonstration caught me by surprise as I was making my way home—it was like a massive wave that swelled as people joined the march from all directions, blocking the major arteries leading to downtown from the Champs de Mars square where the National Palace, headquarters of the Armed Forces of Haiti and police headquarters converge. It was the largest demonstration I'd ever seen in my life. Businesses were forced to close, schools shut down in the wake of such a strong presence and the fear that the crowd would turn out of control. Those against Aristide were clearly outnumbered, but not outarmed.

The courtyard of *Lafanmi* bustled with life, in sharp contrast to the quiet street on the other side of the gate. Piles of sand for construction were scattered throughout the cement courtyard; dozens of boys scrambling down from them to greet me with dusty smiles. They pulled on my hand, touched my hair, asked me who I was and did I want to play with them? Before I had a chance to answer, a middle-aged Haitian woman appeared to take me inside. "*Tanpri, vin jwe avek nou aprè,*" the boys begged: Please, come play with us afterward.

"*Dako,*" I agreed.

I followed the woman across the courtyard into a multistory building. We took the side stairs. At the top she ushered me into a cluttered room with two empty chairs, motioned for me to sit down, and then walked away.

What struck me when Titid entered the room was how imposing he seemed. It didn't come from his build—he was short, slight, almost skinny, and his shoulders, though not hunched, seemed to carry a burden heavier than fit him. But he projected an air of complete and utter confidence—not friendly or menacing, just assured, irrefutable control. Behind his clear spectacles, and despite his droopy eye, his gaze was sharp and commanding and left me feeling small and insignificant, if not inadequate. Before I could extend my hand to introduce myself, he spoke, and his words caught me off guard. "You are not the Kathie I was expecting, " he said and took his seat without any further introduction. I sensed his disappointment that I wasn't this other Kathie, and felt as though I should apologize, though for what I didn't know. I waited, expecting him to dismiss me, or offer some sort of explanation for his statement, but he did neither.

Instead, he began the interview by interviewing *me,* so I sat down. "*Kilès ou ye?*" he asked in Creole: Who are you? And upon hearing me struggle to respond in Creole, agreed to do the rest of the interview in English. Although his English wasn't great, it was far better than my Creole. "Why are you in Haiti? What brought you here? What do you think you are going to accomplish during your stay?

"Do you know that many foreigners are used by this government?" he asked. "Do you know that Americans think they are doing good when they come here, but very often they are doing harm? That their information can be misused?"

He fired questions at me like rapid pellets, one after the other, and then answered many of them himself. I barely had a chance to catch my breath. I thought he was aggressive, but I wasn't naïve enough to believe he didn't have reason to be so. He remained heavy-handed for another few minutes, but seemed satisfied with my responses, when I could get them in, and finally he agreed to let me ask a few questions.

But by then I was frazzled. "I'm here as a journalist," I started, then got lost in an explanation about the street kids that I knew well, kids that used to be part of *Lafanmi*, but whom Aristide had kicked out because of their bad behavior—Ti David, Ti Claude, Wawa, brothers Fatil and Eril, and the ringleader, Ayiti.

The boys must have been only twelve or thirteen years old when I first met them. It was a fluke. Ritva and I had walked downtown one Sunday morning to see what, if anything was happening at St. Jean Bosco after the 1988 attack that had killed more than a dozen parishioners and sent Aristide into hiding. The boys were gathered in a cluster behind a makeshift barrier they'd set up with old pieces of wood, aluminum, and cloth. There was no informal service in the church, as we had hoped to find—instead we found the boys playing tag with a cloth that they snapped at each other. They didn't know what to make of these two sweaty *blan* any more than I knew what to make of them. They were several years older than my nieces, but it didn't seem right that they were there by themselves without family, home, or shelter. Or that this was how they spent their Sunday, how they probably spent every day.

Ayiti was the first to approach us—a tall, lanky kid with ripped pants and a shirt that he wore like an extra layer of skin. His impish grin was full of the devil, but he disarmed me by grabbing onto my hand, as if to ensure that I wouldn't leave. The only people that came into the courtyard, he later explained, were guys trying to run them out of there. These men, some of whom were members of the gang *San Manman* (Without Mothers) realized that by attacking the street kids associated with Aristide, they were striking a blow even more weighty than going after the priest himself.

"*Saw pote pou nou?*" Ayiti asked: What have you brought for us?

"*Anyen,*" Ritva answered: Nothing. "If we didn't know you were here, how could we have brought something for you?"

This amused the boys, who, with that remark, decided we were okay. We sat down with them in the shade—they offered scraps of cardboard so we wouldn't get our clothes dirty, and gave us a list of things they could use—shoes, shirts, a mattress, food, cooking utensils. We promised to return the following Sunday, but only, I bargained, if they agreed to teach me Creole. They loved the idea, and so it was, for the next two months, that Ritva and I went religiously, every Sunday, like regular churchgoers, to St. Jean Bosco and hung out with the boys.

They taught me phrases they thought were important to my survival: "*Ou pa gen dwa fè sa*: You're not allowed to do that," or "*Kitem, monchè*: Leave me alone, man," and "*Wap tiye mwen, mwen pa ka peye tout sa*: You're killing me, I can't pay all that."

We brought things for them to eat, *pate* (meat pies) and *fritay* (fried dough, plantains, yams) and occasionally gave them money, but never very much. They knew we wouldn't let them starve, but neither Ritva nor I had the kind of resources it would take to really make their lives better.

One Sunday when we arrived the boys were asleep. We gently nudged them, but unlike previous weeks, they didn't seem excited to see us.

"*Sak pase?*" I asked: What's going on?

"*Ayiti, Eril ak Fatil disparèt*," said Wawa, who was a master pickpocket and contributed to the kids' survival: Ayiti, Eril, and Fatil disappeared. "A guy we know came by with a car, they got in, and we haven't seen them since."

Their chagrin made the visit unbearably glum. Even though we'd brought a deck of cards and dominos, along with something to eat, they were lethargic and disinterested. Nothing we did cheered them up, and we left feeling as depressed as they felt.

After the end-of-the-year holiday, Ritva and I returned to find them jumping up and down in anticipation of our arrival.

"*Se vre, tout sa yo di, se vre,*" shouted Ti David, an artful soccer player: It's true, everything they said, it's true. The friend who had picked up Ayiti, Eril, and Fatil had driven to the border of the Dominican Republic and sold the three boys for $15 a head to cut sugarcane. Skinny, gangly Ayiti was too little to cut cane, so he stayed back at the camp and prepared pitiful meals cooked in tin cans on burnt leaves to nourish Eril and Fatil. Their escape from the camp was executed with the same abandonment as their being sold in the first place. When I eventually ran into Ayiti after he made it back to Port-au-Prince, he laughed and laughed at the story, retelling it each time with new embellishment. Soon it became legend.

Shortly after their return, one lazy winter night, armed men scaled the wall of the church and woke the boys from their sleep. They demanded to know where Aristide was, and of course the boys had no idea. But they understood the threats. "*Nou se Titid,*" the men yelled at the boys, who cowered in the darkness: You are Aristide. The men left without harming the boys, but the kids said they didn't feel safe sleeping there anymore. They found a place, rent-free, in Cité Soleil, the urban slum just a few kilometers north, but didn't have anything to sleep on, so I bought them some straw mattresses and cooking utensils and helped them set up house. They lasted a week in their new place before an older gang confiscated everything and kicked the boys back out on the street.

I explained a condensed version of this history I had with the street urchins nervously to Aristide, chastising myself for how inappropriate it was that I was sharing this with him, particularly since he knew these boys far better than I did. Besides, he was the one who had kicked them out of *Lafanmi* for fighting and stealing, but once I started explaining the story to him, I couldn't stop. I'd never interviewed such an important person before, and the interview wasn't going exactly as planned. Titid listened intently, nodding at the appropriate time, but said nothing, then answered my questions for the article. Halfway through my list, he suddenly stood up, and with a kinder expression than he had shown in the beginning, said it might be a good idea to spend some time talking to the boys who were actually living at *Lafanmi* now to round out any impressions I might have gathered from the boys he'd asked to leave. Then, without another word, he turned and walked through the door, down the stairs, and out of sight.

Shaken, I gathered my things and slowly worked my own way down the stairs, only to find the group of boys I'd seen earlier clustered around the door waiting for me. Two of the younger ones grabbed my hand and pulled me over to a dusty pile of cement bricks, where I sat in the sun trying to compose myself. It was hot and muggy and I was feeling unsure of myself, but the eager looks on the young boys' faces helped me focus. I folded my backpack into a little ball and rested it on my knees, using it as a prop while I took notes on what the kids were saying.

"*Papam te bat mwen,*" one of the boys said: My father beat me.

"*Mwen pat we manman depi li ale ak lòt neg là,*" said another: I haven't seen my mother since she went off with another man.

Many of these boys had families they left because of abuse or neglect. Young and confused, they got lost on the streets of the capital before entwining themselves into drugs, gangs, and a life of crime. The more fortunate found their way to *Lafanmi*, comforted by its emphasis on community. *Lafanmi* offered academic as well as vocational classes, with courses in mechanics, carpentry, and electronics. It provided language lessons and rotating shifts for the boys at a *Lafanmi* carwash on the National Highway so they could earn pocket money.

Their other campus, an agricultural center in nearby La Plenn, taught them how to raise plants and animals.

I was so engaged in what the boys were saying, and concentrating so hard on understanding their Creole, that I didn't see Titid appear at a downstairs door close to where I was sitting until I heard his voice. I looked up and saw his face—tight, frosty, and piercing. He let out a litany of something in rapid Creole, but it was utterly unintelligible; the words blew by like the encircling dust clouds. Before I had a chance to ask him to slow down and repeat himself, he'd disappeared behind the door he slammed shut.

Confused, I sat quietly for a moment, trying to figure out what to do. Even the boys stopped chattering long enough to allow me to hear myself think; they watched me with curiosity but never left my side. I waited to see if Titid was going to reappear, and when he didn't, I picked up my notebook and resumed my conversation with the kids.

Just a few minutes later, the original Haitian woman who led me to Titid's office approached us. She stood with an air of importance and hostility and the boys stopped fidgeting to hear what she had to say. "*Fòk w ale*," she said: "You have to go." The tone and meaning were so definite that I didn't think to question her. "*Dako*," I said: okay, and tucked my pen and notebook inside my backpack. I walked over to the gate, waiting patiently for the guardian to repeat the laborious process of unlocking the gate and removing the chain to open the door.

The boys I'd been speaking with followed me onto the street, where a vendor with a wooden cart was working his way door to door selling *fresko*, Haiti's version of the snow cone: a large block of ice with flavored syrup in brightly colored bottles that surrounded the sides of a wobbly wooden cart. A swarm of bees hovered over the sticky syrup bottles. The boys gratefully accepted my offer to buy them each one.

As they chose their flavors, a Frenchwoman who worked for *Lafanmi* emerged from behind the metal gate and with a smile walked over and said to me, "*Ou pa oblije rete deyò. Ou met antre, chita pale ak timoun yo andedann lakou nou an:* You don't have to stay outside. Come in and speak with the children in the courtyard."

She spoke clearly and slowly, with such articulation that there was no confusion about her invitation to return inside. But I was thoroughly confused because her invitation contradicted what I'd just been told. Before I had a chance to react, the metal barrier opened yet again, and this time Titid himself came out, obviously agitated. There was no hesitation in his step and, as he approached, he seemed to tower over me, even though he was just inches taller.

His anger was so great, I thought it was going to knock me down. His lips pursed in a snarl around his teeth, his skin tightened around his eyes and his cheeks hardened like baked clay. His quick, harsh words flew past me like bolts of lightning, too dangerous to grab on to and too accelerated to understand. I held out my hands in a futile attempt to catch the words, slow him down, but he kept going, picking up speed and hostility as he continued. When I did catch a phrase or two, I doubted myself because they made no sense. Why was he accusing me of being CIA? What would lead him to believe I had drugs in my backpack, and that I was distributing them to the boys?

I was lost in his tirade against me and helpless to defend myself. It was all I could do to remain upright, as his barrage of insults drowned the street and all of us standing there.

"*Mwen pa konprann,*" I finally muttered when Aristide took what I was sure was his first breath of air in several minutes: I don't understand. I was loath to speak, humiliated, embarrassed, and sure that my Creole would fail me completely. Everyone was staring at me; I didn't know where to look. "I thought you said it was okay to stay and talk to the boys," I said, struggling to control the quiver in my voice. "I can't understand what you are saying. Please, slow down. Would you explain this to me in English?"

"I told you before that I don't want you around these boys." Aristide said, speaking in English now. "If you didn't understand my Creole the first time, it's because you didn't want to understand."

And with no further explanation, he firmly placed his arms around the shoulders of two boys I'd been speaking with, and led them inside. The barrier closed behind him, forcefully shutting me out. I felt the world turn upside down. The most important man in the country had just berated me publicly, and I didn't know why. Was it possible that he'd just heard the rumor about my being a CIA agent? Or had someone just told him something damning and untrue about me in the short time that had passed since I left his office? I shook from confusion and humiliation. My face flushed and my eyes couldn't focus from the puddle of tears that welled up. With as much dignity as I could muster, I picked up my sack, paid for the *freskos*, and walked away. I couldn't think of a thing to say to the street kids who stood silently, staring after me.

That night I dreamed I was traveling—on airplanes, trains, and cars; I didn't know when to dismount. Friends from my world in the States and Haiti passed each other in the aisles. I didn't know where home was.

That following weekend I went to the Esso gas station at the corner of Grand Rue and Delmas. I'd heard that's where Eril and Ayiti were sleeping at night, and I wanted to tell them what had happened. The boys had worked out a deal with the gas-station attendant to allow them to sleep in the back of a truck that parked there each evening. The station was also a hangout for kids who worked the traffic, wiping windows for a gourde, which they too often spent on glue that they sniffed from the inside of discarded plastic juice containers.

The boys slapped their sides with delight, rolling with laughter as I relayed the story of *Lafanmi* to them. "*Uh-oh, pa ankyetew, se konsa li ye,*" they said: "Uh-oh, don't worry, that's just how he is." They promised to ask Titid about it the next time they saw him. Then they broke into street theater, mimicking Titid losing his temper, something he did with them frequently. Ayiti played me, twisting his shirt into little balls and pretending he was going to cry.

Eventually I wrote Titid a letter and included a copy of the article I'd submitted on *Lafanmi*. I said something to the effect that there must have been a misunderstanding. Composing that half page took longer than writing the three-page article.

What I didn't say was how hard it was to reconcile the behavior of that day with the first time I heard him preach. It had been a sweltering spring Sunday in May 1988, during my third visit to Haiti. I had decided to see for myself what made this Catholic priest so popular. I didn't know where his church was, but I had no problem finding it. I followed the steady stream of people moving on foot, bicycle, and in wheelchairs down Delmas to Grand Rue. Some women carried children in their arms; others had merchandise on their heads. The strong steeple, a soggy, mustard color, was the highest thing around. As I made my way forward, swept up in the current, a young girl in a yellow satin dress took my hand and gently led me forward. When we got to the entrance of the church, the carpet of people turned into a massive sea of bodies, three to a seat. Determined, the little girl with yellow bows maneuvered her way down an aisle, where she motioned to a group of people to make room, and somehow they did, with a smile and a welcoming gesture.

Father Aristide was preaching with a voice too powerful to be contained within the church walls. I didn't need to understand what he was saying to understand his impact. The energy was extraordinary, as people listened attentively, nodded in agreement, clapped in unison, and sang with gleeful abandon. It was the same energy, only transformed, that I felt that afternoon in front of *Lafanmi*, when he deemed me persona non grata.

My note to Aristide was simple, and of course said nothing of this experience I'd had in his church. The note the boys delivered to me from him months later, crumpled up in the back of their pocket, was even simpler: "You are welcome back here anytime," he wrote in a handwritten scribble.

I was relieved that there was some closure to this mystery after all these months, but it was hardly satisfying. I wanted an explanation for his behavior, I wanted to know what had caused the tantrum in the first place. But, like so many things in Haiti, it left me with more questions than answers.

I went for more than a year without any personal contact with Aristide, though during that time he was becoming increasingly more visible. His popularity grew at a rate parallel to his criticism of the government. The political situation was dicey; the international community insisted that the interim government hold elections for Haiti's new "democratic" rebirth. The Electoral Board postponed voter registration twice; crime and killings increased—nearly a murder a day in August 1990, though it was hard to say if they all were politically motivated. Elections originally scheduled for November were delayed until December 16. The United States and Canada committed themselves by providing more than $5 million for electoral expenses.

Meanwhile five ministers of the Haitian cabinet resigned in September and the Council of State, which had been set up as a counterbalance to the interim president, cut all ties with the executive branch. It also called for the resignation of Interim President Ertha Pascal Trouillot, accusing her of "fraud, nepotism, carelessness, incompetence, favoritism, and corruption." Serge Villard, the Council of State member who had been wounded when Jean-Marie was killed, died from his injuries.

There were plenty of people hoping to take Trouillot's place, but none had widespread popular support, and Aristide's silence and refusal to endorse anyone impacted popular opinion. The United States was rumored to favor Marc "Mr. Clean" Bazin, a former World Bank consultant. The more progressive parties backed Victor Benoit, a rotund, bumbling schoolteacher who lacked charm and experience but was honest and had good intentions. The Tonton Macoutes holdovers—those that supported the Duvalier dictatorship, bankrolled Roger Lafantont. No one seemed to care that there was an outstanding arrest warrant for this former leader of the Macoutes; not only did the government disregard the warrant, it provided Lafontant with a police escort wherever he went.

Despite the historic possibility of Haiti's holding its first democratic election in its nearly two-hundred-year history, and the United States government's interest in making it happen, Haitians were cynical. Voter registration was extremely low.

About six weeks before elections, I set out to interview "ordinary Haitians" for a preelection piece for the *Christian Science Monitor*. I drove to the marketplace, and parked on a side road, away from the mounds of garbage that had become so compacted with foot traffic it was hard to differentiate it from the dirty streets. I liked going to the market; I felt at home among the organized chaos of the vendors and the buyers, the hawkers and the voyeurs, the red of the tomatoes, the oranges, greens, purples of the fruits and vegetables interspersed with the wide-brimmed hats, easy bartering, and aroma from the mélange. It was far more entertaining, though admittedly more tiresome, than wandering the aisles of Winn-Dixie or Publix.

I headed toward a group of market women whose trays of garlic and wilted lettuce were displayed in woven baskets in front of them as they squatted. I started out with friendly banter, hoping that would warm them to me, before I broached the subject of elections.

"*Eleksyon an?*" one woman questioned from under the brim of her wide straw hat: The election? "I don't know when it is. I don't even know who the candidates are. It doesn't matter. They don't represent me. They are just the blah-blah-blah politicians."

Her friend poked her in the side and told her not to talk to reporters, that only bad things could come of it. I put my notebook back in my backpack, not wanting to make myself more conspicuous than I already was, and wandered a bit farther into the square. The smell of the sun beating down on the stalls selling chicken made me nauseous, and I turned in the opposite direction.

"*Volé, tout se volé,*" said a man peddling little plastic bags of unidentifiable pills that he'd stapled on a cardboard sheet: Thieves, they are all thieves. He wasn't shy about his distrust of politicians and disinterest in supporting a candidate. "Not one of them cares what I think, not one of them is going to make my life better."

"Don't talk to us," said another street vendor, who carried a three-foot cardboard sheet full of sunglasses. "We don't have anything to say to you about the elections or this government. We don't want trouble. Go away."

After another fifteen minutes of similar responses, I gave up, discouraged. It was generally hard to get people I didn't know to say anything political, but this day's attempt left me feeling hopeless about Haiti's future, too. How would things ever turn around if there was no one who could rally the support of the population?

I climbed into my car, and before writing the quotes in my notebook, took the rag I had left on the passenger's seat and wiped the sweat from my face, neck, and chest. It was starting to cool down after the brutal summer heat, but still the days were hot and long; only late afternoon offered a whisper of relief from the sweat. As I pulled out into traffic, I turned on the news out of habit, but was thinking not about what was being said but how to outline my upcoming story. Suddenly I heard horns honking on all sides. I looked around and saw nothing unusual, then heard Aristide's name on the radio. Instantly I focused on what the reporter was saying, and sat dumbfounded as the broadcaster announced that Aristide had entered the presidential race.

The impact was immediate, as though someone had just plugged in an electrical cord. The last time the country had seen such a surge of energy was four and a half years earlier, when dictator-for-life Jean-Claude Duvalier was forced to leave the country. This day, as then, the entire nation lit up. A disinterested population, unaware and unconcerned with the slate of candidates, was suddenly turned upside down. By 5:00 P.M. the next day, there was a 77 percent leap in voter registration.

Aristide named his campaign *Lavalas*—the flood, the avalanche, the torrent. Although it was a Creole word, it wasn't a popular one, and English-speaking journalists bickered among themselves about how best to translate it so that there was some consistency. Aristide explained that he chose the word because it was time for a "*lavalas* of unity. When it goes down, it goes in the same direction. If you have a million people behind you, you have a *lavalas* in the same direction." He denied seeking out the candidacy, insisting that he was just responding to the demands of the people, and if it was their will for him to represent them, he couldn't say no.

It wasn't just the Haitian population that showed a sudden interest in the elections. Suddenly the press wanted to learn everything they could about this little man who had mobilized the country. Foreign correspondents descended on Port-au-Prince like dogs on a bitch in heat. I received a call from Howard, the *New York Times* correspondent for the region. Several months before he'd been in town and asked me to meet him for a drink on the balcony of the Oloffson Hotel. I had no idea why—we had never exchanged more than a few words. I put Howard in the same category as the journalists from the *Washington Post* and the *Los Angeles Times*—experienced, worldly foreign correspondents whose only interest was flying in, getting the story done, then flying out again. Since it was shortly after Jean-Marie's death, I wondered if somehow he had heard that we'd been friends and wanted some inside information.

Howard was a tall, thin man, so light-skinned that, despite tight, curly brown hair and full lips, people often failed to realize he had African blood, something he was proud of. He had serious eyes that rarely smiled and that self-confident, contained aura that fit the stereotype of a *Times* reporter. It turned out that Howard had been reading my articles and was impressed with my reputation of knowing the country, the language, the culture. "Would you like to be my stringer?" he asked.

"Yes," I said, too embarrassed to admit that I didn't know what a stringer was, but thrilled that the *Times* wanted me to work for them in any capacity. As soon as I got home, I called my journalist friend Mike, who was working for the *Washington Post*. "A stringer? It means you cover the region for him when he's not here," Mike explained. "You're like his eyes and ears. He could be in Cuba and something happens here, so he'll ask you to report on it.

"The *Times* is a bitch, though," he added. "If you aren't on their payroll full-time, they'll never give you credit. They'll just leave the byline blank, but expect you to do all the work."

I was flattered that Howard wanted me to work with him but I was ill at ease. He was nearly a foot taller than I was, but it wasn't just inches that created a distance between us. From the beginning I felt more like a secretary than a reporter. One of the first things he did was ask me to set up an interview with Aristide after Aristide entered the race.

Security was still tight at *Lafanmi* the day of the interview, but once Howard and I passed through the metal gate, I was heartened to hear the chatter and laughter of the boys inside. Although the piles of sand were gone, the courtyard hadn't changed much. A group of young boys played while another sat in the shade reading, serenaded by sounds of welding and hammering from the new workshop in the back. As opposed to the harsh and baffling treatment I received the last time, this time a friendly woman ushered us through the front entrance, a cast-iron grille that let in the sunlight.

She then escorted us to another room, where we waited patiently for about fifteen minutes, while I wondered what Aristide's reaction would be when he saw me. Was he thinking of the other Cathy, the American anthropologist he had expected instead of me that first time I made an appointment to interview him? Would he remember what happened and acknowledge it, or pretend we never met before?

When Aristide did appear, he smiled cordially as he entered the room, a more polished politician now, and he held out his hand. Neither of us made any reference to our last encounter, but we shook hands with an unspoken acknowledgment that this was not our first meeting. The interview was uneventful but frustrating. Aristide's flowery language, full of metaphors and parables, made quotes difficult if not impossible. Aristide was not someone who talked in sound bites. Well aware of Aristide's particular way of speaking, Howard didn't expect much from the interview, but asked me nonetheless to try to pull a usable quote from the taped interview that I was translating. It wasn't the language that gave me trouble, but finding a cohesive passage that would make sense to an American reader.

Interviewing Roger Lafontant several days later was as different as oil from water; both were slippery, but in their own unique ways. It was just after the Electoral Council—Haiti's ruling body that made all decisions regarding elections—rejected Lafontant's candidacy for president on a technicality, decreasing the number of candidates to fourteen. The government's July arrest warrant for Lafontant was still outstanding.

Howard and I were given a rendezvous point at an obscure clinic near the National Palace. We baked on the sizzling street, unsure what it was we were waiting for, until a driver and an armed guard pulled up in a four-wheel-drive, air-conditioned Toyota with tinted windows and told us in perfect English to get in. The driver took off on a series of back roads—done, I suspect, to confuse us. I assumed he thought we were foreign journalists who knew little or nothing about Haiti—so they would have had no way of knowing that I could understand their running conversation trashing Aristide—"the voice of the devil;" the international community—"ignorant exploiter"; and the United States—"sticking its ass where it doesn't belong." They insulted the Haitian people for their smell and their stupidity. I pinched my thumb between my first two fingers to calm myself and stayed silent.

A half hour later, we arrived at a typical nouveau riche house in the area of Delmas 31, known to be an area where former Macoutes lived. This suburb was completely different from my green area of Pacot. In Delmas, houses were white cement blocks arranged in asymmetrical, jarring patterns with irregular balconies, tinted glass, and small, scattered courtyards filled with plants and patio furniture—all hidden behind expansive metal gates, in contrast to Pacot's wooden gingerbreads with sprawling porches and porticos.

We pulled up to a large house and waited for the large metal gate to open. Just inside were clusters of men walking around with weapons—sidearms and bigger—the kind I had seen only on the television or movie screen before I came to Haiti. They were extremely impressive, and I stood a little closer to Howard. The air smelled stale despite the bougainvillea crawling along the front gate.

We walked through a heavily guarded, thick wooden doorway into a large-tiled foyer where a man with a rifle told us to wait, pointing to a row of wicker chairs. A few minutes later, Marjorie Robbins, a robust, gregarious Haitian who was responsible for setting up the interview, received us. She wore heavy makeup and her hair looked like starched straw, but she flashed us a warm, welcoming smile. In beautiful English, she offered us something to drink. "It's been so busy that it's hard to keep track of things," she chattered as she poured us the proverbial cup of Haitian coffee in tiny demitasse cups. "Everyone wants a chance to interview Monsieur Lafontant, and he wants to accommodate them, but his schedule is already so full.

"You know what it's like when you're so important." She winked.

Insisting on first names, Marjorie led us past another heavy wooden door into the living quarters, where we walked by more clusters of muscled young men sporting sunglasses and carrying even bigger weapons. They lined the stairs like balustrades, straight sentry-looking men who didn't blink as we passed them. Two of the biggest, meanest-looking guys stood guard outside a door just down the hall from the top of the stairs, one that I correctly assumed led to Lafontant. The former Macoute leader was sitting with his hands folded behind a large oak desk, dressed formally in a suit and tie. I expected him to look thuggish, like a gangster or something from Puzo's *The Godfather*, but the middle-aged man was all saccharine charm, and I distrusted him from the moment we walked in. His face was pumpkin shaped, wide in the middle, squarish on top—he had big white teeth that he flashed each time he smiled, but there was little that I found amusing. He laughed when we questioned him about his arrest warrant. "They've no right," he said dismissively. "It's all a plot."

"What plot would that be?" Howard asked.

"To ignore the will of the people," he said in typical double-talk. "In this election process, nothing is fair." We took that to mean that he—rather than "they"—plotted something to ensure his own victory, but like the interview with Aristide, there was little substance that came out of it. I kept waiting for him to pull out a machete or expose a pirate hook for a left hand. I left with the feeling I had as a kid when there was a bully on my team that I knew was toying with me but I had no wiggle room to escape. I couldn't wait to brush my teeth.

Tens of thousands of people gathered when Aristide hit the campaign trail, a stark contrast to the apathy the population had displayed just a week before. One day I drove the round-trip six-hour distance north to the seaside town of Gonaives just to confirm what other reporters were saying about the size of the crowds. I think the entire population of the country's third-largest city was there, and then some. It was the same elsewhere around the country—in Cap Haitien, Jacmel, Aux Cayes, and particularly in Port-au-Prince. People continued to crowd the streets just to get a glimpse of this divine intervention, the man who they believed would suddenly make it all right.

On December 5, just eleven days before the election, people were dancing in the streets after a political rally for Aristide when the lights suddenly went out. This wasn't uncommon, so there was little reaction and certainly no cause for alarm until there was an explosion and shots were fired. Panic ensued as people desperately fumbled in the dark trying to figure out what had happened. I was having dinner at the Oloffson Hotel with some other journalists, and didn't hear about it until later that night. Radio reports described how people fled the scene, screaming hysterically, but others flocked to help the wounded, stopping taxis and buses to transport the injured to hospitals. When there weren't vehicles available, kind citizens carried the victims on their shoulders and backs to get them medical assistance. The grenade killed seven people, wounded more than fifty others, and cost nearly a dozen people their limbs because the hospital didn't have the equipment to save them.

This was the first outbreak of violence since Aristide began his campaign one month earlier, but there was genuine concern that more could follow in the days leading up to the election. It was unclear who was behind the attack, though Aristide continued to ask for the enforcement of the July 10 arrest warrant for Roger Lafontant, who in turn accused Aristide of sabotaging his own rally. I didn't expect the investigation of this incident, if there even was one, to be any more judicious or successful than others that had occurred while I'd been living in Haiti.

The morning after the attack, Howard asked me to go to the hospital with the photographer and interview some of the victims for the *Times* while he collected other information for his story. It had been a while since I'd been to the State Hospital, but the smell of the sick brought back images of the dead I'd seen following the April uprising the year before. The photographer and I wandered into the main building, down a long, dark corridor into a ward filled with patients. We spotted a young man who appeared to be in his late teens, propped up against a pillow, a ratty sheet drawn over his legs. His hair was matted and his face looked tired, but his eyes were alert. He was wearing a once-white T-shirt with an image of Aristide now splashed with swatches of dried blood. The young man's hands, heavily bandaged in white gauze, lay at his side. When he saw the cameras swinging over the photographer's shoulder, he smiled slightly, beckoning for us to come closer.

His voice was soft, barely audible amidst the clatter in the ward. Around him visitors moved in and out of the room indiscriminately; patients moaned in distress. I bent down to get closer to this young man and his smile widened.

"*Pa gen danje,*" he said: No problem here. In a smooth, steady voice he talked about the horror of the grenade attack. "No matter what kind of weapons these assassins use—guns, bombs, grenades— they can't kill us all. There are too many of us and we are stronger than them."

This young man was racked with pain but I didn't detect any sign of distress—rather, his injury seemed to provide him with comfort. "Aristide's the key to our future," he said, and held up his bandaged limbs where his hands used to be, as if in victory, before pressing them against his heart as the photographer snapped one photo after another, capturing the blood, bandages, bravery.

As I wondered silently what would happen once the press left town and this young man, like so many other victims of this attack, realized he faced a future with no hands, a young man in a kelly green doctor's robe came into the room. A long line of people followed him—family members of victims wanting counsel, comfort, and advice. He walked over to the bed of one woman who had been whimpering since we arrived. He picked up her chart from the bottom of the bed and snapped for a nurse to assist him, before realizing that there was none. With a sigh of resignation, he walked out of the room, then returned with a plastic bag of alcohol swabs. He dabbed at the bloody wounds on the young woman's arm, creating a sterile spot. Then he pulled out a vial, inserted a clean needle, and filled it with a yellow liquid before inserting it in the woman's arm. I waited until he was done before speaking to him.

"How difficult is it to work under these conditions?" I asked, stating the obvious.

"Do you see any other doctors here? Nurses? Someone to sweep up the debris on the ground, get me bandages, sterilize the needles? We can't take care of the sick under normal circumstances; how can we respond in a crisis? Do we have the space to care for these new victims? Do we have the medical supplies we need? Do we have a way to protect ourselves from infection? Contamination?" He held out his hands, pointing to his doctor's gown, stained with medicine and blood.

"We are trained to help people and we can't. There are doctors who wouldn't set foot in the general hospital, but I do, and I try my best to help my patients. Sometimes I feel that amounts to nothing." He pointed to the woman he had just treated. "She's going to have severe burns over most of her body. There's little I can do for that, but there's no medical reason for her to lose her foot. Since we can't take care of her here, we should fly her somewhere that can. Who is going to pay for that? How am I going to sleep at night knowing I performed an amputation on a limb that could have been saved?"

He turned toward his patient as she let out a cry of pain. Her body shuddered. Her burns were so severe that she couldn't move without disturbing the skin, immobilized further by a makeshift traction device that kept her right foot suspended. When the doctor looked back at me again, something had softened. His eyes were heavy. "All I can do is give her a shot for the pain and something to help her sleep. What kind of doctor am I?

"And what kind of father am I that I work without any gloves, without any protection to make sure that I don't become infected with who knows what?"

I watched him walk away to treat his next patient, the trail of people still behind him, and left the photographer to capture the story that might best be told by pictures.

On Election Day, I left my house while it was still dark. Jean Raymond was in a sound sleep, heaving big, cavernous, grunts that came deep within his belly. I kissed him on the forehead and left a note that I wouldn't be back until much later that night. I drove through deserted streets toward the downtown Holiday Inn on the Champs de Mars Square where Howard was staying. I passed other journalists who were padded down with notebooks, cameras, lenses, tripods, and other paraphernalia required in our line of work. They were also filling their pockets with croissants and their canteens with water, gulping coffee as they headed off to do their job of reporting.

Howard asked me to visit some polling stations in select parts of the city. In the quiet of the dawn, I noticed more than the lack of activity and a stray voter moving toward a polling place. The mounds of stinking garbage that had polluted the streets for months were absent. I rolled down my window. Instead of smelling the stagnant piles of sewage water, I inhaled the crispness of the morning air, the freshly washed streets, a scent as welcoming as an unexpected shower on a hot summer day. All around me were altars of painted rocks, tree branches, paper banners, and other homemade decorations. Telephone polls, tree trunks, sidewalks, gates, and brick walls shone with fresh layers of red and blue paint, the color of Haiti's flag. Murals of Titid and his rooster emblem, alongside fluttering flags, were as plentiful as the piles of garbage had been. The rising sun shone its first ray of hope on the voters as they made their way to the polls.

The difference in the streets of Cité Soleil, the largest urban slum in the Western Hemisphere, was as dramatic as a tree blooming overnight. For the first time ever, I could actually see the surface I was driving on. The houses along the main road were lined with more altars, and the words *Titid, nou renmen ou, Kòk Kalite* (Titid, we love you, Quality Rooster) were spelled out in brightly painted pebbles, tin cans, cardboard, and dominoes. Candles and oil lamps threw dancing images on the miniature shrines, lining the way for the voters queuing at the Center Square.

"We'll stay until we vote, no matter how long that takes," said one woman whose gray hair was pulled back in a bandana made from a Haitian flag. "I'm an old woman and I've never voted in my life. Today is the day for *Kòk Kalite*."

"I left my children at home with my sister. I'm older, so she's letting me vote first," said the young man in front of her. "I got up at 4:00 A.M. this morning so I could be first in line, and still there are dozens of people in front of me."

Workers at the Cité Soleil polling station were frustrated because they hadn't received their ballots, but the voters didn't seem to mind the wait. I got back in my car and drove to other stations to see the voting process; some had workers but no ballots, others had ballots but no workers, but there was no dearth of voters. Many electoral employees were using candles to unpack their equipment; others had stoked lanterns or thrown open wooden shutters to let in the creeping sunlight. Some already had their ballot boxes set up; others had workers behind screens helping voters fill out the complicated five-part ballot where voters had to choose a president, two senators, a deputy, a three-person mayoral slate, and a local representative. I traveled up and down the northern highway, taking side trips down long dirt roads in search of *BIV* signs, Voter Registration Bureau.

Along the way I passed international observers and other journalists with their large *LAISSER PASSER* (allow to pass) permits pasted on their windshields. Some of the more cautious journalists had used tape to spell out PRESS on the top and sides of their car, others wore necklaces of press identification. There was still the lingering fear from the violent 1987 elections, when the military shot first at voters, then at journalists. But I wasn't fearful, in part because things had been so bad for so long, and now, for the first time since I started reporting in Haiti, there was something to be really hopeful about. I didn't feel the need, as other foreign journalists did, to travel in groups because I didn't have a sense of imminent danger. Over time I had gained confidence—whether or not it was justified—of my read of a situation and the risk of danger. I always made sure whenever I parked that I had an exit plan mapped out before I even stepped out of the car; and because of what happened to Jean-Marie, I paid close attention to the vehicles around me. This was a skill that I would have had no need of acquiring in the States, but was invaluable in Haiti. As in the old Western movies, I always sat with my back to the wall, faced the door of any public place I was in, and was hypersensitive to where the exits were. I didn't expect other journalists who hadn't worked in Haiti or other war-prone countries to behave like this, and selfishly I didn't want to be responsible for other journalists. I didn't know how someone else might react in a crowd that could inadvertently put me in danger. I was more at ease than ever on my own, swept up in the same stream of goodwill and positive energy that blanketed the voters, the pollers, and some of the Haitian journalists.

As I continued my rounds, I returned periodically to Cité Soleil. Each time, the line was longer, the sun hotter, and the central polling station still hadn't yet opened. But smiles and patience were in abundance that day; voters were determined to cast their ballot for democracy.

I headed back to the Holiday Inn about 1:00 P.M., feeling rather pleased with how the morning had gone. The restaurant was crammed with observers and journalists trading stories, filing information on their computers, talking into their tape recorders. This was the hub where observations would be transformed into news for the rest of the world to consume later in the day, tomorrow, in the weeks and months to come, when the viability of democracy would be challenged. Overall the reports were the same: minor irregularities but no sign of organized fraud.

I was on the *New York Times* payroll that week, but was also filing for the *Christian Science Monitor* radio and newspaper. Between bites of a green bean-and-tomato salad, I joined dozens of other journalists who were compiling radio reports. After lunch, Howard had me work the phones, gathering figures and recording official statements, then sent me back out to see how things were progressing. In Cité Soleil, voters were finally exiting the polling stations, holding up their ink-stained finger as proof they'd completed the voting process. An older gentleman wearing yellow flip-flops and a guyabara winked when he saw me writing in my reporter's notebook. "*Kòk Kalite*," he said, repeating the most oft-used phrase of the day. I smiled along with him.

Howard had to file his story at the same time the polls closed, so I was free to work on my story for the *Monitor* newspaper the rest of the day. I left the Holiday Inn and headed toward Mache Salamon, a congested district just south of the hotel. The streets had emptied but were still clean and fresh. I chose a polling station where the counting process was just getting underway. The sun was barely visible when I got there, but as the hours progressed and the natural light disappeared, election-day workers used flashlights and candles to go through the complicated tallying process. At the front of the room, electoral officials stood behind five different boxes, one for each office: president, senator, deputy, mayor, and local representative. On the other side of the small, cramped space were the delegates from the political parties, electoral observers, and one other Haitian journalist. A designated electoral official took each ballot from the box and held it up for the party proxies and observers to see. Then he called out the result, while another official recorded it. The process was continual until the box was empty; then another box was brought forward and the whole procedure repeated from the beginning. When the results were all in, the tally sheet, boxes, and ballots were carted off to the departmental electoral station. I stayed until this process was complete, recording the results. In this polling station of 404 registered voters that I observed, Aristide was the winner.

I was weary, tired, and hungry when I got home. Jean Raymond was out, but he had left me a salad and a tall glass of freshly squeezed grapefruit juice. I nibbled while I wrote my *Monitor* piece, scribbled a quick note of thanks to Jean Raymond, changed the batteries and cassette in my tape recorder, and fell into bed with my clothes on, too tired to shower away the day's grime.

The sun and I were up together. The news was full of electoral stories from across the country—minor irregularities, but overall elections were declared free and democratic, the first in Haiti's 186-year history. Estimates of more than 70 percent of the population participated. I took notes, then began writing the first of several radio pieces I was scheduled to deliver that morning.

The first radio station called promptly at 9:00 A.M. I stared out the open window at the gently swaying almond tree, intoxicated by the previous day's success. I recited my piece without missing a beat. It was unusually quiet as I delivered my second radio spot with equal ease. The text flowed as easily as warm honey. In contrast to the majority of pieces I wrote, nothing about this story was complicated. It was as straightforward as sewing a seam. And for once, it seemed to have a happy conclusion.

At 10:00 A.M. I received a call from a small Haitian radio station in New York that wanted an interview in English for their listeners who didn't speak Creole. Just as I started, I heard a noise through the window that was hard to identify. It sounded like the swell of a wave—the approach of a storm—but the skies were clear and the sun was out. I tried to concentrate on the questions coming over the phone line but was distracted by the crescendo. It wasn't that I couldn't hear myself speak, but my curiosity made it hard to concentrate. As quickly as I could, I finished the interview, grabbed my tape recorder and notebook, and headed downtown.

I didn't get very far. The roads were so congested with people that I had to ditch my car on a side road where I got caught up in what can truly be called a *lavalas*. From treetops, rooftops, telephone and electricity poles, men, women, and children chanted "*Titid, Titid, Titid*." The noise was deafening. It was like being in the middle of a tidal wave. There were toothy smiles, toothless smiles, one-sided grins, and high-fives of congratulations. I had no choice about the direction I wanted to go; the force of the crowd pushed me along like a pebble in a whitewater rapid.

Someone yelled, "*Hey, blan*" and stuck out a hand from an open window. I grabbed it and hoisted myself up into a living room, where a young man led me out the side door and up onto his roof. There was no more street, sidewalk, or city—just a massive sea of people, tens of thousands of them dancing in celebration. Many had broken off tree branches and were waving them as a symbol of delight, in the tradition of Mardi Gras. Old men who could barely walk pumped their hips, front and back, side to side. Market women abandoned their wares, their straw hats, their reserve, wiggling their bodies with a newfound freedom paralleling the new liberty of their country.

From windowsills and treetops music blared amongst Haitian flags and slogans in support of Aristide. I couldn't distinguish one sound from another, but the cumulative effect was breathtaking. This was their day of victory and they were going to make it count. I high-fived the young man who gave me the bird's-eye view and climbed back down the roof to join the crowd. I wanted to smell the sweat of success, of hope and optimism. I didn't care about being an impartial journalist, at that point I just wanted to celebrate, too. I joined arms with a weathered old man who walked beside me crying tears of joy. "I can die in peace now," he said with a broad smile. "I've cast my ballot for democracy."

I wandered back to my car with a smile that filled the street. Americans never feel that way when they vote, and to be a part of this euphoria was as powerful as a volcanic blast. The collective energy carried me like a magic carpet; blues and greens dominated over the dank, dark pockets of poverty and destitution that had just a few days ago seemed institutionalized, permanent. Now the country was awash with hope. For the first time since I came to Haiti, I thought, maybe—just maybe—things might get better.

In the early hours of January 7, 1991, just three weeks later, I woke to the sound of the telephone ringing. Had I been in Haiti, I would immediately have suspected a coup d'état, but Jean Raymond and I were on vacation in the States on a much-needed break after the intense hours I'd been working covering the election. But I should have known that a call in the middle of the night could mean only one thing now that I was involved with Haiti. It was a friend wanting me to know that Roger Lafontant and like-minded Duvalierists had just forced Ertha Pascal Trouillot to step down as interim president before Aristide was to take office. Armed thugs had taken control of the government's few available armored vehicles and were driving around shooting at people. Lafontant proclaimed himself president on national radio.

I immediately called friends and fellow journalists in Haiti, who by then were reporting that people had spontaneously taken to the streets to quell the coup. In a massive outpour of support, millions rushed to set up burning barricades all over the country. The army waited several hours and reacted only after barricades every few hundred yards had paralyzed the entire country.

Two days later, we saw some of the damage the crowd inflicted as we flew into Port-au-Prince. The mob had destroyed hundreds of businesses and private homes of leading Duvalierists, the papal nuncio, and the Interior Ministry. It also burned Haiti's Old Cathedral, built in 1761, because the protestors thought that the right-wing archbishop was hiding there. At least thirty people died and twice as many were wounded in just three days. This destruction was something I couldn't understand. In a country with so few resources, it seemed criminal to dismantle what was there. But that was looking at it from the perspective of someone who had—there was no way I could get into the mind of someone who grew up not having. The rage that the majority of the population had against the wealthy was only beginning to be expressed.

Months later, Roger Lafontant and twenty-one others went to trial for conspiring against the State for that January 7, 1991, attempted coup d'état. Lafontant and seventeen others were sentenced to life imprisonment with hard labor, even though the maximum penalty for such a crime was fifteen years. Four others received ten-year sentences.

Marjorie Robbins, the only woman who was arrested in the palace at that time, was granted a separate trial. She argued that when Lafontant telephoned her to come to the palace in the middle of the night, she was only doing her job by following orders. The judge ruled that her story wasn't credible.

The day after Jean Raymond and I returned from our brief vacation in New York, Aristide gave a press conference. In fact, he gave four consecutive ones, thirty minutes each, in Creole, French, English, and Spanish. Looking presidential in a suit and tie, he winked at me as I sat in on three of them. "*Jodi-a wap pwofite,*" he said to me in reference to my language skills: "Today you have the advantage."

There was considerable difference in the atmosphere and content of each press conference. I didn't attend the Spanish one, but the Haitian journalists asked questions that were provincial and personality oriented. The English-speaking journalists were confrontational and provocative, focusing on the relationship between Aristide and the U.S. government. The French-speaking journalists posed questions that were more philosophical than practical. The answers were all of the flowery, vague genre, full of parables and symbols, leaving much for interpretation. Aristide was not easy to translate or decipher.

On January 14, three days before the legislative runoffs for those candidates that did not receive 50 percent of the vote in the first round, the Electoral Council released the official results. They were no surprises—the unofficial results had been obvious since the day after the election. Aristide received 67.48 percent. His closest rival, Marc Bazin, obtained just 14.22 percent.

"Use the symbol of the bouquet of flowers on the table," Aristide said at his victory press conference the next day. "Draw the parallel to a well-watered garden. That's what happened with *lavalas,* and the flowers stand as a tribute to that and the approaching democracy. Flowers of mobilization, flowers of democracy, liberty, justice, and solidarity that will never be absent again."

▲ ▲ ▲

Less than a week before the inauguration, the phone rang again in the middle of the night. I silently congratulated myself on getting in the habit of placing the cordless phone next to my bed, so habitual were these routine interruptions from a solid night's sleep. "It can't be another coup," I said to Jean Raymond before answering. "Who would be behind this one?"

"It's Haiti, Kathie," he said, and put a pillow over his head.

"Fire at *Lafanmi Selavi*," said a journalist friend of mine.

I jumped out of bed, thinking I should rush over to get firsthand information, but Jean Raymond persuaded me to wait until morning. We had recently learned that I was pregnant, and therefore subject to many Haitian superstitions about having a baby. "*Pa fèm sote pandan map domi pou Bondye pa deranje pandan lap fè travay li a*: Don't startle me from sleep or you will disturb the area that God is working." Before I drifted back to a fitful sleep, Jean Raymond warned me not to roll over him during the night. If I wanted to get up on his side of the bed, I had to walk around it; otherwise I would transmit my labor pains to him. I tried rolling over him just to make a point, but I never succeeded—even in a deep sleep, he sensed my movement and held me in his arms to keep me still. Haitian folklore aside, the thought of my pregnancy was enough to keep me awake regardless. I was nervous and thrilled at the thought of having a child. I had the sense—as I assumed most pregnant mothers did— that my life was about to change permanently, but given how unpredictable things in my life had been and how planning for anything in Haiti was impossible, I tried to let go of any anxiety. I also had enough sense to know that I had to be willing to do most—if not all—of the parenting on my own, despite Jean Raymond's insistence that he was going to be an active parent. Men in general, and Haitian men in particular, were not, as far I could tell, reliable when it came to picking up the parental slack.

Early-morning radio reports provided only sketchy details of the attack. I dressed quickly, making sure not to tie a belt around my waist, so that the fetus wouldn't feel pressure and be crippled. The damage to *Lafanmi Selavi* wasn't visible from the front of the building—the arsonists had thrown the firebomb into the dormitory in the rear. In the dark of the night, exacerbated by a blackout, the boys struggled to find an escape route while the rescue team groped to find a way in. Four children died. When I learned this, I rubbed my stomach, all the more grateful for the life I was carrying. The charred building was an eerie reminder of Aristide's church, St. Jean Bosco, which had been burned just two years earlier. Aristide's face was tight with pain as he surveyed the damage and offered words of support and condolence to the boys, their families, and neighbors. Most of the boys wandered around with dazed looks of confusion and shock.

The funeral was held a few days later at the Sacre Coeur church, halfway between my house and *Lafanmi Selavi*. Ayiti, Eril, Ti Claude, and Ti David, unsure of their role but wanting to be part of the memorial, skulked around outside, looking as stunned as the rest of the crowd. The *Lafanmi* boys living there shuffled inside en masse and ushers led them to the pews in front. Floral wreaths covered the coffins that lay before them in a neat row, one after the other. The boys stared at them indiscriminately, chatting idly, picking unconsciously at their hair, their clothes, each other. Aristide sat in the front near the pulpit, the military commander to his left.

Serami, a sixteen-year-old boy from *Lafanmi* that I'd befriended, beckoned me over when I walked in, planting a warm kiss on each cheek.

"*Mwen kontan wew,*" he said in the traditional greeting: "I'm happy to see you."

"*Mwen menm tou,*" I answered: Me, too. "I looked all over for you that morning and couldn't find you. I was so worried. Are you okay?"

"I'm lucky," he answered. "I was sleeping in another room."

Serami used to live in the other *Lafanmi* residence of Tabarre, a rural area northwest of the capital, but after a recent knee operation the doctor recommended that he recuperate at *Lafanmi*'s Port-au-Prince dormitory rather than the rural domicile.

"Look at these kids." Serami rubbed his hands together nervously. "Some of them are so messed up they don't understand what's going on. For them the firebomb is just one more fucked-up event in their lives.

"But for those kids who do understand, it's worse," he continued. "They know that the best way to attack Aristide is to attack us." The same thing that Ayiti had said to me a year earlier. Didn't anything in Haiti change?

Nothing, however, stopped the inauguration. The cleanup that took place December 16 was foreplay for February 7. No part of the country was without a mural, a poem, a portrait of Aristide. Red and blue paint decorated everything, from houses to rocks to fences and metal gates. Port-au-Prince even benefited from long hours of electricity, something it hadn't had in months.

The daylong procession started at the Legislative Palace, worked its way up to the Port-au-Prince Cathedral, then continued to the palace. It was serious and festive at once, with speculations about Haiti's future. Journalists from all over the world came to witness Haiti's first democratic government take office.

I took my place among them, in part feeling like an impostor. I was only part journalist. With the growth of a baby in my stomach, my future was forged with that of Haiti's. I held my secret tight as officials herded us to a designated area on the grassy palace lawn. I was not to tell my parents or friends I was pregnant because if I did, the *lougawou* (werewolf) would suck the blood of the fetus. Tired of standing, I bent my knees to sit, only to remember "*Nan premye mwa fòmasyon timoun nan, pa chita ba paske van ka antre epi fè tèt timoun nan gwo:* Don't sit too low because wind can enter you and make your child's head big." I couldn't stop the litany of advice from playing like a broken record in my head: don't eat *graten,* the scrapings at the bottom of the pot, considered a delicacy in Haiti or I would have a bald-headed child, *tèt kale*; if I eat salt, my feet will swell. I was told to drink out of only things with small lids so my child would have a small, delicate mouth, but Haitians winked at that one and said they didn't do this, which is why so many of them had full lips.

Tens of thousands of people lined the streets around the palace on February 7, 1991, five years to the day after the departure of the Duvalier dictatorship. They were unconcerned by the intense midday sun. Vendors hawked flags, buttons, and plastic-covered wallet-sized pictures of Aristide that doubled as key chains. Aristide broadcast his inaugural address over a loudspeaker system so everyone outside the palace courtyard could hear, rattling off the names of key army generals he wanted removed. He played a game of musical chairs with lower-ranking officers, transferring those who were known human-rights abusers to isolated areas around the country. He promoted officers and privates who had suffered abuse while serving under former military President Avril and upgraded the head of the Electoral Security Committee, Colonel Raoul Cédras, to major general.

Seven months later, on the very day that I went into labor, General Cédras led a military coup that killed several hundred people, sent President Aristide into exile, and consolidated his power for what turned out to be three long, violent, and devastating years of military rule. The coincidental timing just further solidified my bond to Haiti.

Chapter VI

Motherhood

Omlet pa fèt san kase ze.
Omelets aren't made without cracking eggs.

While Aristide was fighting for his political life, I was giving birth at a hospital in San Francisco, where I'd decided to deliver. I hadn't trusted the medical care in Haiti, and I wanted to be close to my family in the States. I also wanted a chance to get used to the whole business of mothering in the comfort of my San Francisco home, so I'd terminated the contract with the woman subletting my house so I could finish up the last six weeks of pregnancy there.

Sucking his fist, my son weighed in at eight pounds, twelve ounces. He had fair skin, brown eyes, and a head of curly hair. His name was Kadja, taken from a Vodou chant I'd learned from Jean Raymond. Although I didn't understand the meaning of the text as I sang to him while he suckled—*Kadja, Kadja, nou tande, Kebyesou danle*—it

seemed right that our child should have such a name, lyrical and spiritual, and that it be sung to him no matter where we were living.

That first night, as I wrapped Kadja in his white blanket with baby
blue and powder pink stripes, General Raoul Cédras and his men
assassinated the chief of Aristide's Presidential Guard in Port-au-
Prince. International diplomats negotiated to spare Aristide a bloody
death as the military forced the president from the National Palace to
their headquarters before exiling him to Venezuela. That same night
Roger Lafontant was killed in his jail cell; others, including Marjorie
Robbins, escaped.

The next few days were a blur. I was overwhelmed with the joys
and responsibilities of motherhood, but it was impossible not to be
distracted. I woke up at 3:00 A.M. unsure whether it was from Kadja's
whimpers or my anxiety about Haiti and those we'd left behind. Jean
Raymond changed from an anxious father to a depressed exile.
Choosing the name of our baby was, in fact, the last carefree thing he
did. While I had hoped to be a happy family unit, we were anything
but. Isolated from his country and all that was familiar to him, he vac-
illated between joy and depression, but I felt his anguish more than his
elation. He went through the motions of being a father, but he was
distant, his behavior erratic. The first weekend home from the San
Francisco hospital, he went for a walk and returned eight hours later,
unable to say where he'd been. We lived miles from the Pacific Ocean,
but his shoes were covered with sand. He threw a fit when he wasn't
able to watch a particular boxing match because we didn't have the
right cable connection, or when we ran out of the kind of rice he preferred in making *diri djonn djonn*, Haiti's traditional rice-and-mushroom
dish. He didn't express what was going on in his head and didn't want
me asking. This wasn't unusual, but in Haiti we had a rhythm for
dealing with our problems; we knew how to maneuver to get around

them so that we could function and work through them. It was a maze we'd navigated so often that it had become routine. But in San Francisco we had none of that. Jean Raymond was like a palm tree slowly dying from the fog, the winds—a tropical bud unable to bloom. Haiti was his oxygen, and without it he was suffocating right there in front of me.

He handled Kadja like china, worried that if he applied too much pressure our son would break into a thousand shards of glass. "So tiny," he said, as he plucked Kadja from the bureau drawer I'd set up as his makeshift bed; and then, as though he couldn't help himself, he added, "and so white."

Kadja was closer to my Mediterranean olive than Jean Raymond's coffee-cream skin, but everything else was from his dad; his curly hair, short waist, short nose, exceptionally small fingers and toes. Oddly enough, I hadn't thought about his skin color—I wasn't particularly anxious about anything regarding the pregnancy other than delivering a healthy baby, and after several years of being with Jean Raymond, the difference in our skin tone was as inconsequential as the color of our eyes. So it was a shock to me when my sister warned my nieces and nephews: "Don't be surprised if the baby doesn't look like your aunt." It was a poignant reminder that we were, indeed, a biracial family.

When Jean Raymond wasn't holding Kadja, changing diapers, or helping around the house—at my constant prodding, rather than his own initiative—he was on the phone. He craved news directly from Haiti, and getting it was nearly impossible; phone lines were constantly busy. When we did get through, calls were often interrupted or the line went dead. A film of paranoia sealed Haiti overnight—even my closest confidants didn't want to say much for fear of reprisal from tapped phone lines or newly paid informants on the military payroll that now lurked in the shadows. I spoke with Gisele frequently, but fear dripped across the wires. Normally upbeat and positive, her voice was an octave lower and filled with an anxiety I could imagine. Fortunately, she and her family were safe, but she didn't know about the store or its employees. She hadn't been able to get downtown and said she thought it would be a while before she'd be open for business again. I ached in sympathy with her pain.

Editors from various radio stations and newspapers from the States and Canada that I had been working with before I left Haiti called me in San Francisco asking for news and names of those who might be sources for them. I felt frustrated and resentful. This period of giving birth to a precious, healthy, and happy baby boy should have been the most extraordinary period in my life, but it was cut short less than twenty-four hours after delivery because of the coup. While I was thrilled with the wonders of being a mother and took delight from such simple pleasures as watching Kadja breathe in his sleep, I begrudged the world that I was missing the biggest story since Duvalier's departure. The stress took its toll. I lost forty pounds in a week and barely slept more than three hours at a stretch.

Jean Raymond continued to share Haitian folklore even after the birth, encouraging me not to eat avocados, tomatoes, mangoes, eggplant, peanut butter, and white food (like milk and the whites of eggs) because the leftover tissue and lining from the pregnancy might leak out as white secretion. He cautioned me about the first bath for both Kadja and myself.

"You have to use special herbs," he insisted, but I didn't know how to translate the names he rattled off, and I wasn't inclined to visit the local botanicas in San Francisco's Hispanic Mission District. I sensed his disappointment when I ended up taking a bath with plain old city water. Even that was a fight. He wanted to wash Kadja in cold water because he believed it would make his skin strong and tough, but I feared Kadja would catch pneumonia. On a routine house visit arranged by the hospital, the midwife persuaded Jean Raymond that warm water had its own merits and supervised us closely as we held our son's tiny body over the bassinet and sprinkled water over his soft cafe latté skin.

"I'm a man without a home," Jean Raymond complained one morning, a few weeks later. It was the start of winter; the days were short and often cloudy. The nights were nippy, requiring clothes we didn't have to keep warm.

"Aren't we your home?" I asked, my feelings hurt.

"That's not the point." He wanted sympathy, not logic. "San Francisco isn't where we're supposed to be."

We had planned the timing of our trip back to the States to give birth with precision. I'd made arrangements with my San Francisco tenant to move out by August so that we would have the house to ourselves; in October she was to take it back as we were going to my younger sister's wedding in New York, then planned to continue directly to Port-au-Prince. Factoring in the coup made our immediate future unsettling. I didn't know just how long it would take for things to stabilize in Haiti, and until I felt comfortable with the news I was hearing, I wasn't willing to risk moving to such uncertainty with a newborn.

"Since there's nothing we can do about that, the least we can do is make the most of our time here." But my words were as vaporous as passing clouds. No matter what I said, I couldn't reach Jean Raymond. He shut a door, bitter and lonely in his new surroundings. He was grumpy and ill-tempered more often than not. I felt as lost with him as he felt in the States.

Our three-month stay in California turned into sixteen months as disturbing news of what was going on in Haiti continued. It was challenging enough to cope with the newness of being a mother; I couldn't see complicating that with all the inconveniences Haiti normally presented, to say nothing of the new dangers posed by the military dictatorship.

The nicest part of being back in San Francisco was reconnecting with my family. My mom was now living just a few miles from my sister in Los Altos, an hour's drive south, and I saw both of them frequently. They walked me through the diapering process, breastfeeding, nail clipping, and swaddling. They listened when I complained about Haiti and shared in my motherhood joys. Reacquainting myself with my nieces and nephews took no time at all—for them, Kadja was their newest toy.

I was able to return to work part-time for the nonprofit I'd been involved with before I left for Haiti three years earlier. Caribbean Exchange had morphed into Global Exchange. And I was able to spend a lot of time with my close women friends, who, while unfamiliar with Haiti, understood how hard the whole adjustment was. They were available for me during the frequent trips Jean Raymond made to New York, where his fellow band members had settled, and understood when I didn't call for a few days each time he came back, usually refreshed but never satisfied. I wanted to be able to fix his angst, but I was helpless. He woke each morning itching for fresh mangoes, ripe avocados, and eggs that had real flavor—not the oversized tasteless variety from the local Safeway. He wanted to warm up the engine of his jeep, wipe the proverbial Port-au-Prince dust from his windshield, and drive to Bas Peu de Chose, the neighborhood where he'd grown up, to chat with his friends. His day started best when he caught up on the gossip of the night before, and found out what the word was on the street. Happiness for him was being able to continue this routine, simple and familiar. But it was impossible to do anywhere other than Haiti.

Therein lay the ultimate conflict because, instead of having Haiti, he had just Kadja and me. Although his resentment wasn't aimed at us, it felt like a rash that wouldn't go away. I urged him to get involved in something, anything that could provide him relief from his own thoughts, which were consuming him; but the more I pushed, the more he rejected. His face became drawn, his shoulders slouched; he wore the same clothes for days at a time. Despite our efforts to find common ground, it was growing increasingly apparent that the only way our relationship would survive was for us to return to Port-au-Prince. Life in the States proved too much of a challenge for him—not just with the language, but also with overcoming his feelings of utter isolation. His lovely face aged with despair.

"What can I do to make it easier for you?" I asked after one of his habitual three-hour afternoon naps. I knew it was hard for him to be thousands of miles away from anything familiar, in a country where he had no friends and family outside Kadja and me and didn't speak the language. He had no musician friends with whom he could jam, no gigs. He felt alone and lonely most of the time. Sleep was a respite, and while I understood that, I also had to be careful that I didn't act resentful, because in the end I was carrying more than my share of parenting, driving, translating, shopping. He shut me out when I complained, not wanting to acknowledge that he was negligent, or suffering from depression.

"Nothing," he said, turning away.

"But it's not normal, how much time you spend sleeping," I said, like the nagging bitch I didn't want to be.

"Not normal for whom?" he said, slamming the door on his way to the garage, where he had set up his drum set. The only time he seemed happy was when he was drumming. Or painting. Though he'd never handled a paintbrush in his life, he took to design and color as though it were a rhythm, exploring and manipulating until he achieved just the right balance. He painted his way across the canvas with the same confidence a miner feels in the dark. His paintings reflected Vodou in their theme and colors, a manifestation of the ceremonies he wasn't playing in, the services he wished he was participating in, the country he wished he was living in.

There were periods when we forgot our troubles, though they were sporadic and short-lived. We spent a week in the Bear Valley mountains north of San Francisco, where we went on early-morning hikes and late-night stargazing picnics. We drove over the Golden Gate Bridge to Sausalito for Sunday brunch, where we lost ourselves in mimosas and bouillabaisse, Kadja cooing contentedly at our side. We took the ferry to Alcatraz Island and had a picnic of crusty French bread and Napa Valley wine. We drove along the coast for short overnights at Big Sur, Pescadero, Mendocino. Gisele came for a week, and we took her on a tour of the city, letting her rest in a way she hadn't been able to since the coup. She bonded with Kadja like a cat with her kittens, and helped us feel a little bit closer to Haiti and what was happening there.

On days we stayed close to our San Francisco home, we put Kadja in the stroller and explored local coffeeshops, used bookstores, and secondhand baby stores. Rollerblading was a bust, but Jean Raymond mastered miniature golf and developed an insatiable craving for Thai food.

Kadja and I spent a lot of time together when Jean Raymond was physically away, or emotionally withdrawn. He was an easy baby, and I had no complaints about motherhood. I surprised myself by how much I reveled in it, and was grateful every single day that I was able to provide my son with everything that he needed, from kisses to Kleenex. Never far from my thoughts, however, were the street kids—Ti David, Ayiti, Eril, Fatil, Wawa. I couldn't imagine what their lives were like, where they were living, how they were surviving. I cried when I heard the news that arsonists destroyed the records and carpentry shops housed in the main building of *Lafanmi Selavi*. The wooden administration building was completely ravaged. The room where I interviewed Aristide burned to the ground. About 125 boys were sleeping on the premises the night of the arson but no one was hurt.

Exiled President Aristide, who eventually migrated from Venezuela to Washington D.C., toured several cities on the West Coast in the beginning of 1992, including Oakland. He didn't travel frequently, but he was trying to gather national support that he could translate into effective diplomatic pressure on the American government to take a more active role in ending the Haitian crisis. Ironic, really, that the man who had been such an anti-imperialist zealot was now dependent on the U.S. administration for his survival, politically and physically.

The Bay Area's Diaspora, along with a group of concerned citizens and like-minded activists, formed a host committee to plan Aristide's visit. The committee asked me to speak at the main event, albeit for three minutes, but I was thrilled to be selected; Maya Angelou and Danny Glover were also part of the event.

Aristide's entourage was large and official-looking when it arrived in San Francisco International, and the energy was high from a wild crowd of boisterous, chanting supporters who came to greet him. But there was something surreal about his being there, too. He seemed smaller than before, his stature deflated. He waved to the crowd, his drooping eye juxtaposed against his wide, ebullient, but still-sad smile. He barely had time to wave to the crowd before the organizers shuffled him off to a meeting with local leaders, then the press. There, we greeted each other, he addressing me by name and in Creole—on many levels, that pleased me, not the least of which was the status it gave me among the local journalists, but also that I could converse easily now with Aristide in his native tongue. And that, despite of or because of our history and the current circumstances, we had a relationship of some undefined nature that had transcended time.

Over 800 people attended the evening reception the next day. I was nervous. I'd never spoken before a large crowd before and was unsure what tone to set. I tried to strike a balance between being a professional journalist and an American witness to the country's transformation when Aristide announced his candidacy. I memorized my speech and got through it without a single blip. Afterward, I shook hands with everyone on the podium, including Aristide, who pulled me closer as I approached him. He whispered to me, quietly: "That was beautiful. I am so grateful." And softer still he added: "I will never forget how wrong I was the first time we met at *Lafanmi Selavi*."

"That was many years ago," I replied, shaking from the excitement, the applause, the president's words. "Something we can put behind us."

"Yes, behind us," he said, and we never spoke of that incident again.

It wasn't just the country's insecurity that kept us from returning to Haiti. Kadja had developed a breathing problem, which in the end was not serious; but until the test results were complete, we couldn't go anywhere.

There was another problem—Jean Raymond's visa, which had expired a few months earlier. We were aware of the expiration date when we left Haiti, but because we had every intention of returning immediately after Kadja's birth, we hadn't taken care of it before we left for San Francisco. Now, with the coup and subsequent closing of the U.S. consulate in Port-au-Prince, we faced a different situation. Returning immediately after the birth would have been irresponsible, I thought, given everything that was going on, and as time lapsed so did Jean Raymond's visa.

"I could just go back to Haiti," he said. "That way there's no problem when I reapply."

"And when would that be?" I countered. "The consulate could be closed for months—there's no way to know when it will open. Are you that anxious to go back that you don't care how long it would be before you see Kadja and me?"

"Don't take it so personally," he said defensively.

"Don't take it personally?" I replied. "Is there any other way to take it?

"What other option do we have? Marriage?" he asked.

The question took me by surprise. I didn't know if he was being cynical or serious. Given how tumultuous our lives had been, how uneven our communication, I had no idea if this was something he'd been thinking about before or was a result of the visa situation. It wasn't something we ever talked about. I'd never been that interested in marriage, in part because I didn't see the purpose of Church and State sanctifying my personal life. But we were living in exceptional circumstances, and the more I thought about it, the more sense it made. Although it was far from a romantic proposal, if that was indeed his intention, it was a practical solution to our problem.

Jean Raymond balked when he learned that in order to get a marriage license he had to have a physical examination and AIDS test. "*Non,*" he said and turned to walk out of the room. "*Se racis, bay sa yo:* That's racist, that kind of thing."

"It's not," I explained, trying to sound more understanding than I felt. "It's required for everyone in the United States."

"*Pa vre:* Not true."

"Yes it is," I said, infuriated that he would think he knew more about this than me. "Ask anyone else and they'll tell you the same thing."

"Look, either you get it done or we don't get married. It's as simple as that," I said and walked out of the room before he had a chance to.

At that time, I didn't know that Jean Raymond had never been to a doctor before. When he finally explained what his real fears were, I found a sympathetic Chilean doctor who, with great tact and understanding, cajoled my soon-to-be husband into his office. When Jean Raymond walked out after the exam, he looked like a sheepish pre-schooler post–temper tantrum. The doctor had a huge smile on his face and was holding one of Jean Raymond's CDs. They spoke to each other on the phone after that several times, as if they were old friends.

The day of the ceremony I wore a floral silk skirt and a royal blue silk blouse, Jean Raymond a long-sleeved shirt and casual sports jacket, his dreadlocks cascading over his shoulders. He was as handsome as the day I met him, and my heart fluttered. My best friend Mary, who was our witness, helped out with Kadja, who in a one-piece black-and-white velvet tuxedo, outshone the bride and groom.

It was a mild February day as we drove to City Hall for our civil ceremony. We were one of a half dozen weddings that morning, and because renovations were taking place in the main hall none of us was able to stand on the balcony overlooking the winding marble steps and grand foyer below, a main attraction for holding ceremonies there. Instead, we were shuffled into a dull gray side room filled with chairs, a table, a VCR, and stand-up screen for slide shows. Hardly romantic. While we waited for the other couples to finish their vows, Jean Raymond and I held our own private rehearsal. Because his understanding of English was still halting, we worked out a foot signal where I tapped his shoe just at the point he was required to say "I do." The justice of the peace never caught on, and afterward we shared a soft, warm kiss to cement the vows, wrapping Kadja in the middle of our embrace.

Neither of us felt particularly euphoric afterward. The setting wasn't conducive, and there were so many other things on our minds; but we held hands as we drank a celebratory glass of champagne with Mary before scurrying off to the airport to pick up my mom, who had been visiting my sister in Cleveland. She took the news of our marriage in stride. After all these years, Mom was used to me. My sister Karin, in Los Altos, was sorry to have missed the event, but understood the circumstances and sent us a beautiful bouquet of flowers.

The same day that Jean Raymond got word that his residency status was secure and that he could resume traveling outside the country, he booked a flight to Haiti. I was happy for him because he was so happy. Still, I felt a pang of regret when the plane lifted off from the tarmac. In the big scheme of things, I knew Jean Raymond loved me, but Haiti was a tougher challenge than a rival woman. Haiti provided an unconditional comfort and security that was fundamental, nonnegotiable, and complete, and if he had to choose between the two of us, my money would have been on Haiti. While that ate away at me, it was something I had to accept, because to fight it would have consumed more energy than I had to give.

When he called to say he'd arrived safely, I could hear the difference in his voice; the tenor of his "*bonjou*" caught me by surprise. It was the first time in months that I heard the sweet melodic tone he had often used to soothe and seduce me. I'd almost forgotten what it sounded like. Gone was the edge, the stress, the angst of feeling misplaced. Despite the dangers he confronted in Haiti, he was sleeping on the soil that nourished his soul with a peace he couldn't find in San Francisco, a feeling he radiated through the telephone wires.

After he returned from Haiti to San Francisco, he was a changed person. His face filled out, returned to its natural color, his shoulders were straight, and his spirit was recharged. I knew he'd slept soundly, drank juice straight from coconut shells and ate grapefruits from his mother's trees. He didn't say it, but I knew he would be going back frequently.

And then one morning in the end of 1992 I, too, woke up ready to return. I was tired of my staid life in San Francisco, and yearned for the easterly winds off the Port-au-Prince Bay, not the ocean chill from the Pacific. I craved the demitasse of strong Haitian coffee and crusty French bread, not pseudo-croissants from my local San Francisco bakery. I loved my Noe Valley home, the view of the foothills, and the comfort of close friends and family, but I also longed to return to the lifestyle I'd left behind in Port-au-Prince, in spite of the insecurity, violence, and hardships imposed by the coup. It didn't make sense—I knew that and didn't try to explain it so my family and friends could understand. Instead, I spoke of the other part that was drawing me back. Professionally I was wilting in the States and needed to resume my place as a field reporter. I needed to resume my relationship with Jean Raymond in Haiti, where it had a chance to survive. If we spent much more time in the States, it was going to die a quick death.

Kadja also deserved to have two parents, and I couldn't squelch that nagging thought that if Jean Raymond were forced to choose between Haiti and us that eventually, for his own sanity, he would choose Haiti. The adjustment he would have to make to stay in the States demanded more than he had to give. Still, I didn't want to put a time frame on how long I would stay in Haiti so I decided to rent, rather than sell my house in San Francisco. I worked out a deal with the renter that allowed me to return for a month at a time provided I gave ample notice. That assuaged my mom, who was diplomatic enough to ask what she could do to help me organize, rather than express her concern about the danger I was returning to and her sorrow at seeing me go.

My oldest sister, with whom I had so easily reconnected and saw frequently, was more upset than I expected when I said we were moving back. "If you leave, you won't be part of our family anymore," she said.

She didn't mean forever, of course, but she took my decision to return to Haiti personally. No matter what I said, she couldn't resolve her own sense of loss and unconsciously began to withdraw emotionally. I felt badly and told her so, but in her mind the damage was done. It wasn't that I didn't feel conflicted about leaving my friends and family behind, but I wanted to start building a foundation for my own family, and for the time being, at least, that meant living in Port-au-Prince. What I was unable to communicate effectively was that I wasn't doing this *to* anyone, but rather I was doing something important *for* myself. I knew the inherent risk of raising Kadja without a family-support network, and all the other inconveniences and hardships that Haiti would present, but I was willing to try it, at least for a while, because I also knew what Haiti had to offer that I couldn't find in San Francisco. Some of those things were tangible—meaningful work, for one, and improving my relationship with Jean Raymond; but the intangibles were equally as important—pushing myself to define what was important, what I could do without, and what I really needed to live a complete and fulfilling life.

Once I'd made up my mind, I immediately began negotiating for a particular house in Port-au-Prince that I'd seen during a trip there a month earlier. It was an old gingerbread with sprawling porches that lined the front and side of the house, and had a two-person swing in the garden. There were trees and plants and views of the ocean, along with large, airy rooms and big wooden shutters. I imagined myself rocking Kadja to sleep under the rustle of the mango tree. I was thrilled when the Haitian owner, who was living in Philadelphia, agreed on a rental price. She promised to fax me an inventory list of what was currently in the house along with a contract, which I said I'd review, then sign and return to her with a check. The next day we discussed logistics. "Who else will be living in the house?" she asked.

"My husband and our year-and-a-half-old son."

"Do you work?"

"As a freelance journalist and translator."

"Journalism," she replied. "It's always intrigued me. Whom do you work for?"

"I'm freelance, but my main strings are the *Christian Science Monitor* newspaper, Monitor radio and the *San Francisco Chronicle*. I was also the local stringer for the *New York Times* before I left Haiti, but I don't know if I'll be able to get that back."

"I bet it's fascinating, reporting. Is your husband also a journalist?"

"No. Musician."

Pregnant pause. "Oh. What kind of music does he play?"

"Drums—he's a percussionist."

"Does he play with a band?"

Something in her voice signaled a change, so I replied cautiously. "Yes, maybe you've heard of them. Foula. They've been around a number of years. Do you know them?"

"I think so. They have a saxophone player, Theodat, and their music is sort of jazzy."

"Uh-huh. It's traditional Vodou rhythms with a jazz beat." I hesitated. "You don't have to be concerned about rehearsals at the house; they have a place where they practice in Laplèn."

"It's not that I don't like music," she said with a slight edge, "it's just that it's a quiet neighborhood."

"My son can wail louder than the band can play," I joked.

She laughed, and the conversation continued without another wrinkle. "My dad lives just two doors away and has an extra set of keys. Since your husband is in Port-au-Prince already, he can pick them up tomorrow. That way he can get things ready before you and your son arrive," she suggested.

I didn't know very much about this woman, but I'd been told she was a contemporary. We had mutual friends in Haiti, and they all said she and her husband were nice, progressive. So I spoke frankly.

"How about if I pick up the keys when I get there? It's probably nothing, but since your dad doesn't know my husband, and my husband has dreadlocks, it just might create a better impression if I stop by for the keys myself.

"Not," I added quickly, "that I'm saying dreadlocks would be an issue for your dad, but I know that sometimes people are uncomfortable with things like that. Especially since your dad hasn't met either one of us."

"No problem," she said, and upon our hanging up, I immediately called Jean Raymond and gave him the good news. That night I dreamed of soft almond leaves caressing the side of the house and wooden shutters creaking in the wind.

My mom came to the city to spend my last day with me, helping me put things in order, advising me on last-minute items. We had a late-afternoon lunch in a neighborhood café, where she held in check her fears about my safety. We kept the conversation light but still I choked up saying good-bye, and insisted that she come back to the house for a final cup of tea. As I set down my packages, I automatically hit the blinking message button on the answering machine.

"Hi, Kathie. Listen, I'm afraid that I won't be able to rent you the house in Port-au-Prince. I'm sorry for such late notice and wish you luck finding something else."

I looked at the machine as though it could offer an explanation. "What's going on?" my mother asked.

I repeated yesterday's conversation as best I could remember while I rewound the answering machine and played the message again to see if I had missed something. Hers was the only one on the tape. "Call her," my mother said, seeing the look of panic on my face.

I reached her on the first try. "I just received your message," I said. "Would you explain what's going on? It sounds as though you're reneging on the contract."

"I'm sorry," she said, "but I just don't think it would be a good idea to have you and your family move into the house. It's a quiet, conservative neighborhood. A Haitian military officer lives on one side, my dad on the other."

"And?" I said, waiting for an explanation that made sense.

"With your husband being a musician and having dreadlocks, well, I just don't think it's a good mix."

"You must be kidding," I said.

She sounded embarrassed. "I'm thinking of you as well as of my father. It's a decision that would be best for everyone."

"You haven't even met us. How can you say that?"

"It's nothing personal. I'm sure your husband is a lovely person, but I just don't want to disrupt things in the neighborhood, especially when I am so far away and my dad is getting old.

"I am sorry, but I am not going to change my mind," she added.

As I hung up the phone, I shook my head in disbelief. "I should have known better," I vented to my mother. "Class and social standing are everything in Haiti." I stomped around the house trying to calm myself. I wasn't sure how much this was a response to the coup or how much it reflected deep-rooted class division in Haiti, but it was not a good omen. Had things changed that much since the coup, or was this just a manifestation of Haiti's historic social problems? We'd experienced discrimination before, but this was a real blow. And the timing couldn't have been worse. I'd counted on having this wonderful place to ease the transition back to our old life. Not knowing where we were going to live brought to the surface an unease I didn't know I had. Was I being totally irresponsible by taking a fifteen-month-old into this situation? As soon as that thought crossed my mind, Kadja felt my tension and started to cry, forcing me to focus on him instead of my own concerns.

I didn't tell Jean Raymond the real reason we lost the house. "Nothing positive would come of it," I said to my mom. "He'll just get worked up. It'll only stoke the anger he already has for the bourgeoisie. I don't need to contribute to that. It is what it is," I added with a sigh before calling him. I offered a vague explanation about how the conditions had changed and the landlord wanted more money than we could afford. He promised to resume a search immediately.

From the window of the plane, the Port-au-Prince airport looked curiously unchanged. But at the balcony terminal, where friends and family used to elbow each other for a sight of those deplaning, there was only empty blue sky and a row of armed guards. The welcome band squeaked out the same, monotonous tune, but it lacked the zip that made the campy experience fun. They played like robots, stiff and perfunctory. The air was oppressively hot. Inside the immigration room hung a large TOMORROW FOR HAITI sign.

In light of the horror stories coming out of the country, it was hard to reconcile how quiet it all seemed. Everything appeared routine:

immigration officials stamping passports, undisciplined porters retrieving luggage, young boys swarming outside the terminal gates to beg, and then the heat. Always the heat.

As before, the streets were crowded. There was a constant flutter of movement, a scurrying of cars, carts, feet, bicycles, and scooters. Yet the tension in the air was palpable, and I held Kadja tight to shield him from it. The random groups that used to hang out on the street corner were now members or cronies of the military. There was no public curfew, but a self-imposed one where nearly everyone scuttled inside after dark. There was no open resistance, but underground there were small localized groups organizing to destabilize the military. All hush-hush. All very James Bond 007. All very real. Everyone kept tight control on who was following whom, when, and where.

I arrived at the familiar Oloffson Hotel with a heavy heart and even heavier suitcases, but brightened up after seeing that it hadn't changed much in my absence. Jean Raymond had booked us a suite, so we weren't so cramped. I spread my things on the wooden benches and flung open the wooden shutters to let in the smell of the warm Caribbean air, the frangipani blossoms nearby. On the verandah I fed Kadja while sipping coffee, grateful that there was just enough distance between the streets and me to soften the transition. Between the sounds of honking horns, crowing roosters, and random gunshots, I turned to Kadja. "*Byenvenu,*" I whispered in his ear. "Welcome home."

Chapter VII

Living in Darkness

Kote sole bwiye, lalun pa vini.
The moon doesn't belong where the sun shines.

Within days of our return, we found a new place to live, someone to watch Kadja, and I was busy at work. My British journalist friend Mike generously handed back my main strings, the *Christian Science Monitor* and *San Francisco Chronicle*, which he wrote for in my absence; he had decided to leave journalism in order to pursue a job with the United Nations. A Scottish journalist, Andrew, was now working for Howard of the *New York Times* and although I was sorry to lose that job, I was plenty busy. Even with full-time help with Kadja, it was a totally different thing being a reporter *and* a mom.

The conditions in the country shocked me. During my absence, the military dictatorship had spread its roots like wild anise. Months of repression morphed into a year, and then some. Fear of the de facto government's unilateral power was so widespread that it spooked the most innocent. One didn't dare say Aristide's name out loud. If it was pronounced at all, it was whispered in the company of trusted friends and families in a back room, in the brush behind the house, away from peering eyes and overamped ears. Tens of thousands of people went into hiding to escape the wrath of the lawless local officials, who thought nothing of beating or torturing a suspected Aristide supporter. Or settling a personal debt. Reporting on this required a new level of sophistication and surveillance, and I found the challenge exhilarating.

Correspondents in Washington reported on Aristide, where he continued to work the political scene to bring the crisis to an end. But he had little luck on that front and almost none on alleviating the fear and violence at home. Although the Organization of American States stepped in quickly after the coup and placed an embargo on imports and exports from Haiti, including petroleum products such as gas and diesel, the only real impact the embargo had was greater economic hardship for the population.

Part of the problem was that the OAS sanctions were not compulsory for nonmembers and not enforced for members; so more than a dozen countries in Europe, Africa, and Latin America (with the Dominican Republic being the worst offender) routinely ignored the sanctions. The elite and the military were able to obtain all the oil and other necessities they needed to maintain their accustomed lifestyle. In 1992 I visited the Port-au-Prince wharf on a quick trip to Haiti and counted eight ships from six member countries of the Organization of American States docked there. More than a million barrels of petroleum products were shipped to Haiti in the first six months of the embargo alone.

It wasn't until twenty-one months after the coup, on June 16, 1993, that the UN Security Council got seriously involved. By then I was well settled back in Port-au-Prince and reporting full time. I followed closely as the UN voted to impose a ban on all petroleum and arms sales to Haiti. It also ordered a freeze on the foreign financial assets of top Haitian officials and businessmen. The resolution was binding for all UN members and scheduled to take effect June 23.

Four days later, President Aristide and his team, along with de facto leader General Raoul Cédras and his delegation, converged on Governors Island, New York. Negotiators hoped that they would be able to hammer out a solution acceptable to both parties, but things didn't go as planned. Although the two groups were housed just minutes from each other, ate the same food, slept in identical rooms, and met with the same negotiators, they never met face-to-face. They saw images of each other on television and in newspapers but they were never in the same room at the same time. Harried diplomats tried desperately to work out an agreement, but in the end only General Cédras signed the document that came to be known as the Governors Island Accord, confident that it was tilted in his favor. He returned to Port-au-Prince cocky and triumphant, gloating to the crowd of opportunists who were at the airport to meet him.

The agreement called for Aristide to nominate a prime minister. After Parliament ratified that nomination, the accord called on the international community to suspend sanctions and resume foreign aid. It called on the Haitian government to grant amnesty to those involved in the coup, and for Cédras to retire before Aristide's arrival. Other key members of the high command were to be transferred. The president agreed to appoint a new military commander, who in turn would select a new general staff. Aristide's scheduled return was set for October 30, 1993. Nothing in the agreement mentioned the purging of the military.

The military was clever. It brought Aristide to the negotiating table before the impact of the new United Nations sanctions were felt. It also bought the military four months' time to stockpile and strategize.

"There's movement," I said to my mom, who was beside herself with worry for Kadja and me. "But this Governors Island Accord hasn't really done much to help Aristide."

"From what the press says here, it looks like it's backed him into a corner," she said. I wanted to reach out and hug her. I knew I could depend on her to be closely covering the events in Haiti, and willing to speak about them with me even when I knew she just wanted assurances that I was fine. "He's relinquished any leverage to enforce the conditions leading up to his scheduled return date," I explained. "If he doesn't sign, he risks being ostracized by the international community for his lack of good faith. And people here will eventually start to criticize him because that just means a delay on lifting the embargo."

"What does that mean for you?"

"Honestly, Mom, I'm in such a privileged position that it's hard to complain. I've got money to purchase whatever's available on the black market. It doesn't make for easy living, but—"

"Are you safe?" she asked, knowing I wouldn't tell her otherwise. "Just promise me you'll be careful and stay away from all those military types."

I promised, but then promptly broke that promise. My editor at the *Monitor*, Faye Bowers, wanted a quote from Cédras about the Governors Island Accord. I had yet to interview anyone from the military— the truth was that I was terrified of them, but I put aside my personal fears by reminding myself that I was a professional, and on assignment. I also wanted to be a top-notch reporter. My personal goals were quite different than when I started working as a reporter five years previously—it wasn't enough to just get the 800-word story out or the 60-second radio piece. I wanted these stories to be unique and hard-hitting. I wanted them to have a special insight, a certain style and a memorable impact. If that meant pushing myself out of my comfort zone, I was willing to try it—I just didn't think it was necessary to tell my mother how far I was willing to go.

Armed only with my notebook and a pen, I made my way downtown. I had a queasy feeling in my stomach as I approached the *Quartier General,* military headquarters. The building itself was charming, with pristine white paint and bright green shutters, a structure reminiscent of New England. But its appeal was immediately eradicated by the sheer number of firearms, rifles, automatic weapons, and pocket pistols in the hands of the men standing outside the building. The group at the nearby street corner had a similar cache, as did those on the second-floor balcony. The setting was very male, very macho, and very threatening. "You're a professional," I reminded myself again, keeping my gaze straight ahead, ignoring the leers, the curiosity, the posturing. "You're just doing your job," I consoled myself as one of the soldiers bumped into me deliberately when I entered into the building. I inhaled slowly to keep myself focused.

An equal number of tough, well-armed men milled about inside the building, crowding the glass reception booth along the right wall. The officers in the booth were overrun from the front by people like me trying to get close enough to make a request, as well as from the side, by officers trying to get entry passes to the building for their friends. Off to the left, in the small reception area with tattered chairs, sat several chic young women sporting *talon kikit,* stiletto-heeled shoes and tight, short skirts. They carried Haitian-style "to go" containers for their boyfriends—stacking aluminum bowls held together by a long handle attached at the sides: one for rice, one for sauce, and another for fish, meat, chicken, or vegetables.

It was chaotic and frightening and my impulse was to turn and run, but the voice of my editor was like a nagging earworm. I could feel my armpits sweating and the beads of doubt dripped down my back like wet dew. A few years earlier I might have given in to my anxiety, but I was resolute to push on. It was going to take more than a bunch of men with guns to deter me if I wanted to be the journalist I said I was going to be, so I moved forward, one step at a time. "Get the interview first," I said to myself. "*Then* you can run."

Behind the glass booth, a door led to a dark row of rooms through which lower-ranking officers shuffled in and out. Off to the left was a heavy metal gate with a Y-shaped staircase leading to the second-floor offices of the military high command. There was also a waiting room with a television. The only thing that played was static.

That first day I waited downstairs for nearly thirty minutes before a young man escorted me to the second-floor waiting area. Madame Nicolas, the first uniformed woman I had ever seen in Haiti, sat at a desk in a small room off the top of the stairs. She was in her thirties, petite and official looking, with a severe bun at the base of her scalp. Her eyebrows were pinched so tightly they looked as though they were stitched together. Her mouth was pursed as if she were sucking on sour limes. She told me in a stiff, well-rehearsed voice that for an interview with General Cédras, I must receive clearance from General Jean-Robert Gabriel, who was in charge of public relations.

"He is in a meeting right now. Please, have a seat," she said and pointed to the room around the corner. "I'll call you when he comes out."

There was a copy of the daily newspaper, *Le Nouvelliste,* sitting on the only table in the waiting room, but it was several weeks old and I finished it within five minutes. There was also a wall framed with pictures of Haiti's former presidents that I studied to pass the time. Aristide was included along with his "successor," Supreme Court Judge

Joseph Nerette, who had been appointed by the military after the coup. An hour later, I returned to Madame Nicolas's desk. She was just as polite as she had been an hour earlier, and as she was one hour later. I was not as polite. "If he can't see me, is there someone else who can?" I demanded, my timidity evaporating with each waiting minute, my hunger pains and boredom adding to my impatience.

"General Gabriel is in a meeting right now. Please, have a seat," she said like a windup toy. After two more hours, I gave up, knowing this was precisely what she had intended.

I returned the next day and waited only fifteen minutes on the first floor, but once upstairs, Madame Nicolas said, "I am sorry but General Gabriel hasn't come in yet. If you have a seat in the waiting room, I'll call you when he arrives." This time I limited myself to two hours and brought a *New Yorker*, along with a written request for an interview that did me no good. Days three and four were a repeat of day one, but on the fifth day I got lucky and bumped into General Gabriel on the stairs. He wasn't thrilled when I planted myself firmly in his path and recounted my week of waiting just to speak with him, but he promised to discuss my interview with General Cédras later that afternoon.

Madame Nicolas called me three days later to inform me that I had an interview scheduled for the following morning. I could hardly believe I'd succeeded in what seemed like a battle of wills. I'd long forgotten the original story for which I needed a quote, but getting the interview was a personal victory, and I figured that I'd take from it whatever I could get, since I might never be granted another. I arrived early and was escorted upstairs immediately. I asked permission to wait on the balcony, a lovely little porch that I'd always admired from the square below. I imagined, on a better day, in another era, that if it could somehow be cleared of the military men who hung out there flaunting their weaponry, it would be a perfect movie setting for a romantic love story. After some consultation and mumbling, the officer in charge granted my request. As a matter of protocol only military have the right to stand on the balcony but they may have thought it would be good public relations to have a foreigner's face visible. After all, there weren't that many *blan* seen in the company of the Haitian military—at least, not in public.

I didn't care what the reason was. I was sick of the waiting room, and wanted a chance to enjoy the view. The balcony overlooked the Champs de Mars, the park encircling the National Palace. The statue of the *Neg Mawon*, Unknown Escaped Slave—a rebel blowing a conch shell to signal the start of the slave revolt and Haiti's independence—was off to the right. The irony didn't escape me.

General Cédras's office was physically the same as it had been when I interviewed the head of the military two years earlier, but that was before Aristide was president, before he was exiled in a military coup. There was, however, something fundamentally different. The air was heavier, mustier, more oppressive. The carpet was tattered, the thick, dark curtains fusty. This juxtaposed with General Cédras, who although smaller in person than he appeared to be on television, was handsome in an austere way—his jaw square and weighty, his face lean with slightly sunken cheeks and deep-set, serious eyes. But he was also slimy, someone my mother would surely have told me to stay away from.

Cédras was big on protocol, and in English made sure that I was settled with my demitasse before we got started. He introduced me to Darryl Reaves, an American who came through a side door. I suspected Reaves might be the translator, which wasn't that surprising, despite Cédras's proficiency in English, but I said it was perfectly fine to conduct the interview in Creole. This seemed to delight Cédras, who wasted ten precious minutes of my time by asking his own questions about how I learned Creole and why I was living in Haiti now. When I eventually turned around the direction of the questions, he said nothing original, a trait he shared with Aristide and Lafontant. Was this endemic to self-important people? He was also righteous in his defense of the coup, terming it "absolutely necessary" and accused Aristide of being an antidemocratic ruler.

"Why are demonstrations systematically crushed?" I asked.

"Now is not the time to demonstrate, not when an agreement has been reached that includes a date for President Aristide's return," he answered.

"Why did the military not only tolerate, but participate in a demonstration for your departure and return from Governors Island?" I asked.

He laughed. "That was not a demonstration. I have a large family, and they were all there to greet me."

Then Reaves looked at his watch and told Cédras that he had another appointment. I wasn't disappointed. I'd learned over time that this was part of the game. As a reporter, I was at the mercy of those granting the interviews. Sometimes I never even had the opportunity to pose a question, so in this instance I was lucky to get a few useful quotes. And hopeful that now that Cédras knew who I was, a second interview sometime in the future might not be so hard to obtain. As I prepared to leave, Cédras shook my hand. "When I retire as commander-in-chief upon Aristide's return, perhaps I should take up something more lucrative, like selling handicrafts, so surely our paths will cross again."

I nodded and smiled politely. There wasn't anything appropriate to say. I hated this man who pretended that he'd done what was best for the country when it was wallowing in misery. It was hard not to hold him responsible for the inequities that engulfed Haiti—the freedom with which the military and police ruled and the terror in which the population lived. When I got home I took a long shower, anxious to wash away any remnants of my experience.

About 10:55 P.M. the following evening, the phone rang. It was a blackout and the only lamp lit cast just enough light for me to read. It was rare to get a call anytime because of the erratic phone system, but even more so to get one that late at night. Jean Raymond was already asleep. I gently pushed him aside, walked over to the desk, then hesitated before lifting the receiver. "Is this the *Christian Science Monitor*?" asked a voice I didn't recognize in English.

"Who's calling, please?"

"Darryl Reaves. Are you the journalist I met yesterday with General Cédras?"

"Yes," I said, not at all sure I should be admitting this. Even though my article, which mocked Cédras, hadn't yet run, I wondered if he had such extensive intelligence that he knew what I was going to say. Could he already be plotting my demise? I sat down, my legs wobbly.

"How are you?"

"Fine, thank you," I answered, knowing he hadn't called to inquire after my health. "What can I do for you?"

"I'm calling to invite you to have breakfast with Michel François tomorrow morning. Nine o'clock. Can you make it?"

"Nine o'clock?" By now Jean Raymond had woken up and looked over at me inquisitively. I shrugged my shoulders, trying to figure out what was going on.

"Breakfast? Where?"

"Nine o'clock. We'll pick you up at the Holiday Inn," he said conclusively. "See you in the morning, then. Have a nice evening."

Only after he hung up did I realize that I had just agreed to have breakfast with the notorious Michel François, alleged drug trafficker and human-rights abuser, who declared himself head of the police after the coup and gotten away with it because no one dared to cross him. He had been elusive ever since then, never once showing his face in public. I'd never even seen his photograph. While meeting him was surely a unique opportunity, Jean Raymond was skeptical.

"Come on, Kathie," he said, now fully awake. "You know the reputation of this guy. You have no idea why you've been invited. You don't even know where you're going or who is going to be there. You didn't ask any of the questions you normally do. What were you thinking?"

I wasn't thinking straight, that was certain; the call had taken me by surprise. The darkness of the night, the darkness of the period we were living in, it was a setting ripe for distrust, plots, and conspiracies. The horror stories I'd been hearing over the last eighteen months made me suspicious of just about everything. This could easily be a setup, but I couldn't imagine why I would be targeted.

I thought of Jean-Marie and wished, as I had so often in the past few years, that he was around to talk to. I missed him in many ways, and knew that he would have figured out the right way to handle this unexpected wrinkle. Over the last year I'd become exceptionally good friends with another Haitian, a radio journalist who had great politics and a sound mind. I woke him up to ask his advice. He repeated the same warning as Jean Raymond. "*Fè atansyon,*" he said, warning me to be careful if I decided to go. I was too spooked to decide whether or not to go; I felt like a child standing on the edge of a diving board, scared to jump, scared to climb back down.

The descriptions of tortures linked to François were chilling. Just a few weeks ago I'd met with a human-rights monitor, one of the several dozen who were part of the United Nations/Organization of American States International Civilian Mission (MICIVIH), who showed me a photo of a paramilitary thug swinging a stick; he had a machete strapped to his waist. He was beating a peasant in the presence of one of the foreign observers, a young man who was wearing the standard white T-shirt with blue lettered *Misyon Sivil Entènasyonal* on the front. The observer's blue hat had white OEA letters, the French acronym of the Organization of American States. Another photo showed the peasant's buttocks exposed, the skin ripped raw. That the paramilitary had the audacity to beat someone in front of a monitor illustrated the thugs' impunity.

My human rights monitor friend also told me about a young man who, after hiding in the Central Plateau for eighteen months, decided to return home because it was the planting season. He thought things would be safer with MICIVIH's presence in his hometown, where he was known as an Aristide supporter. He was back only a few days when the military came for him at 2:00 A.M. and beat him more than 300 times.

A professor living in Haiti's extreme northwest town, Mole St. Nicolas, was arrested for having "photos" of Aristide in his home—photos that appeared mysteriously out of the socks and shoes of those who came to arrest him. They made him cut the photos into small pieces and swallow them with water. After that, he was paraded through the streets carrying a photo of Aristide and forced to say, "*Se papam*: this is my father." Finally the military shaved his head and made him eat his hair with bread.

It didn't matter that it was physically impossible for François to be responsible for the atrocities in the countryside—I believed he or Cédras could have put an end to the torture if they wanted. And the fact that they didn't, that so many people lived in absolute fear, condemned them both in my mind.

As these thoughts ran through my head, I glanced at the clock. It was after 11:00 P.M., but I looked up the home number of Faye Bowers, my editor at the *Christian Science Monitor* in Boston. "It could be a setup—what kind, I am not sure, but I find the whole thing odd," I said after excusing myself for calling so late. "Why is he doing this, and why did I get the call so late at night? François never goes out in public and never speaks to journalists. And it's not as though he frequents restaurants like 'normal' people; I've never heard anyone say that they've seen François in public.

"I don't even know what he looks like," I went on. "The only thing I know about him is his reputation, and that's pretty awful. It gives me the creeps to think I'll be going to an undisclosed place in someone else's car and no one will know where I am."

Faye shared my concern. "The article we have slated to run is strong and can stand on its own," she said. "Given the late hour and the last-minute preparations, don't go. If this guy calls again and offers you a chance to meet with François another time, set up parameters that you have more control over."

Her words reassured me and made Jean Raymond feel better, too. He held me tight but I spent the night tossing and was sluggish in the morning.

Just before 9:00 A.M. the phone rang. Jean Raymond and I exchanged glances before I picked up the receiver. It was Harold, an American journalist who lived down the street. When I first met him, I used to call him Todd because he bore such a strong resemblance to the American tennis player Todd Martin, tall, lanky, friendly. It was coincidental that Harold was just as likable in the journalist world as Todd was reputed to be on the tennis circuit. "Hey, Kathie, what's going on?" he asked. I was so relieved to hear his voice rather than that of Reaves that it took me a minute to respond.

"Not much, how 'bout yourself?" I asked.

"Well, listen, I'm down at the Holiday Inn with Darryl Reaves and he said you were going to be here, too. Aren't you part of this group that has an interview with Michel François?"

"Oh my God, Harold—I thought, well, yes—I mean, uh, I'm coming. I'll be right there. I'm on my way. Tell them I've left already; I'm out the door. Don't leave without me."

I hung up without saying good-bye and jumped in the shower, brushed my teeth, combed my hair, and threw on a dress. Jean Raymond promised to come to the Holiday Inn in an hour to make sure I was okay. I grabbed my tape recorder and notebooks, kissed Kadja good-bye, flew down the stairs and raced to the Holiday Inn, arriving at 9:12 A.M. Reaves, a coffee-colored, round-faced guy who I later learned had been a legislator in the state of Florida, was waiting outside. He looked like a nice enough guy on the surface, but the mere fact that he was associated with François was enough to warn me not to annoy him, so I immediately went up to him and excused myself for being late. He made an appropriately sarcastic retort that journalists were worse than politicians, but smiled when he said chauffeurs were the worst of the lot. "Mine hasn't even arrived yet."

My heart fell into my stomach when I realized we weren't staying at the Holiday Inn. I looked over at Harold for reassurance. He smiled halfheartedly. When I took him aside and told him about the mental gymnastics I'd gone through to get there he burst out laughing, then toned it down when Reaves looked our way.

"He called me last minute, too, but I wasn't as paranoid," Harold said playfully, poking me in the arm. Jose, a thick, short Mexican cameramen who worked for the Spanish television station Telemundo said there was safety in numbers. Still, we were only three. I wondered if more had been invited but had declined.

When a four-wheel-drive vehicle with tinted windows pulled up,

Reaves motioned for us to get in. The three of us squeezed in the back; Reaves sat in the front.

After a few minutes of silence I couldn't stand the suspense. "Where are we going?" I asked.

"El Rancho," he said, referring to the five-star hotel in Pétionville. "It was François's anniversary last night and he was out late, so we are a little behind schedule this morning." He lapsed into silence for a few minutes, and then turned back around. "Have any of you ever met or seen Michel François?"

"No," we said collectively.

"Well there's something you should know about him," Reaves said in a serious tone, his voice dropping. Dead silence from the backseat. "A few years back he had a pretty nasty accident that burned the left side of his face. He has had hours of reconstructive surgery and the tissue has healed nicely, but it left some pretty heavy scarring on one side of his face. He's really sensitive about this so don't stare at him. He hates that."

None of us said a word. This description wasn't far off from what I imagined François to look like given everything I'd heard about him. Just as I was trying to envision how I would conduct an interview without looking directly at him Reaves let out a whopping roar.

"You believed it, didn't you? God, what's wrong with you guys?" He laughed heartily as he turned back around. "You really think François is a monster? He's just a regular guy. Lighten up back there!"

We forced a laugh, but I was no less convinced that I was about to meet one of the most sinister characters in all of Haiti. We spent the rest of the ride in silence and I used the remaining time to pull together some questions, chiding myself that I hadn't done so the night before. When we pulled in to the El Rancho, Reaves repeated again: No questions allowed until François has his breakfast.

Reaves escorted us into a private dining room with five chairs. We left the seat at the head of the table empty. I kept my tape recorder in my purse while I reviewed my questions again, conferring with Harold to make sure we covered all the relevant points. Ten minutes later, we heard clicking heels approach on the walkway and four bodyguards came in surrounding Michel François.

François had a round pug face with a large lower lip and a slightly protruding jaw. His body was the classic military stereotype, dense and firm. His jeans and dark green shirt fit tightly on his muscular torso. He took short but precise steps as he walked around the table to shake our hands, gripping firmly. His hands were meaty, and his fingers left marks in my flesh. His bodyguards stood at attention next to each of the doors.

A waiter came in with a pitcher of water and menus. François and Harold ordered French toast; Reaves and Jose ordered ham-and-cheese omelets. I couldn't think of eating and ordered the Continental breakfast just to have something in front of me. Holding the coffee cup steadied my nerves, but I didn't want to drink too much caffeine because I was worried that my voice might tremble. I was jittery enough as it was.

François opened the conversation with light banter. Hearing his perfect English reminded me that he had trained in the United States where, I thought cynically to myself, he probably learned all his torture techniques. He talked about his anniversary celebration and having too much champagne and then the conversation moved to wine, beer, and sports. I contributed little, thinking instead about the guy with the torn buttocks, the man who was forced to eat pictures of Aristide, and that Jean Raymond was going to get to the Holiday Inn and wonder where I was.

When the plates were cleared, Reaves set the ground rules. "Each of you will conduct your interview one at a time. You will complete your questions before the next person begins their interview. You will not ask any questions about drug trafficking, human-rights abuses, or François's involvement in the coup d'état."

"And no filming," he said to Jose, who then asked why he'd been invited.

The rules eliminated all my questions. I flashed Harold a smile and told him he was welcome to go first.

As Harold and I pulled out our tape recorders, François pulled out a small notebook from his front shirt pocket, and cupped it discreetly inside his left hand. From time to time he flipped through it, almost unconsciously, then lifted his head. He cocked his neck to the side as if he needed a moment to reflect. His replies were as mundane as a kindergarten primer, elementary and scripted.

"Do you feel the country is safer than it was under Aristide?"

"My job is to ensure law and order," he repeated several times.

"What are you going to do to bring unity back to the country?"

"I can't answer that. I'm not a politician," he replied a half dozen times.

Harold was unable to pull anything useful from him; I came up with even less. François never said that if the Governors Island Accord was respected, he would step down. "I can give my collaboration to a new police force but you are not going to kick me out, say you don't need me anymore," he said. Obviously, he'd been coached to answer the questions without saying anything relevant, just like Cédras and Aristide.

He accused the International Civilian Mission of committing human rights abuses so they could justify their presence. "If everything were quiet in the country, then they would have no reason to stay here. So they encourage people to have demonstrations so that they can have the police beat them, make the police nervous so they do bad things."

Jose sat quietly, squirming in his chair from time to time. The bodyguards stood impassively. When the tapes ran out, so did our time. François smiled. "See, that wasn't so bad," he said proudly. "Now I want to ask you something. After meeting me, do you think I am a monster?"

I mumbled something incoherent, unable to look him in the face. Harold just laughed and Jose stood up with his camera and said, "Can I get that or something on tape, please? Anything just to prove that I was here?"

"The press can make Michel François a monster," he said, ignoring Jose's request as he prepared to leave, "but they can also make me an angel. It depends on the purpose. We do not beat people in prison." Just kill them, I thought as François led the way out, followed by his bodyguards and then Reaves. With a heavy sigh, Jose slung his camera on his shoulder and trailed after them.

Harold and I were putting away our tape recorders when I noticed, on the floor next to the chair where François had been sitting, the small notebook he'd been holding. "Look," I whispered to Harold in my quietest voice. We stared at each other for a split second before I dropped down and picked up the notebook so quickly Harold wasn't even sure I got it. I tucked it in the inner pocket in my purse, and then, like two bit actors from a C-grade film, Harold and I bumped into each as we skirted the table to catch up with Reaves.

I was so nervous about having the notebook in my purse that I was afraid just my eyes would give me away. I cast them downward and sat on my hands so as not to fidget while Reaves made small talk with the others. Harold tried valiantly to keep his cool and the attention away from me, chatting about his most recent vacation and his favorite

French food. I was so worried I was going to be discovered that I almost peed in my pants, grateful I hadn't drunk that second cup of coffee.

As soon as we arrived back at the Holiday Inn, I made a fast excuse to part company with Reaves, who seemed pleased that his public-relations event had been such a success. Harold said he didn't need a ride home, that he was going with me, and we dashed out the back entrance to my car. I didn't even think of stopping to see if Jean Raymond had asked for me at the reception desk for fear of being surrounded by François's towering, menacing, powerful bodyguards.

"Quick," Harold said, "let's go back to my house and have a look."

While I tried to steady my nerves by holding on to the steering wheel, Harold played scout and made sure no one was following us. We didn't think we were being paranoid, we were genuinely afraid of the consequences of getting caught with the little spiral notebook. The country's justified paranoia was part of our daily routine, too.

Safely inside Harold's house, I pulled the notebook from my purse. The second half of the four-by-two-and-a-half-inch notebook was blank, but the beginning was filled with scribbles. Some were simple geometrical doodles; others appeared to be floor plans. Some pages contained names, telephone, or license-plate numbers. We speculated about the stories behind the references. One page had an address and phone number for Radio Cacique, *"Reunion Frequente des Lavalassian— a controler,* Busy Meeting for the Lavalassian—control it." Soldiers destroyed the equipment of Radio Cacique the day of the coup, September 30, 1991.

There were nearly a dozen French phrases, each on a different sheet of paper. *Je commence à compter,* I begin to count; *La Force est calme,* Force is calm; *Tout ou Rien,* All or Nothing.

They weren't particularly enlightening, but we continued, hoping to find something, anything that could tie François to some of the current crimes: *Goutez Pas Laissez*, Don't Leave Anything Behind; *Rien à Perdre, Tout à Gagner*, Nothing to Lose, Everything to Gain; *le new PN sera la responsibilité de la politique extérieure*, the new National Police will be the responsibility of the external policy; *Pauvre!!!?* *Il est innocent*, Poor Person!!!? He is innocent.

But the sad truth was that there really was nothing of significance, at least as far as we could decipher. The final pages had only trivialities, vacuous statements: *Oui, Elle est Mauvaise*, Yes, It is Bad; *Oui, il a eu peur, mais il a été préssuré*, Yes, he was scared, but he had been pushed; *Oui, les informations se paient chère, i.e. en argent et en nature*, Yes, information is costly—i.e. in gold or in kind, and finally, *Désolé, Désolé, Désolé*, Sorry, Sorry, Sorry.

In English, we found the phrases he used for our interview. I imagined Reaves sitting in a high-priced hotel room paid for by the Haitian government, coaching François over a shot of imported whiskey. "I'm not a politician. Only one man is authorized to do politics in the army, General Cédras. They make me bigger than I am. High class. Lower class. Powerful man. Honor."

On another page: "Why are you so powerful? Because it's not easy to find a man who is not afraid to die. Job of a Chief of Police is to maintain order, to give peace, to protect everybody's property." And finally: "We have to avoid excess in whatever we do. Excess always bothers."

As our initial glee of snatching the notebook wore off and reality set in that we were in possession of something belonging to Michel François, our anxiety heightened. I broke out in a sweat, yet again. We fed each other's panic as we listed the possible consequences once François realized he didn't have his notebook: He might send one of his bodyguards to the El Rancho to look for it and then throw a fit when he discovered it wasn't there; he could fire all the hotel employees who had access to that room, or worse. Finally, that he suspect us and plot a way to get rid of us that wouldn't be linked to him.

"I'll go back," Harold offered in a moment of weak desperation, "and discreetly drop it on the floor." But we rejected that idea, thinking that it would be even more suspicious if they'd looked for it already and then it turned up later. In the end, we decided the damage was done, and I promised Harold I would do away with the notebook as soon as I got home. I dropped it back in my purse and put everything else on top of it.

I looked both ways cautiously when I left Harold's house and, rounding the bend of my driveway, I checked one more time to make sure no one was loitering before I pulled in. I ran up the stairs, unlocked the door, and hurried into the bedroom, where for the first time since I moved into my new place, I locked the bedroom door behind me. I stood on a chair to reach for a shoebox on the back shelf of my closet, emptied it, placed the notebook in the bottom, and dumped everything else on top. I hoped the Haitian military hadn't seen too many American movies, or that would be the first place they'd look.

I also hoped Harold wouldn't ask me how I'd disposed of the notebook because I didn't want to lie to him. My gut was telling me that I might eventually be able to use the information in it in some valuable way, and that alone offset the danger of holding on to it.

I called my editor in Boston. She had a good laugh over the burned-face joke and agreed we didn't need to devote too much space in the article to François.

In the article, however, I talked about how instead of bringing relief, the Governors Island Accord brought the worst wave of politically related violence since the coup. Between early July and mid-September 1993, hundreds of people disappeared. In Port-au-Prince alone there were over 100 killings. Pro-Aristide activists were repeatedly intimidated, beaten, and arrested, sometimes in full view of international monitors, who, when I interviewed them, relived the emotional trauma they felt at the time. Automatic weapons disturbed the night and raids were a common practice in the poorer sections of the city, where residents supported the ousted president. It seemed increasingly clear that the military had no intention of allowing Aristide to return.

Jean Raymond, Kadja, and I flew to Miami for a few days' respite in September. I wanted some light, literally and figuratively. I was totally drained from the constant pressure of the insecurity, the lack of progress on restoring democracy, the pressure to be a good mother, wife, and journalist. I didn't feel as though I was doing well on any front and took long walks on the beach to center myself. I called my mom and sisters and had lengthy conversations, catching up on their lives and making sure that they knew I was thinking about them all the time. Kadja grabbed the phone and smiled into the receiver as his cousins shouted their greetings collectively. He nodded, as if he understood.

My mother tried to persuade me to come for Thanksgiving when it became clear that no one had any interest in coming to Haiti to visit me.

"With things as volatile as they are in Haiti, I can't make plans that far in advance," I said, knowing I was reinforcing my family label as unreliable. "The political situation is so unstable that even thinking about making plans next week seems stupid."

"Well, you do what you have to do," she said, though I didn't believe she really meant it. I was still dealing with the conflict I felt about taking the short Miami vacation, even though I needed it, and it wasn't something

I could easily explain. I'd become entrenched in Haiti in a way not dissimilar to Jean Raymond—when I wasn't there, it was all I thought about. I recognized that I could leave it behind physically at any time, but mentally it dominated my thoughts. I felt schizophrenic in not being able to fully enjoy the conveniences and beauty around me in Miami while it was the very thing I craved. It wasn't that I wanted to immediately return to Haiti but in some way it was though I hadn't left.

During our Florida vacation, Robert Malval, a decent and honest businessman with no prior political experience, was nominated and ratified as the new prime minister, under the Governors Island Accord. Cabinet positions were filled, though no one was sure how easy it was going to be getting anything done.

At the same time religious leaders organized an anniversary memorial service for the victims of the 1988 attack on St. Jean Bosco Church. It was, in part, a test to see if the military was really going to let Aristide return. There had been no "prodemocracy" gatherings since the coup nearly two years earlier.

The mass was at the Sacre Coeur Church just minutes from my house. There were about fifty people, including several well-known priests and a progressive, wealthy businessman, Antoine Izméry, whom Jean-Marie had spent a lot of time with before he was killed. There was no sign of the military, but *attachés*—thugs who were informally on the military payroll to do their dirty work—were visible inside the church and on the surrounding streets. There were some observers from MICIVIH, but they stayed in their cars. The air was thick with tension.

Father Antoine Adrien was speaking to the small group of parishioners when suddenly there was some commotion coming from the back part of the pews. People turned around in time to see *attachés* forcing Izméry from his seat. They encircled him and pushed him out the door. For whatever reason—uncertainty, or determination or just plain fear—Father Adrien continued with his sermon. Just as he was saying it was time to end the flow of blood in Haiti, a solid round of shots were fired, close range. People panicked and began running outside, only to see Izméry's body slumped on the sidewalk, right next to the church. Father Hugo Triest, a Belgian priest, walked slowly over to the body, then bent down to confirm that he was dead, murdered in cold blood. A truckload of expressionless policemen watched from their flatbed less than a block away.

The United Nations Special Envoy, Argentinean Dante Caputo, blamed metropolitan area police chief Michel François. Since our interview, François had been *pwen disparèt*—a Creole phrase meaning he had used his Vodou powers to disappear. Not that there weren't signs of his presence all around, with the killings and tortures and disappearances, but he remained invisible to the public. Cédras's response to Izméry's murder was in character: "It is regrettable that the constant efforts of the military institution and its goodwill to do its job passes in silence."

We came back from our peaceful vacation to more bodies littered in the streets. Many were thought to be the victims of a newly emerged paramilitary group, the Front for the Advancement and Progress of Haiti, FRAPH, or strike, in Creole. Sixteen corpses were found in a week. FRAPH was audacious in its demands, including the resignation of interim Prime Minister Robert Malval, who hadn't even been in office one month. The paramilitary group gave Special Envoy Caputo an ultimatum to leave the country within seventy-two hours. No one seemed to know much about this group other than its leader, Emmanuel Constant, was a crazed, English-speaking alleged drug addict who craved publicity as intensely as he did crack.

By mid-September, the United States was getting nervous. The

Clinton administration sent a high-level delegation to meet with Prime Minister Malval and other cabinet members.

On September 23, the UN Security Council unanimously approved Resolution 867, calling for the immediate deployment of 567 United Nations police monitors and a 700-man military construction unit. The 1,300-man team had a six-month contract at an initial cost of $55.2 million and was scheduled to arrive in early October. UN Special Envoy Caputo was chosen to coordinate the mission.

The primary focus of the technical team of 700 unarmed technicians, trainers, engineers, and doctors was to work on repair and construction of roads, schools, and clinics. Such work was welcome, but there was extensive criticism about the police monitors, because they were going to be working directly with the police force led by Michel François. The UN registered fifty killings in the capital alone the first three weeks of September, with an even higher number of people disappeared. It was hard to think about living my life when there were so many dead all around me. Although Kadja was too young to understand, I worried, every single day, if I was being an irresponsible mother. I checked in with my own mother frequently, trying to reassure her that we were fine but I don't think she believed me. I was fine, though, in my own sort of now-Haitian way. I knew that leaving would make me safer, but not happier. It was almost too complicated for me to understand, so I didn't try to explain it to anyone else.

The first group of Canadian police arrived October 7. They were unarmed and wore their country uniform along with the United Nations badge and blue beret. The same day the emerging paramilitary group FRAPH called a strike to protest the arrival of foreign troops; it paralyzed the capital.

A documentary Canadian television crew from a show called *The*

Fifth State hired me for that week; they were researching the misuse of U.S. aid money. I hired as our driver Sergo, Jean Raymond's mechanic friend whom I had become friends with, too. Sergo's quick wit, good humor, and common sense were the perfect qualities to have for such a high-risk situation. The day of the strike he plastered our vehicle with PRESS stickers and raced through the empty streets, pedal to the floor. Only FRAPH members were outside, taking potshots at a few defiant citizens, but they didn't aim for us. They did, however, throw a tear-gas bomb at the few brave merchants selling in Pétionville's outdoor market. Everyone else went indoors, out of sight—not because they supported FRAPH, but because they were terrified of the gang's firearms. It was as though a giant vacuum had inhaled all forms of human life, leaving only the skinny pigs and desperate dogs to feed off the proverbial piles of rotting garbage.

The next day people resumed work, but FRAPH was back shouting anti-UN slogans and waving the black-and-red Duvalier flag. Gone was the red-and-blue flag that the liberated Haitians flew after Duvalier left in 1986. Sitting next to the thugs in their pickups and flatbed trucks were uniformed policemen providing security.

The military was also there when FRAPH antagonists stormed a local hotel looking for the mayor, who had left minutes before. The uniformed soldiers fired random ceiling shots. Almost all of the cabinet members, including Prime Minister Malval, were working at home for fear of being attacked in their offices. Pro-Aristide legislators had already gone into hiding or fled to the United States. I made sure that Kadja stayed well within the confines of our home and played fun, silly games with him every evening in an effort to maintain some sense of normalcy even when I knew life was anything but. Jean Raymond continued with his daily routine of music rehearsals and hanging out with his friends as much as possible. He seemed better suited to adapt than me, something that I shouldn't have found surprising.

The initial deployment of U.S. troops, some 200 of them, were scheduled to arrive on the USS *Harlan County* on October 11. It was the first of what was earmarked to be a 1,600-strong troop dispatched as part of the UN peace accord. Already two dozen American military advisors, mostly doctors, engineers, and linguists, had arrived along with 50 Canadian policemen.

On the morning of October 11, Sergo loaded the CBC's equipment in our four-door Pajaro and we piled in on top of it. It was exceptionally humid—despite the air conditioning, we dripped sweat as we drove along the coastline to the Port-au-Prince wharf, where offshore we saw the USS *Harlan County* waiting for an empty berth to dock. Dozens of journalists milled outside the padlocked gate that led to the wharf area. An American embassy car with tinted, fully drawn windows sat like a black anchor in the eye of a whirlpool as it waited for the gate to open so it could drive down and greet the troops. The level of anxiety in this small area in front of the port was as potent as fumes from a fire—thick, intense, undeniable. A small group of wild-eyed, arms-toting men swaggered about in a manic fashion as they pushed and shoved the journalists and shouted death threats to foreigners and Aristide.

"We'll kill Aristide if he comes back!" snarled a young man as he waved his arms up and down.

"We'll roast him piece by piece!" shouted another. "We're going to do to them what they did to the Americans in Somalia!"

Sergo turned the car around to park in the direction of the quickest exit. "I'll wait here," he said to everyone, then added in Creole: "*Voye je-w yo, Kati, bay la pa dwat*: Watch out, Kathie, something's not right."

The majority of the foreign journalists there didn't understand what the men were saying because the rantings were in Creole, but the tone of their message was as clear as the water in front of us. Like psychotic warriors with wild, demented eyes, the men blasted their way through the crowd, brandishing their weapons and shouting insults.

My heart pounded as I walked through the chaos and tried to assess the situation. I had on a skirt, as was my habit when I was working, but lamented that I hadn't worn pants, even though I knew that a longer layer of clothing couldn't possibly protect me from the danger I sensed. There were more journalists than protestors, but the thugs' tenacity and anger overwhelmed me. It was quite possible that one of them would randomly pull out a knife or a broken bottle or worse. With some trepidation, I worked my way through the crowd to the gate to try to get a better look at what was happening on the wharf side but a man with a machete waved me back, spitting as he shouted: "*Ale ameriken, ale:* Go, American, go."

I backed up, but kept my gaze in his direction. I didn't want to get hit from behind. I smoothed my skirt, wishing again I had worn pants. The CBC producer caught up to me, sweat dripping off his upper lip. "Gather the crew, stay close to them," he said just as a journalist shouted something in English, a cry of alarm barely decipherable over the screaming mania of the Haitian thugs. I couldn't make out the words but they created a chain reaction. First was a shuffled commotion around the embassy car, then the sound of its engine. A mob of angry men banged and pounded and beat on the car as it backed up and pulled into the street. It sped south as someone fired shots. The crowd scattered like loose marbles. The CBC crew made a beeline for the car and I threw myself on top of them as Sergo peeled into the street, dodging the dozens of other cars desperate to get away.

Even as the international community condemned the violence,

Emmanuel "Toto" Constant and Louis Jodel Chamblain, the infamous leaders of FRAPH, announced a vigil to ensure that the USS *Harlan County*'s troops and heavyweight equipment might never reach Haitian soil. By the end of the day, they'd set up camp in front of the port, barricading street access.

U.S. press secretary Dee Dee Meyers said: "The president does not intend to let the troops sit on the ships offshore indefinitely," but added, "The president is not going to send [troops] into an environment that isn't secure."

Without consulting or even notifying the United Nations, President Aristide, or Prime Minister Malval, the United States withdrew the USS *Harlan County* from Haitian waters the next day. At the time of the retreat, I was several blocks away and heard a deafening round of automatic weapons. An old man walking next to me stopped, shook his head back and forth, then looked straight at me. "*Ale yo ale, kòm ti sourit. Sak pral rive nou koulye a?* They've gone, just like little mice. What's going to happen to us now?" he asked.

The only action the UN Security Council took was to reimpose sanctions.

The CBC crew finished their filming and, within hours, packed their bags to take the first flight out. Standing off to the side, I imagined the collective sigh everyone on the plane uttered when the wheels lifted off the tarmac and Haiti faded away behind steamy clouds.

The streets were as empty as an abandoned mining town. Nightlife came to a screeching halt. No one—not even the rats—ventured forth after dark. Local foreign correspondents, a group that didn't need an excuse to party, tempered their late-night festivities at restaurants and nightclubs, gathering instead at the bars of local hotels. The most popular was Hotel Montana, headquarters for Special Representative Dante Caputo and other high-ranking UN officials. Perched on the side of a hill halfway between Port-au-Prince and Pétionville, the Montana transformed from a poolside resort to a bastion of security. On the winding path leading to the hotel I passed armed guards, stiff like sentries. Just inside the hotel grounds dozens of men toting sidearms and rifles flanked Caputo's private security corps. The biggest, beefiest guys had long black bags that resembled golf bags, but everyone knew what was really inside. The only thing missing was men talking into their sleeves instead of cumbersome walkie-talkies.

I didn't want to bring my work home with me, but it was impossible to separate what I was reporting on from what I was living. We were already into the second week of the academic year, but most parents were too scared to send their kids to school. I wasn't scared in the sense of something awful happening to Kadja at school, but I was on heightened alert to the possibilities of things happening and was nonetheless impacted by the panic. I'd wanted to send Kadja to a preschool close to home but I didn't like the few choices I had—what I did find was a Montessori school, in Pétionville, a half-hour commute. The first day was fine, but the second and third there were strikes and shooting, and I didn't want to take the risk of removing Kadja from our protected environment at home. The fourth day was fine and he had a wonderful time, but the following day was again dicey, and I wasn't going to take any chances. Over the weekend I spent a lot of time with him and knew he was ready for some interaction with other kids his age by the time Monday rolled around. But when I drove him to school that second week, I found it closed, boards nailed onto the shuttered windows. There was no one around to give me an explanation as to what happened or why, and no one answered the phone. Eventually I learned that the owner, a Trinidadian, had decided that Haiti was more than she wanted to take on, and so she'd just up and left. I scrambled to make sure that I had someone to watch Kadja, since my days were consumed with reporting.

On Thursday of that week, October 14, 1993, fifty-one Royal Canadian Mounted Police, members of the UN technical police force who had arrived less than a week earlier, pulled out. I heard the news on my way home from Gonaives, the country's third-largest town, north of the capital, where I'd been interviewing peasant groups and international human-rights monitors for a CBC radio journalist who had hired me for the week. Everyone we spoke with was discouraged by the news of the *Harlan County* and the departure of the RCMP, and Sergo, who had by now become my driver, confidant, bodyguard, and best friend, encouraged us to leave early so that we could get back to the capital by dark. Although the distance wasn't great, the road was littered with giant potholes, and it took nearly four hours to go less than 100 miles.

We arrived in Port-au-Prince just before twilight. "*Pa gen moun,*" Sergo said: There's no one around." His round, pleasant face turned down at the edges when he worried, and his full cheeks went taut. There was almost no traffic heading down the Pan-American Highway. As we turned toward Pacot and the Sacre Coeur Church, I felt a sudden chill and shivered involuntarily. "Something is wrong," I said.

Sergo nodded. "*Pa gen machann,*" he agreed: There are no vendors. "Or traffic. No people, no cars. Everything is too quiet. Why are all the shops closed already? Where is everyone?"

He turned on the radio in time to catch the end of a sentence: ". . . *te anile a kòz de asasinay minis jistis la Guy Malary ki te fèt apre midi a, anfas legliz Sakre Kè.* . . . has been canceled because of the assassination of Justice Minister Guy Malary that took place this afternoon in front of the Sacre Coeur Church."

We sat stunned, speechless. Tears welled in my eyes as I thought of the last time I'd seen Malary and remembered him saying that he was determined to see change in the country even if it killed him. The radio reporter continued: "Malary, his bodyguard, and his driver had just left the Justice Ministry, down the street from the Sacre Coeur Church, when they realized they were being chased by assassins, who killed the two men at the exact spot where Antoine Izméry had been murdered the month before."

We drove by the church in silence before heading up the hill to my house, both of us lost in the sad silence of our thoughts. Too many good people were dying. How was the country going to be able to recover from this sad period, I asked myself? How do Sergo, Jean Raymond, and so many other bright, well-intentioned Haitians, reconcile what is happening to Haiti when they see that it's going down the wrong path. They know there's a better way. I wanted to offer some word of comfort, some pearl of wisdom, but I stayed silent, because in the end there really wasn't much to say.

Cédras was scheduled to resign the following day, but he didn't. Instead, members of the International Civilian Mission left. The UN announced that for the safety of its staff of nearly 300, it was evacuating all personnel to the Dominican Republic. The observers I'd interviewed in Gonaives the day before had new worry lines around their eyes, at the corner of their mouths as I watched them get out of their UN vehicles and board the bus for the DR. As the buses rolled away and out of sight, they took with them Haiti's last chance for a quick resolution.

I went to speak with the CBC radio correspondent, who was staying on the second floor of the Montana. His picture window faced the bay; the airport runway was visible off to the right. "I have everything I need for my report," he said awkwardly, fumbling for a way to explain his early departure. "I'll still pay you for the week, but there's little reason for me to stay any longer."

I smiled. "Have a safe trip home," I said warmly. I understood, and didn't let on that his eyes held the same fear I saw in the faces of the workers at the Montana, the people I knew on my street, the vendors in the market—even my own. We shook hands. "Whenever you want to come back, just let me know," I said sincerely. "I'll still be here."

Thirty U.S. Marines stayed behind to fortify the U.S. embassy and protect the interests of about 1,000 other American citizens, but Belgium and Canada recommended that their citizens go home. Most did. Visibly bobbing in the bay was a mixture of UN destroyers and frigates, along with eight U.S. Coast Guard cutters. Their job was to patrol the waters as part of Able Manner, the U.S. program charged with controlling the threat of boat people. Ironically they were not there to control the people who were really out of control, paramilitary groups like FRAPH, the police, and the governing de facto military regime, but rather those who were trying to escape the terror that had engulfed their country.

The weekend was one of quiet disappointment. Thousands of Port-au-Prince residents flocked to the public bus stations to get out of town. Over the next two weeks, human-rights groups estimated that more than 10,000 people had fled the capital, but things weren't any safer in the countryside. Rural sheriffs and FRAPH members freely extorted, raped, tortured, and killed people. I wondered how people paid for their tickets—bus drivers had raised their rates three- and fourfold, and *machann* sold their entire stock of goods for a pittance. Supermarket shelves were only half full, even though the Malval government indicated that the sanctions would not be felt for at least a month.

Nighttime shooting was routine. Where there used to be security behind barred doors, every morning I heard stories about people beaten, robbed, and disappeared from their homes. The radio reported eight bodies in the capital streets Sunday morning alone. The *attachés* who committed the crimes weren't strangers to the victims, they were often power-hungry, desperate, devious men who wanted to take advantage of the vacuum of law and order, right old wrongs, collect old debts. Far too often, they lived next door to the people they attacked, and the victims were unable to defend themselves. Parents kept their children home from school. The government postponed the official opening of the State University. Kadja's school was still boarded shut. How was it that I had become a person who understood violence to be routine?

U.S. Embassy spokesperson Stan Schrager, who was the most accessible diplomat of the time, held daily press briefings. He repeated the official line that "the Governors Island Accord is still the best formula for transition from military to civilian rule," and although he had the reputation of being the king of sound bites, it was obvious to all of us that his heart wasn't in it with this one. He had trouble looking us in the eye and wasn't as available for informal chats as he used to be. He announced that the United States had frozen the assets of Cédras and forty other military and coup supporters, including FRAPH leaders Toto Constant and Louis Jodel Chamblain, but said nothing about the men's removal.

I spent long afternoons outside Malval's house, along with several dozen journalists, on a routine basis. We were on a permanent stakeout to see if Malval or Cédras, who often came to secret meetings inside, would make a statement. I had plenty of work, with three to four articles a week for the *Monitor* and numerous freelance jobs for visiting media, and these lazy afternoons were part of the job, even though I felt as though I wasn't doing a thing. It was hard to concentrate on anything. I brought books I never read, a laptop I never opened. The most I could handle was a word or card game; other journalists caught up on their sleep, gossip, and the latest rumors.

By October 30, two weeks after Cédras was to have resigned, Port-au-Prince degenerated from a ghost town to a morgue. Instead of celebrating Aristide's return, as had been agreed to in the Governors Island Accord, Haitians spent the day hiding from the armed thugs who patrolled the streets, which were littered with unclaimed bodies. The day was relatively quiet, but the night was marked by gunshots and barking dogs. All U.S. spokesman Stan Schrager said was: "By impeding the return of President Aristide on October 30, the Haitian military has won a battle but not the war."

On October 31, Constant held a press spectacle. The entire press corps showed up and waited on Toto's sprawling lawn for the conference to begin. It had the air of a circus, complete with cameramen and photographers jockeying for the main attraction, which was Constant reveling in the power he had over the media. I tried to force myself to pay attention to the dog-and-pony show, but couldn't concentrate, so instead of taking notes I just turned on my tape recorder. "FRAPH represents more than twenty political parties," Constant bragged, but was unable to name which ones they were.

I haggled with Faye Bowers at the *Monitor* over how much space to give FRAPH. "You have it too far down in the article," she insisted. "It is the lead in almost all the other stories."

"Toto Constant's only power is his gun," I replied, irritated that I had to change my copy for someone I didn't feel deserved any space at all. "He has no real following, and the more credibility we as press give him the more power he believes he has."

We compromised; his quotes stayed in the article but weren't the lead. Faye understood my frustration. I knew that FRAPH was important—it owned the city, ruling by gunshots at night, terror tactics during the day. On rue Champs de Mars, between rue de la Reunion and rue de l'Enterrement, FRAPH set up headquarters next to an innocuous blue-and-white bar/restaurant, the Normandy. No matter what time of day or night, there was always a crowd there, mostly macho men parading with heavy artillery in one hand and a bottle of booze in the other. Even Sergo, whom I thought of as my fearless hero, stopped the car a block from headquarters and asked to switch places whenever we drove by the Normandy because he didn't want the crowd outside to identify him as a driver for the media for fear of retaliation.

Five days after Aristide should have returned, Caputo set up a tripartite meeting between the UN, the Malval government, and the Haitian military. Along with dozens of journalists, I waited in the conference room of the Christopher Hotel, a moderate, middle-of-the-road lodging just off the Pan-American Highway. Inside the conference hall was a long table surrounded by chairs, Caputo at one end, Malval the other. Cabinet members, parliamentarians, and foreign diplomats fanned one side but the other—reserved for the Haitian military—remained empty. Forty-five long, tense-filled minutes after the designated meeting time, during which we sat in stiff, sticky silence, a courier delivered a letter to Caputo from General Cédras, declining the invitation to that meeting. "It is unacceptable that the internal security of the meeting is assured by foreign armed civilians," he wrote by way of explanation.

That closed the chapter. Caputo led the exodus; the next day, he flew to New York to talk to the UN Security Council, taking with him his sexy, strong bodyguards. One by one the journalists packed up and by the second week in November, the Montana Bar was as empty as the Normandy was crowded.

Now I had real time on my hands. I spent one twenty-four-hour period reading Donna Tartt's *The Secret History*. I wrote overdue letters to my sisters, trying to describe how I spent my time, knowing that even as I wrote they wouldn't be able to imagine it. I visited with friends I'd neglected for the last few months. Gisele's store was just a few minutes away, and when I didn't have gas, we'd walk over there. Kadja rearranged her shelves while she and I drank coffee and talked politics. I installed a modem I'd bought the previous August. But with the shortages of electricity, I rationed my time on the computer so that if there was ever an emergency, I could use the reserve battery to complete a story.

I stayed close to home. Kadja's innocent joy and delight in my company gave me the lift I needed to get through my own dark mood about the black cloud suffocating the country, but it was a challenge to be creative about how to fill our time. Just a minute from our home was a small bridge over a ravine where people dumped their garbage. It became a feeding ground for the livestock, so at least once a day, we went to visit the neighborhood pigs who feasted there. We adopted the fattest, most oversized pig I'd ever seen. Kadja called her *"ti bèf"*—little cow; and squealed with delight as he chased her down the street. She paid him no mind, strutting regally down the street as though she owned it.

Walking was preferable to driving anywhere—the fuel supply was low and contraband prices were high. I pitched a story to the *Monitor* on the contraband fuel coming from the Dominican Republic. They agreed to pay my travel fee, which was helpful, given the rising cost of gas. Several journalists friends, Andrew from Scotland, along with Greg from England joined me—Andrew because he craved a cold beer and Greg because it was something to do. Sato, a Japanese photographer I knew from San Francisco, hopped in the car at the last minute, hoping to take some interesting photos.

I took the thirty-mile, two-lane highway to the border, racing along one of Haiti's newest and finest roads. I was sure it had been built specifically to help the Haitian military get access to Dominican fuel. Nothing—certainly no road—had ever been constructed so quickly in Haiti, and never so discreetly. The road was as smooth as a silver platter, smoke- and traffic-free, and I closed my eyes as I pressed my foot on the gas pedal, unconcerned about having to break for potholes, garbage, or even cows. For a very brief and delicious second, I forgot where I was.

We knew we were getting closer to the border as activity increased on nearby Lake Saumatre, the body of water straddling the border between Haiti and the Dominican Republic. Gasoline runners stapled together small pieces of wood to serve as rowboats upon which they transported gasoline in everything from liquid dishwashing containers to five-gallon drums. Their only limitation was the size of the container—anything bigger than five gallons would sink the rickety wooden platforms.

Gasoline at the Dominican pumps sold for about $1.50, but was resold at the DR dock for $3 and again on the Haitian side of the border for $6. An organized Mafia sold it in the capital for anywhere from $8 to $10. I knew plenty of people who'd bought what they thought was contraband petrol on a stretch of the highway in Port-au-Prince known as Gasoline Alley from one of the many vendors there who set up makeshift mom-and-pop "gasoline pumps." Too often it was watered-down gas or avocado oil or something in between, and it burned out car engines. We smiled in anticipation of a full tank of real gas, cold beer, and a lazy afternoon away from the repressive fog we were living in.

But we ran into trouble right away. Greg and Sato hadn't applied for a Dominican visa and, as a Japanese citizen, Sato also needed a Haitian visa to go in and out of Haiti. We avoided the first crisis by paying the customs officer a small bribe, known as *woulman*, to fix Sato's papers. Confident that he would have no problem with his documents because he was British, Greg told me to continue on, so we did, driving directly across no-man's-land. We could taste the cold beer, it was so near. With the lack of electricity, an ice-cold anything in Haiti was as rare as a gallon of pure gasoline.

"I can feel the foam on my lips," said Andrew, in his pronounced Scottish burr.

"A brewski," said Greg, "now that's my idea of a Sunday afternoon."

But after two hours of standing in lines at Dominican immigration, we were beginning to wonder if even gasoline was going to be a possibility. Immigration officials sent us from one window to another, one agent palming us off on the next until Andrew, who was starting to foam at the mouth in a way he hadn't expected, barged unannounced into the director's office. He emerged ten minutes later with a wide grin. "If we buy Dominican car insurance for $60, we'll be allowed in."

We walked in the hot midday sun to another building ten minutes away, paid our fee, and then returned to the first building— only to find that the immigration desk had closed for lunch. One hour turned into two before we were given our papers. We piled back in the car, but didn't get more than 100 yards away when a Dominican sergeant on a motorcycle pulled us over, for no apparent reason. When he discovered that Sato and Greg didn't have an official stamp, he escorted us back to immigration, where he read us the riot act. Sato and Greg were forbidden to leave the immigration area, but Andrew and I were free to go. We promised the two of them that we would make a quick trip to find gas and then, cold beers in hand, return to pick them up. It was already past 3:00 P.M., and the border was set to close at 5:00.

The nearest gas station was 60 kilometers away, so rather than risk using up our limited time, we headed toward the nearest border town, La Descubierta, just 24 kilometers away. We immediately noticed a Haitian officer loading a ten-gallon gasoline container into his car from a house right off the main street. We waited until he pulled away before taking his spot.

The odor of gasoline permeated the air—I felt as though I'd just bathed in it. Inside the open door of the small home where the Haitian officer had emerged were dozens of five-gallon drums and rubber hosing lining the room. In the center a corpulent one-eyed Dominican sat quietly in his rocking chair. He heard us approach and called gruffly for his wife, a querulous woman who agreed to sell us gasoline for six dollars per gallon. Even with the cost of the visas, border fees, and insurance, I was still buying for less than the asking price in Haiti. Dynamita, or Dynamite, as the one-eyed Dominican called himself, manipulated his makeshift system of tubes and hoses and filled my tank. Fully gassed, we bought beers and headed back to retrieve Sato and Greg, making it back to Port-au-Prince just before dark.

But the gas didn't last long. By the end of November, I had only ten gallons left in my car and another fifteen in reserve. Rumor had it that the military had stockpiled enough fuel to last another six months; coupled with their control over the stock on the black market, they didn't have anything to worry about. The only improvement in the country was a slight ease in the amount of repression—triumphant in spoiling Aristide's October 30 return, the paramilitary eased up on repression.

Like many of my friends, I was at a loss as to how to spend the holiday season. The only ones in Haiti who had anything to celebrate were those who supported the coup, had enough gas to run their generators, or were buying contraband. Like most of my *blan* friends, I decided to take a minibreak for a few days and go to the States. As we descended onto the snow-covered runway of New York, Kadja looked out of the window. His eyes grew wide and he gripped my hand tightly. "*Woyoyo, manman, gade sik la,*" he said in awe: "Oh my goodness, Mom, look at all that sugar!"

Chapter VIII

Trekking Along

Espyon bon, men li tire anpil gouvènman.
Spies are good, but they've toppled many a government.

In the spring of 1994, Jean Raymond's mother came in from the countryside to stay with us for a few days. Her visit coincided with a call
from Mike, my tall British journalist buddy who wanted to know if I
was up for a three-day Haitian-style "backpacking" trip to the mountains. Agnes, my mother-in-law, pushed me out the door, thrilled at
the chance to take care of her grandson. Two and a half years into the
coup, with little forward movement politically, minimal freelance
work, and even less electricity, this was a welcome diversion.

"How about Parc National La Visite?" Mike suggested. The timing
seemed just right: the weather was still in transition from the fresh
winter air, the temperature moderate, and the rainy season just around
the corner. La Visite was one of four national parks that struggled to

survive Haiti's proverbial lack of management, rural sprawl, and the peasants' stubborn use of timber for charcoal. Something like less than 3 percent of Haiti's land was now forested, in contrast to the time the island was so lush it was known as the Pearl of the Antilles. Mike thought we might find animals and birds in La Visite that weren't living anywhere else in Haiti, including the endangered mongoose. "We could climb one of the three peaks, or visit the waterfall. Someone said there are some limestone caves and a 1000-meter limestone cliff surrounded by a virgin forest."

"When do we leave?" I said.

"Stick a poncho, long-sleeved shirt, and shorts in your backpack, and we're off," Mike said. "I've got an extra sleeping bag and canteen. Don't think there's anything else you need." Except to speak with Jean Raymond and make sure it was okay with him. I thought carefully about how to broach the subject so that he wouldn't take the invitation in another context. We'd come a long way in our relationship, but jealousy was still an issue. Other than Jean-Marie, which had come in the beginning of my relationship with Jean Raymond, I hadn't had even the slightest interest in another man since we'd been together, but the question of his fidelity popped up from time to time. It was like the odd allergy that caused a runny nose, watery eyes, and sneezing for no apparent reason. If he was interested, Jean Raymond was going to cheat on me regardless of whether or not I was in town. He hadn't given me a reason to be concerned, so I wasn't. And I certainly hadn't given him a reason to be concerned, but my going away with another man for three days might give him pause if not presented strategically.

"Mike suggested going hiking in the mountains for a few days." I said when he got home from one of his rehearsals. I was sitting at my desk writing; Kadja was playing with his Batmans on the floor next to me. "He thought about going to La Visite. Are you interested?"

For years, Jean Raymond was cordial to Mike, but suspicious of him. Even though he wouldn't admit it, he was threatened by Mike. As colleagues, Mike and I spent time together covering events, conferring on political matters, and sharing information on articles we wrote. Mike and Jean Raymond were always pleasant to each other, but they weren't friends, and I didn't think they ever would be. I tried hard to show Jean Raymond that I had no romantic interest in Mike and often said so, but I wasn't sure he believed me.

"Why would I want to do that?" he responded.

"To see another part of Haiti, do something different."

"Can't," he said. "Got some things to do, the band is rehearsing and I'm working on a new song."

"Well, if you'll be that busy, it's probably a great time for me to go."

"Hmm."

"Plus your mom is here, and I know she'd be really happy for the chance to be with Kadja. And Rose Andrée will be here, I could ask her to spend the night if you're going to be out late. I will be back the day after tomorrow." Rose Andrée was like a member of our family, a young, warm, competent girl who had started working for us when we moved back to Haiti the year before. Kadja adored her, and she him— my only hesitation with her had been when she started proselytizing the philosophy of Jehovah's Witnesses, of which she was a devoted member. When I heard Kadja say *"Mèsi, Jeova,"* before eating his meal, I intervened quickly. Since then, she kept her religious practices to herself.

"Yeah, why not?" he said and I turned back to my computer, smiling.

Three friends were at Mike's the morning of our departure, Haitian musicians from the popular band Boukman Ek Speryans, who had stopped over unexpectedly the night before and wanted to tag along. If Jean Raymond had known that, he might have objected to my going, now that it was his wife and four guys, not just Mike. I thought about calling him to let him know, but discarded that idea as soon as it popped into my head. Why look for trouble? I turned my attention to their backpacks. "How come yours look so empty compared to mine?" I asked, suddenly worried that despite my meager packing I was still taking too much.

"Because you *blan* (foreigners) always overprepare," said Lolo, the tall, affable bandleader. I'd known Lolo for several years, a bushy guy with a wide smile hidden behind a full beard. His short dreads stuck out of a small leather cap and his bulky body didn't seem up for a trek, but set out we did, leaving Mike's car at the bus stop where downtown we boarded a rickety, overcrowded Haitian bus to the mountain town of Kenscoff. The road, a windy, tree-lined two-laner had more bumps and potholes than an egg carton; what should have been a quick fifteen-minute ride took forty-five. The houses, which grew in size and comfort as we progressed upward, used to be for the wealthy, but as I gazed out the window, desperate for fresh air and fearful that I might otherwise vomit on the passengers in front of me, urban sprawl was evident by the growing number of shacks built irresponsibly on the hillsides between the mansions.

Just minutes onto the trail, the sun disappeared and it started to sprinkle. At first the rain fell like gentle rice flour sprinkling through a sifter, soft and fine, but suddenly, without warning the skies opened up. Mike and I barely had time to put on our ponchos before the rain fell like pellets, heavy and punishing. It was so thick that it was impossible to see five feet in front of us, and hardly worth looking back to see how far behind Lolo and our other friends had fallen. "Not going to get far tonight," I complained quietly, but loudly enough for Mike to hear.

"Don't worry, Kath," he said and gave my arm a squeeze. "We'll get there when we get there; it's not like we have reservations."

Because the initial part of the road was paved, our shoes stayed relatively dry, but as the road broke up, we began trucking through slushy red soil that stuck to our boots in baseball-sized clumps. Every so often I wiped my heels clean with a stick, but the mud balled up again just a few steps later. Eventually I resigned myself to carrying an extra pound of slush on each foot, marveling at the Haitian market women who passed us barefooted, produce piled high on their heads in woven baskets.

We were only halfway to our destination by the time it got dark. "How about reevaluating our itinerary?" Mike proposed. "It doesn't make any sense to keep climbing higher because the weather in the higher elevations is only going to get worse. We could continue walking along the western section of Massif de la Selle and go to Seguin. From there we can head to Marigot and catch a bus back to Port-au-Prince."

All agreed; we turned toward Pierre Louis, a tiny village nestled at the bottom of one of the numerous mountains we'd been traversing. It was too dark to see much, but Davius, the town drunk, spotted us as soon as we arrived and, as luck would have it, made me his mission for the evening. Despite my persistent protests, he insisted on being my chaperon, host, and local tour guide. I also suspected he entertained other plans for me that evening but I made it clear, quickly, that I planned to spend the night asleep in my sleeping bag, alone.

He introduced us to Bòs Mizè, an unemployed carpenter who happily took our money in exchange for providing us with a place to sleep. We were exceptionally hungry but because we'd arrived so late all the *machann* with their pots of cooked food had gone home. We negotiated a deal with our host's sister to improvise an evening meal from rice, cabbage, and *aransel* (salted herring), the only things available at the market at that late hour. She threw in the firewood for free but charged ten times the normal price for the spices and Maggi, a bouillon cube that is to Haitian cuisine what soy sauce is to Chinese. The dinner was tasteless and heavy and on top of that there was no potable drinking water, so I drank Juna, Haiti's most popular locally produced Kool-Aid imitation that just made me thirstier. Still, I was happy to lie quietly on the too-small sofa and quickly fell asleep to the patter of a light drizzle on the tin roof overhead.

I woke to the smell of a charcoal fire and fresh coffee, which Bòs Mizè's sister had made in a *grèg*—a piece of cheesecloth wrapped around a metal wire through which water is poured over coffee grounds. When the *machann pen* (bread lady) came by with a basket on her head I purchased several loaves to entice the boys to life as I wrote in my journal on the crumbling porch and listened to the crickets and scuttle of tree branches sweeping the roof.

Despite our silent partner of mud and overcast skies, I inhaled the scenery once we got going. Over the first hilltop the colors leapt out like shooting stars—emerald green leaves, bright orange carrots brimming from the baskets of the market ladies, blue patches of sky dusted with silvery clouds. Bespattered with mud, we climbed up and over the mountains, the constant drizzle our uninvited companion. We passed through forests and dense thickets until we reached the southeast rock formation appropriately named Broken Teeth—*Kase Dan*—a field of sharp, irregular rocks that created the impression of walking through a cave without a top in the midst of stalagmite spikes reaching to the heavens above. This was a part of Haiti I'd never experienced before, didn't know existed, and suddenly I fell in love with the country all over again, through the sweat, mud, grime, and other unidentifiable layers crusting over my skin. This was the Haiti that I had trouble describing to my family and friends who couldn't understand why I stayed. It was the spiritual side that too often eluded the average tourist who saw only Haiti's poverty, crime, and filth. Outside the city, away from the noise and pollution, there were intense colors, private moments, vast passages that forged an irreversible bond between me and the country I now considered home.

We reached Seguin midafternoon. The market square, located prominently in the town center, was conspicuously empty, normal for a nonmarket day, so I looked around for a place to rest and, hoped against the odds, a *machann* would still have some hot coffee for sale. As I turned to take off my pack, a thin, middle-aged man with a slight limp and pockmarked complexion appeared out of nowhere and signaled to me with his chin. "*Chef la bezwen-w,*" he said: The boss wants to see you. He turned on his heels and limped away, motioning for me to follow. I had no idea who the "boss" was or what he wanted but I didn't think it was good news. Sore and tired, I begrudgingly picked up my pack and joined Mike and the others in a march through the empty, muddy market, down Main Street toward the seedy mustard-colored military post. Just outside the sad-looking building stood a young man who appeared to have nothing better to do than stand there looking for trouble.

I knew the moment he and I set eyes on each other that things were going to get ugly. A military official of some sort, he had a "bad boy" stance designed to intimidate, and when he turned from us he walked with an exaggerated strut, his broad shoulders sashaying back and forth. He was in his twenties, fit, with sculpted features and cropped hair, coal black eyes. His expression was tight and arrogant and his eyes a deep, nasty black, the kind I ran from in my dreams.

He didn't say a word, just flicked his head toward his office as he swaggered through the door. We followed silently, unsure how to handle the situation.

"*Mete bagay ou yo la,*" he ordered: Put your things there.

"*Chita!*" he barked: Sit, and motioned to the long wooden bench propped up by the side of the west wall. Within minutes a crowd of locals appeared at the door; a smattering of curious faces poking at each other through the lone window to see this unusual sight of strangers, until the thin man with the limp, and a slightly beefier man with cropped hair and arched eyebrows, snapped at them in severe, menacing tones and lifted their *fwèt* (whip) and machete to intimidate them. "*Attachés,*" I said to Mike, the word used to describe flunkies and other devious types who were loosely on the payroll of the military. Sometimes *attachés* did nothing more than the military's dirty work, enslaved to the tiny handful of coins they got, not some false ideology that they were actually doing anything moral or for some higher cause. Some *attachés* I knew had been Aristide supporters, but they realized after the coup that the money was in the hands of the military and quickly shifted allegiance. "They look mean and hungry."

"Shhh," Mike said and shot me a look. "Not now."

The officer, who still hadn't identified himself, asked us for our identification. I went limp. It hadn't occurred to me to bring identification. I poked Mike in the ribs regretfully; he shook his head in reproach, knowing already what I was going to say.

The chief started his interrogation with Lolo, and to my surprise Lolo pulled out his identification card. What if I was the only one who didn't have one? I tried to curl my body into itself, hating how exposed I was, like a condemned criminal waiting for my execution. If he wanted to, the officer could use this as a pretext for letting my companions go but keeping me. Despite the cool breeze, I felt my face flush and my hands itch. I started calculating: it would take at least a day for Mike to get to Port-au-Prince and back again either to bring me identification or some other form of relief. I was short of breath just thinking of what might happen to me in the interim. I leaned over to get assurance from Mike, but he was concentrating on what the captain was saying to Lolo and motioned me to sit still.

The room we were in had only the bench we were sitting on, a large chair that the officer was using, a desk, a window, and three doors. One door led to the outside, where the officer had a sweeping view of the marketplace. I imagined him holding court on innocent passersby, controlling them like a king during times of medieval repression. Here in the countryside, his word was law. People responded to his mood and desire, or else. It scared me just to think about.

The door on the left led to a prison cell, and the one on the right appeared to be for private use. As the questioning proceeded, friends of the officer wandered through and greeted him as Captain Louis. I took a little bit of comfort in knowing this man's name; if I was going to be tortured or raped or die at his hands, at least it wouldn't be by someone anonymous. I tried to redirect my thinking, but it was hard to purge the images I'd accumulated over the last two and a half years, of inhumane, barbaric acts executed by the military and police. If the tortures I knew about filled me with fear, I shivered at the ones I couldn't conceive. Even though we were less than 30 miles from where we'd started, we could have been in Siberia. This was like the end of the earth, where all my skills, contacts, and experiences were useless.

As Captain Louis finished with Lolo and called up the next musician, a smart-looking woman in tight jeans and a sheer halter-top strutted in carrying a glass bowl between two checked cloth napkins. She flashed a knowing smile at Captain Louis and without a word entered the room on the right, closing the door firmly behind her.

Captain Louis was reveling in his role as interrogator. I was sure he had newfound fame, two *blans*, and members of a popular Haitian band in his custody. He spit out his questions with accustomed authority: "*Ki moun nou ye, ki sa nap fè la, kote nou prale?* Who are you, what are you doing here, where are you going?" My friends maintained their cool even when told to drop their pants and empty the contents of their packs on the floor. Under orders from Captain Louis, the *attachés* examined everything meticulously—even the lining of our sleeping bags. If they were looking for drugs, something illegal or valuable that they might extract as a bribe, we disappointed them. They found nothing other than underwear, toothbrushes, a few plastic bags, and a flashlight.

When Captain Louis finally turned to me, the last of our group, I felt the final color drain from my face. He brightened when he learned I had no identification. "Against the law," he said, wagging his finger at me with gleeful authority. I looked through his steel-cold eyes and saw the beginning of a scenario I knew I wasn't going to like. "And where is your written authorization from the Minister of the Interior to be traveling in my *komin* (district)?"

This request was bogus, but I kept quiet. The only consolation I had about breaking the law was that it seemed to distract him enough that he didn't ask me to lower my pants. "I have no choice but to lock you up," he said smugly, satisfaction dripping from his mouth like a drooling predator. "You will spend the night in jail and tomorrow I will send someone to accompany you to Cayes Jacmel, where the local commander will decide what to do with you."

A cold wind whipped through me. A night in jail with these men? Miles away from a real road, telephone, any kind of secure, familiar surroundings? Now I really panicked. What would happen to me? What would Jean Raymond think when we didn't make it back tomorrow? Cayes Jacmel was at least another half-day hike, and then we had to deal with an even-higher-ranking commander if and when we got there. I swallowed hard, not wanting to give him the satisfaction of seeing me puke my guts out.

"I have to think where to put you all," he said, and it was at that moment I realized we—Mike, Lolo, and the boys—we were all in this together, that it wasn't just me who was going to be locked up, though the guys could rightfully blame me for our detention. Emboldened by the thought that I wasn't going to be imprisoned alone, something came over me, some unexpected aggression I didn't know I was capable of. Again, the impact Haiti had on me came out in the most unexpected moments, and this was one of them. I was so furious, it didn't even occur to me to swallow my words. I was tired of always being correct in a country where one seldom was, and so I unleashed my fury.

"You can't do that," I said. "We've done nothing wrong. You don't want us, here, fine, let us go. We're not hurting anyone, we're not breaking any laws. Just say the word and you'll never see us again. There's no way we can spend the night here—it's impossible. You'll have to let us go, immediately."

My outburst made him smile, which brought tears of frustration to the corner of my eyelids and spilled over before I could blink them back. Mike, clearheaded and unemotional, intervened in an effort to calm things down, but Captain Louis, egged on by my belligerence, stuck his shoulders back in defiance and beefed up his chest. Mike put his hand on my arm to silence me. I turned from everyone, boiling with rage, and took an oath of silence for the duration of the night.

The dilemma was where to house us. A middle-aged woman with enormous breasts and a waist the width of the door occupied the jail, a single room with no windows or furniture except a chair. According to the *attachés*, she was in jail because her husband, a friend of Captain Louis, wanted to teach her a lesson. She'd been giving her husband a hard time because of his affair with their neighbor. This double standard didn't surprise me any more than the irony of Captain Louis taking it upon himself to be the one to teach this woman the "proper" way to behave. It didn't escape me that this prisoner was spending the night in jail while Captain Louis was planning on screwing someone in the next room. I was sure that this wasn't an exception, but rather the rule in Seguin.

I was worried that they were going to put me in the cell with her while Mike and Lolo and the others slept somewhere else. Or even worse that I was going to be in a cell alone. The last thing I wanted was Captain Louis or one of his *attachés* to come calling. I tried hard to keep my breathing steady, not wanting to even look at Captain Louis or the other *attachés*.

While I stewed in silence, Mike and the boys took a more sensible approach, striking up a friendship with the *attachés*, who were fans of Lolo's band, and delighted to meet the musicians. That was the thing about these *attachés* that was so droll—they bought into this dog-eat-dog system and were willing to play the charade of holding us hostage because they were getting paid, however pitifully, for working for Captain Louis. It was a question of survival: better to be with him than against him. Eventually one of the *attachés* asked the captain if perhaps we might spend the night at his house. Captain Louis rejected the suggestion, saying it was too risky. But finally, after an excruciating silence, he looked around and said, "Why not sleep here?"

"Too public," the *attachés* said, and instead suggested we sleep in Captain Louis's "office," a place where it seemed he spent so much of his time that he had equipped it with a bed, a chest of drawers, a mirror, and a cushioned chair, as well as the young woman in the sexy outfit. She was lying casually on the bed listening to the radio when he opened the door. He made a show of gathering her up and taking her out back to explain the change of plans, then told his flunkies to move the bed from his office into the main room.

It was dark outside by the time the sleeping arrangements were complete. I was hungry and irritable, but my companions were in fine humor with their newfound buddies and after negotiating a price for food, we wrapped up to protect ourselves from the rain and trotted off in the mud, again, to the home of one of the *attachés*, Jorven.

Jorven's home was similar to Bòs Mizè's, but in slightly better shape. It had a living room and a bedroom. We sat around a wooden table on boxes and planks for chairs and gave Jorven a few extra gourdes for a round of *kleren*, which fortunately he kept a reserve of in a small cabinet under a calendar picture of the Virgin Mary. The house smelled like the countryside—wild, earthy, and fresh from the rain. As the discussion moved away from music, Jorven revealed he practiced Vodou, and for the next two hours the *attachés*, Mike, Lolo, and the musicians discussed local customs, rhythms, and rituals. I didn't participate. I was punishing myself with my vow of silence and overwhelmed by my inability to get past the absurdity of the situation. Dinner was tastier than the previous night, with rice and beans and some stewed vegetables, but I didn't have much of an appetite.

It was nearly 10:00 P.M. by the time we returned to Captain Louis's office. We gathered our bags, which had been rifled through during our absence, and followed Captain Louis to our "prison cell."

"*Pa fè bwi!*" he barked: Don't make any noise. You either, I thought, giving him my frostiest stare. He waited for us to light candles before firmly closing the door. I listened carefully and was grateful that there was no sound of a key turning in the latch. I had visions of a fire and us burning to death in the locked room, never identified.

I spread all the extra clothing I had on the floor before sandwiching myself in my sleeping bag, but the thin layer did nothing to stop the cold from seeping through the cement and into my bones. I wadded up my sweater for a pillow, then pulled a section over my head to drown out the buzz of the mosquitoes and the banter of the boys who were yakking it up, finding humor where I saw none. I admired their attitude, but took perverse pleasure in feeling sorry for myself. I stayed in that frame of mind most of the night as I tossed back and forth, in part trying to find a comfortable position, but also bothered by the noises coming from Captain Louis and his girlfriend. It was like being behind the scenes of a tacky porno film. I woke up groggy and stiff, but pleased that nothing "out of the ordinary" had happened. I welcomed daylight, even if the sun was still buried under layers of stratocumulus clouds and there was the proverbial slight drizzle.

Since we had nothing to do but leave we were ready to go as soon as we woke up. But Captain Louis couldn't find the man he'd assigned to accompany us. "*Mawon,*" Captain Louis muttered to himself furiously: Hiding. His eyes narrowed and his mouth pulled back in a snakelike position. He walked with the same conceit he'd displayed the night before but with a little less wiggle. He must have had a tough night, too, and now he was being humiliated in front of us. He had given orders for someone to be there first thing in the morning to accompany us but it looked as though his flunky stood him up.

To kill time we sat and drank coffee. We waited, drank some more coffee, and waited some more. Jorven intimated that the guy we were waiting for didn't want to make the hike with us but the fear of Captain Louis's wrath was so great he would eventually show up. And an hour later, he did, a thin man clad in thinner jeans, muddy boots, and a large straw hat. His face was long and drawn in the middle, pleasant but sad. He listened silently while Captain Louis chewed him out with expletives and head shaking and finger pointing, but no blows. When he ran out of steam, Captain Louis turned to us. *"Ale ave-l,"* he snarled: Go with him. "Make sure there's no problem or you'll have to deal with me."

With no regrets, we turned away from Captain Louis and nodded at our "warden," who was so pathetic that it was hard to take him seriously, and began the trek toward Perodin, where we hoped to catch a bus to Cayes Jacmel.

The trip was unpleasant, a steep, slippery downhill slide that was unforgiving and went on forever. My knees crunched and my thighs ached. The only relief was freshwater from abundant natural sources and for the first time in three days I rinsed off the layers of slime crusted to my skin, nails, and hair. As we dropped in altitude, we found flatter ground, warmer temperatures, and clearer skies. I delighted in shedding layers of sweaty, mud-splattered clothes and at the bottom of the hill I pulled out my only clean, dry T-shirt and gratefully peeled off the wet, smelly one and threw it away. No amount of washing was going to get that thing clean.

It was market day at Perodin. The rainbow of colors lifted my spirits—rows of red plastic containers with yellow tops, piles of carrots, cabbages, pumpkins, and potatoes. There were queues of used goods known as *pèpè:* pencils, shoes, schoolbooks. The boys made a beeline for cold beer. I went off in search of a bucket of water and the market women, taking one look at me, threw in a little soap for free. Cleansing my feet was a religious experience. It would be weeks before I would consider putting on my boots again, if ever.

We knew it would be easy to lose our chaperon in the crowd, but I felt sorry for him because he was going to have to climb back to Perodin that night and he had no money. He was as much a victim of Captain Louis as we were, and since he was kind and rather pitiable, we bought him something to eat while he went to find someone with whom he could trade his machete for a pocketknife. He returned with a smile on his face that grew even fuller as he ate; then we all boarded the crowded bus for Cayes Jacmel. I explained to the driver, in my sweetest and most seductive voice, that we would only be a few minutes clearing up a misunderstanding at the police station, and that we would pay him a little something if he would wait and take us on to Jacmel, just down the road, so that we could catch a bus back to Port-au-Prince. Otherwise, we might be stuck in Cayes Jacmel for hours waiting for another bus to come along, or worse, have to spend another night on the road. I knew Jean Raymond would be sick with worry if we didn't get back on time, and already it was looking pretty dubious that we could make it to the capital that day. It was a good two-hour drive from Jacmel to Port-au-Prince and I didn't want to arrive in downtown Port-au-Prince after dark, especially after what we'd just been through. Flashes of Kadja's curls and chubby arms flashed before me and I longed for one of his hugs.

We didn't arrive in Cayes Jacmel until after 4:00 P.M. Against the protests of the other passengers, the bus driver waited as the five of us got off the bus in front of the military headquarters with our warden, who with great temerity went inside to explain why we were there.

Meanwhile the *attachés* hanging outside the military headquarters recognized Lolo and the other band members immediately. "Maybe we can take advantage of that," Mike said to me, "so don't blow it with your temper." He was right, so I concentrated on reassuring the driver *"n'ap vini koulye a, koulye a menm;* we're coming right now, right now," but I lost all hope when I met the officer in charge of the Cayes Jacmel post. He resembled Michel François. Same mean, husky military type. Intimidating. He listened indifferently to our story, questioned us, and directed yet another search, though this time the boys didn't have to drop their trousers. The bus driver came to the door of the headquarters to fetch us, patience spent, and said he was leaving. I pleaded with him to wait just a few more minutes, knowing there were be no more buses to Jacmel that night, but I had little conviction in my voice.

I had hoped that this was just another shakedown and that once this commander saw we had nothing worth confiscating, he would let us go. I couldn't have been more wrong. With the same supreme arrogance delivered by Captain Louis, this man looked me up and down, undressed me with his eyes, then delivered another harsh reprimand for traveling without identification. "*Emposib,*" he said: Impossible. "You all think you can just travel around the country wherever and whenever you like? This isn't the United States. It is too late to clear things with Jacmel's military supervisor, so you will spend the night in my prison. Tomorrow, I will personally take you to Jacmel's *avan pòs.*"

"No, I can't spend another night in prison," I blurted out. "I have a son who is expecting me home tonight. This is ridiculous. Let us go home. We haven't done anything wrong. I don't understand what is going on here."

Everyone looked at me with surprise. True to my word, except for addressing the bus driver, I had been silent since yesterday's outburst. Mike shot me a warning look, but there was no stopping me now. "You can't keep jerking us around like this. There is no rule that says you have to have written permission to travel in the countryside. Everyone does it all the time. I've been here for six years, and this is the first time I've ever had a problem traveling to the countryside. Haiti has always been friendly to foreigners. And now you're saying we can't travel without written permission. Absurd. I didn't bring identification because we were going for a hike in the mountains. I was worried about carrying too much weight and I didn't want my things to get damp, so I only brought the bare essentials, as you can already see. I didn't bring identification, I didn't bring valuables, and I brought only enough money to get me through what I thought would be a simple three-day hike. This is the third day and my money is running out and I am tired and cranky and I want to get home to my son."

The chief paused. Then, as if I'd just told him I didn't like his outfit, he said, "*Dézolé, Madame*. Sorry, Madame. You will spend the night here. I will take you to Jacmel, myself, in the morning."

At that moment the bus driver tapped me on the shoulder. "*M'ale,*" he said definitively: I'm going.

I spun on my heels like a top out of control. I looked around in desperation to see if there was some solution staring me in the face but all I saw was the piercing eyes of the chief, the sad look in the eyes of my friends. Defeated, I nodded my head and told the others I would gather the rest of our things from the bus. Our warden followed me, and thinking he was going to help me bring our stuff inside I smiled at him gratefully through my tears of utter despair. "*Mwen pa gen senk kòb, madanm,*" he said. "I don't have a nickel to get back to Seguin. Can you give me some money for the bus?"

I smiled at the irony, my first smile in two days, and reached in to pull out the last of my money. At that very moment Mike came running down the path from the police station, shouting to leave our things on the bus. "*L'ap kite nou ale!*" Mike shouted gleefully: "He's agreed to let us go." The *attachés* who knew Lolo and the other band members looked at me and winked.

I didn't ask a single question, nor did I look back. I hopped on the bus and kept my eyes trained straight ahead as we rolled away, only too happy to leave behind Seguin, Perodin, Captain Louis, and the rain. I sat in the front, away from Mike, and Lolo, and the other musicians. I didn't want to know what had transpired in the two minutes I had left them inside with the captain. I didn't care. Those awful, spiteful, cocky military men were behind me now, and that was good enough for me. I nodded off, dreaming of Kadja and a dry night in my own bed.

Jean Raymond was happy to see me, but Kadja was overjoyed. He threw his chubby arms around my neck and smothered my cheeks, nose, and eyelids with kisses. I folded myself around him like a belt, tight and encompassing. I rustled my hands through his Shirley Temple curls and tickled his Buddha belly. That first night home I fell asleep with him gently snoring on my breast.

He was now enrolled in *Collège de l'Étoile,* a private French school with mostly middle-class students. I was happy to have discovered the school not just because it had a good reputation, but also because it was less than a ten-minute walk from our house. Not having to drive alleviated some of my concern about gasoline, given how scarce and expensive it was.

Being in school took care of the first half of the day, but Kadja was home by 2:30; after-school activities continued to be a challenge. We walked home from school slowly, studying the plants, trees, and chasing the sow and her piglets when we spotted them. With the meager resources available, we made up projects and games—designs from the perforated edges of computer papers, houses from playing cards and cardboard boxes. At night we played flashlight tag, jacks, and marbles. And when I ran out of creative juice, I allocated some of the precious electricity we had stored in our batteries to watch videos. Kadja loved Curious George, though he also liked the Sesame Street Sing-Along videos because he played on the drum that Jean Raymond had given him. Clearly Kadja was going to be a product of two cultures. Afterward we piled his books on the bed and read by the oil lamp until we both fell asleep.

We averaged about ten hours of electricity a week; the times that the government provided it were as random as the nightly shootings. When it came on at 3:00 A.M., the whole neighborhood came alive. Lights flooded the streets and the throttle of water pumps was as audible as motors revving for a drag race. I filled my water containers, printed things that had been piling up in my computer, and plugged everything in to charge. Turning the lights on in the bathroom after days of using candles and oil lamps made me feel like a movie star. Even Kadja woke up to watch videos.

Kadja's language skills were coming along—ever so slowly, since there was the combination of three at the same time. He spoke Creole to just about everyone, English to me, and French at school. It was impressive to watch his little mind at work as he switched back and forth between languages. He developed his own system, often translating sentences literally. "*Bouch mwen swaf,*" he said in Creole, then in English said, "My mouth is thirsty." After a fall, he said, "This does me hurt; *sa fèm mal.*" When his friend was hungry, Kadja motioned in English, "It's hungry," not yet aware that the English language delineates the Creole pronoun *li* as either he, she, or it.

One of our favorite pastimes was walking around the neighborhood visiting friends. One afternoon Kadja and I went to visit Andrew, my Scottish journalist friend whose unique sense of humor kept me laughing during some of the darker days we spent. We knocked on the door full of sweat and very thirsty. Andrew offered Kadja a Coke, and immediately forgot to give it to him as the two of us became engrossed in a conversation in the living room. Kadja wandered off to the kitchen and picked up a glass of flat Coke that had been sitting on the counter for days. He innocently walked over to Andrew and offered him the glass, ants crawling from it onto his tiny fingers and around his wrist and arm. "*Eske mwen ka bwe yon koka san bet?*" he asked: "Can I have a Coke without animals?"

Kadja had a kind of sweetness that made him irresistible not just to people, but also to biting insects. Mosquitoes hovered around him the way bees do flowers—nothing I did kept them away. I tried insect repellent, mosquito netting, citronella, eucalyptus. But they always found him. He contracted malaria numerous times, always with the same symptoms: fever, vomiting, and overall achiness. Each time he contracted malaria, he was unable to digest anything, even his medication—he was infected so often that his pediatrician no longer needed a consultation to prescribe the medicine. He just heard the alarm in my voice and said, "Start with the chloroquine immediately."

One evening Kadja was so ill he needed to get the antimalarial medicine injected. Françoise, a French dentist whose daughter was in school with Kadja, lived nearby. "*Map vini koulye,*" she said as soon as I explained how ill Kadja was: I'm coming right now. Within minutes she was there and delivered the shot. Françoise lived in the same complex where my Finnish friend Ritva had lived, but since the coup Ritva had stayed away from Haiti—it had been more than two years since I'd seen her. Françoise was petite but solid, with short black hair, dark eyebrows, and a pinch line above her small mouth that melted away with her quick sense of humor and hearty, honest laugh. I knew we'd get along the moment we met—her energy, as she often boasted, operated on 220 volts, rather than 110. Because of the tenuous situation created by the coup, Françoise also had more time on her hands than she would have otherwise, and so we were able to see each other frequently. It helped that our kids were about the same age and played well together. Developing a friendship with her was a wonderful gift for me, and contributed to my feeling as though finally, after several years, I was developing a community of people I could count on, much as I had in the States. Together with Martine, a Canadian nongovernmental worker who also lived in Françoise's building, my circle of women had grown and my sense of isolation diminished. "*Relem kèlkswa lè, siw beʒwen mwen,*" she said: Call me, regardless of the hour, if you need me and I knew she meant it. Given how difficult things were in Haiti it was comforting having friends that were like family.

The strain of malaria in Haiti, different from the dormant, recurring kind in Africa, meant Kadja could become infected again only if another malaria-carrying mosquito bit him, but that was little consolation watching him suffer. The next morning his fever was down but he was so weak he didn't want to get out of bed. A few times he opened his eyes and asked for water but by the time I brought it back he was already asleep.

Over the weekend he continued to feel better, so Martine, Françoise, and I splurged on our gasoline ration and drove the kids to the beach. It was a warm, clear day and the water invigorated us with new energy. But that night Kadja woke up at 4:30 A.M., trembling and shrieking, "*Gwo bet, gwo bet* (large animal)." His face was painfully red, his teary eyes large and frightened. Jean Raymond took his hand and walked him around the house with a flashlight, opening up every closet, drawer, window, and door to show him there were no monsters. We calmed him down enough to tuck him back in bed and sing him to sleep.

But twenty minutes later he started to scream again, this time crying relentlessly for Rose Andrée, the young woman who watched him during the day. Nothing I did consoled him—again we led him around the house to show him that Rose Andrée wasn't there, that it was nighttime and everyone was in bed sleeping, but it had little impact. I couldn't tell exactly why he wanted Rose Andrée but I was too spent to give it much thought. Exhausted, I left him to sleep with Jean Raymond and lay down on the couch in the living room. He soon joined me, all smiles, an endearing "*Bonjou mami, kijan ou ye?*": Good morning, Mom, how are you?, and a morning appetite. Daylight was just around the corner;

sleep was out of the question so I cooked a large bowl of *labouyi* (Haitian-style porridge) and watched him devour it while I nursed a cup of coffee. Jean Raymond remained fast asleep.

I was convinced that Kadja's outburst was a combination of recovering from an irregular sleeping pattern because of the malaria, and a bad dream. Jean Raymond was convinced that there was *maji*, Haitian-style magic involved, because he himself had also been feeling out of sorts. "A tightening of the chest, coughing, and an upset stomach," he explained. He went to his nightstand to pull out the formula he had had the *oungan* (Vodou priest) from Gonaives prepare for him, convinced that using it would purge the bad spirit from the house.

The container he was looking for wasn't there. I cringed. The week before, while cleaning out the drawer, a white solution spilled from a plastic container. Forgetting that Jean Raymond had had an *oungan* in the house a short time prior, and unaware of the significance of the substance, I cleaned out the drawer, washed the bowl and put it back in the kitchen without giving it another thought.

Jean Raymond believed that this potion, its placement in the drawer, and the role it was meant to play in creating harmony and protecting his family were the key factors to the contrariness, the inexplicable "out-of-sorts" mood that he and Kadja were experiencing. When I confessed what I'd done, he was convinced that my interference and disposal of the potion was to blame for everything that had gone wrong. Arguing the point seemed futile. "It's too late. The damage has been done," he muttered, and walked off grumbling that now he had to find a way to placate the Haitian spirits for my stupidity.

A few weeks later, in the spring of 1994, after seven weeks of near-total darkness, the government resumed distribution of electricity to diverse neighborhoods throughout the capital. The local press said it was because the government finished cleaning out thirty years of accumulated silt and other unidentifiable matter from the Peligre Dam that had clogged the turbines and prohibited it from working at capacity.

Maybe so, but I suspected there was another factor at play. The World Cup was approaching quickly. Fanaticism for soccer in Haiti surpassed the popularity of the Super Bowl, NBA playoffs, World Series, Masters, and U.S. Open combined. Rather than resume diverting a portion of the water from the Peligre Dam to the Artibonite Valley for the rice fields as had been routine, the government siphoned it off to generate power in the capital. It knew if it didn't provide electricity to broadcast the tournament soccer matches, the population could explode. Supplying additional hours of electricity seemed a small price to pay to control the population.

At the same time the blackouts ceased, so did my unemployment drought. Since the time of my trip with Mike to the mountains, there had been very little work because the situation in Haiti had been status quo. But recent events in Haiti had catapulted it back into the news like a boomerang. The United Nations increased sanctions—expanding the six-month-old arms and oil embargo to include the cancellation of visas and freezing of assets of some 600 Haitians, all military officers and coup backers. It restricted all noncommercial flights and sea traffic to humanitarian use only. And it threatened to expand the oil and arms embargo to a complete embargo if General Raoul Cédras, Police Chief Michel François, and military Chief of Staff Philippe Biamby refused to step down.

The United States halted the forced repatriation of Haitian refugees, claiming that it "changed its procedure, not its policy." Of the 40,000 boat people who left Haiti during the previous two-and-a-half years, only 5 percent had received political asylum.

I was getting calls for freelance work from a variety of news agencies: *The Economist, USNews & World Report,* and the *Boston Globe.* Mike decided to stop writing articles to "free up his mind" to work on longer pieces, so I took over his string with the *Houston Chronicle.* That, plus my regular writing for the *Christian Science Monitor* and *San Francisco Chronicle* had my days as full as my weeks used to be.

On May 11, two journalists working for reputable American newspapers hired me to translate an interview with Evans Paul, former Mayor of Port-au-Prince who had been an ally of Aristide's and one of the first people I met in Haiti. He'd been in hiding since the coup, working with others to keep the grassroots movement alive. Getting to him involved various maneuvers and contacts, secret phone numbers, and several security checks.

"Did you hear the rumor that Parliament is going to install a new president today?" he asked me after the interview. While having employed questionable political strategies, the de facto government had never gone as far as inaugurating a parallel government. "It's not the first time this rumor has circulated, but anything's possible."

"Worth heading over there to check it out," I said. Turning to my colleagues, I asked them if they were interested in going with me.

"I don't know," said one of the journalists, looking at his peer for a response. "What do you think?"

"Let's go to lunch," she replied, and with a shrug, I left them, breezing west through the empty streets. I turned down Avenue Marie Jean toward the government building and almost lost control of the car, so great was my surprise at seeing the military band in formation in the middle of the street. Their black pants and white shirts glistened like chessmen in the midday sun, rays reflecting off their brass instruments onto the row of official government cars that lined the street.

I pushed my way through the small crowd of Haitians that had gathered around the metal gate surrounding the entrance. "We're finished with Aristide, he's bad for the country, a rabid dog," a military supporter shouted in my face, his foul breath a match for his words. Past the security guards and in the main chamber men dressed in suits, ties, and wingtips encircled me. I hadn't seen many of these strident putschists and ardent anti-Aristide businessmen, politicians, and military officers since last fall, during the *Harlan County* incident. They looked even smugger this day than they had back then, but I nodded respectfully to the ones I knew.

The ceremony began with the arrival of four military high command and General Raoul Cédras, who appeared to be shrinking beneath the folds of his military uniform. I hadn't seen him in person in many months, and now he looked less the part of stately military dictator than he used to. The skin around his cheekbones was drawn as tight as Saran Wrap, his color a few shades paler than I remembered. A few foreign press thrust themselves forward and shouted to the general, hoping to evoke a reaction from him, but his hard, stone eyes stared straight ahead impassively, ever the devotee of military discipline.

After the military band played the national anthem, the de facto president of the de facto Senate called the session to order. "According to Article 149 of the Haitian Constitution, when the president is unable to carry out his functions, the head of the Supreme Court will replace him until elections are held."

Emile Jonassaint, a tall, thin man with a soft mustache, walked slowly toward the podium. His eighty-one years showed on his leathery, rough forehead. His dark blue suit complemented the pepper gray hair. A dapper young senator in the 1950s, he had been asked by François Duvalier to be on the Supreme Court, but he'd turned down the position. After Jean-Claude Duvalier's 1986 exile,

Jonassaint reemerged, coauthoring the 1987 Constitution that was still in effect. He was appointed head of the Supreme Court after the coup d'état but Aristide's prime minister, Robert Malval, fired him in 1993. This appointment was clearly orchestrated by a group of parliamentarians allied with the army.

"Today, Haiti won't die," he said. "I can't promise miracles because the illness is serious. The sickness was in the hand of the *blan*. Today, it's cured."

If I'd thought he was someone to take seriously, I might have been offended, but in fact he was partially right. Between the French colonizers and the manipulations of the Americans, Haiti had been squeezed tightly. But with leaders like Cédras, Namphy before him, and Duvalier before that, Haitians also seemed to be their own worst enemy.

As the procession left the Legislative Palace, the military band made a weak effort to play some sort of marching song but their success at harmony and synchronicity was as fruitless as trying to stay cool and composed after hours in the grueling sun. I followed the official cars as they made their way to the National Palace, where Jonassaint was sworn in with a twenty-one-gun salute. While Cédras and Jonassaint greeted the Presidential Guard and the small crowd that had gathered outside the palace gate, reporters scurried to their hotels to file before deadline.

It was at least another week before I met up with the two foreign journalists who'd hired me to translate for them the morning of Jonassaint's inauguration. They didn't look me in the eye—rather, they waved their hands to acknowledge me and then turned in the other direction. But by then I already knew they'd been reduced to hanging out at the hotel bar with other journalists to pick up incidentals of the ceremony they couldn't be bothered to attend. Then they complemented that information with what was available on the wires, folding it in to construct a story that hid from both the reader and their editors that they weren't, in fact, really there.

I worked twelve-hour days for the next three weeks: a day trip to the border to track the contraband fuel flowing from the Dominican Republic; a trip to the northern coast to see boats being built for the flood of refugees taking the treacherous voyage; futile attempts to reach Jonassaint, Cédras, Biamby. I never tried Michel François— even though no one had ever come after Harold or me for the little notebook we'd confiscated after our interview with him, I still thought that that day could come. The notebook remained safely tucked away in the shoebox in my closet. I couldn't be too careful. Since our interview with him, he'd never given another. And I never heard another word about or from Darryl Reaves, the American who tried to promote the Haitian military for something it wasn't— professional, competent, classy.

Leading up to this uninterrupted run of work, I'd had only one recent job that was as compelling. Human Rights Watch/America's Watch (HRW) hired me as a consultant for two weeks to work with a bright young woman from their Washington office who was collecting evidence against the Haitian government for crimes against women. HRW's premise was that state agents—police and military—were the ones stealing, raping, and committing sexual abuse, and thus the state of Haiti should be held accountable for these crimes. Prior to the coup, the modus operandi for state agents was systematically beating women on their reproductive parts. After the coup, the trend was rape.

Cases involving arrests and beatings were difficult to document, but far less difficult than rape. It was a challenge not only to iden-tify a victim, but then also to convince her of the importance of giving testimony. Too many women justifiably feared retribution, but the shame/guilt factor they endured also inhibited them from coming forward.

LaShawn, the researcher, was a tall, elegant woman with skin the color of sandalwood. She had piercing eyes and an efficient manner that got in the way of her effectiveness as a field researcher. This was, she admitted, her first field experience, and although she seemed genuinely excited by the project, she had little understanding of the importance of cultural sensitivity, much like an executive of a large corporation twice removed from the blue-collar workers he employs. When she bought something for two gourdes—a mere 20 cents—she peeled a 100-gourde note off a roll of five others. "Be careful with your money," I warned.

"Oh, come on!" she scoffed. "it's only $40."

"More than most people see in a month."

Her lack of understanding about Haiti's conditions underscored my own appreciation of Haiti's resourcefulness and resiliency. "Where's the nearest rape-crisis center?" she asked.

"There isn't one."

"Who are the counselors and what kind of training do they get?"

"There aren't any such counselors in Haiti."

We often ran late for appointments. As we drove from one to another, she said, "Pull over at a phone booth so we can let them know we'll be there soon." There was neither a phone booth in the country nor a phone number to call at the homes or meeting places where we scheduled interviews. LaShawn had yet to understand that the reality she operated in back home had little to do with Haiti's. Country conditions were as foreign to her as Creole. The things she took for granted in America were either unavailable, or available at a very high cost. I was becoming so accustomed to the hardship conditions of the coup and the peculiarities of Haiti that it was sobering to remember how abnormal they really were. I'd become so integrated into the Haitian way of thinking that it was hard for me to look back and know for certain if I would have been any less naïve in asking the questions that LaShawn was.

It also helped me better understand just how strong the women of Haiti were. By now I had become more integrated into the Haitian lifestyle, and while the wives and girlfriends of most of Jean Raymond's friends were not close friends we enjoyed each other's company. I was in awe of how they kept their lives together, finding enough money to cook a meal every day, and bring home enough water to bathe and wash clothes. There was no "leisure" time nor the protocol of making a "date" to get together—their leisure time was spent braiding hair, washing clothes, chopping onions or garlic, or something else to put in a bubbling pot of food.

This wasn't something I could explain to LaShawn any more than I could explain it to my sisters. It was just part of the lifestyle I lived. The point was brought home even further when, after an interview with a thin, attractive nineteen-year-old, LaShawn gave the young girl an unsolicited, heavy-handed lecture on why she shouldn't be seeing a forty-year-old man. That this man was the young girl's sole source of income didn't register with LaShawn, who made a quick and unsubstantiated judgment, labeling the girl a prostitute; the young girl saw herself as resourceful, using the man to get her out of her destitute living situation and affording her an opportunity to educate herself. She was only too well aware of the price she was paying, but she'd decided that it was worth it. The last thing she needed was an educated, financially stable woman from the States lecturing her on something she felt confident LaShawn knew nothing about.

LaShawn was on a mission, and any deviation from it was an

unnecessary diversion and thus a waste of time. She wanted to know, even before the interviews started, that the women were going to fit the profile she was looking for. But because of the sensitivity of the issue and the back channels I had to go through to set up the interviews, I often knew only that the woman had been raped—I wasn't always certain it was by a military or police officer. Each interview was different—like the victims, the circumstances, reaction, even the pace of providing details varied widely. When the victims finally got to the part that revealed who the perpetrator was, LaShawn was often down to biting her last nail. If the attacker didn't fit the profiler LaShawn needed, she cut the woman off. "Thank her for her time," LaShawn said as she began packing her bag to go to the next interview.

"I can't do that. You can't just dismiss her like that, after all the emotional trauma it took to get her to this point. Do you know how hard it was to persuade this woman to speak with us? Relive the experience so you can record it?" I was furious, but curbed my anger because I didn't want to distress the woman we were interviewing. I lowered my voice. "Just because the rapist isn't a soldier or policeman doesn't make the assault less traumatic to recount."

"I'm not saying that it does," LaShawn replied. "I'm just saying that I don't have a lot of time, and I'd rather be hearing the stories of women whose cases I can use in the report." But I drew the line. Although I was being paid to do a job for LaShawn, my allegiance was to the woman I was interviewing, and I circumvented the problem by not translating everything and letting her finish her story in her own time.

At one meeting, two young girls invited us to their home. This was unusual, because two foreigners driving up to a lower-middle class home in a popular neighborhood just north of downtown on a busy street, where *machann* and *attachés* intermingled on the street, usually drew attention. But because this was set up by a mutual friend, she had time to spread the word, telling people members of a religious community from the States would be visiting their neighborhood soon.

The younger of the two girls, thin and nervous, said that a few months earlier she and a friend had gone out one evening with two guys that they knew. "Friends," she said. Both policemen. Her friend was beaten so badly that she remained flat on her back for three weeks. There was no explanation. The attack came out of nowhere and no motive was apparent. "My friend left me alone. I don't know why. I just know I'm lucky," she said with tears in her eyes.

The other woman we interviewed, who was not present at that incident, was a large, busty girl with permed hair and small, scared eyes. She was not as lucky. She was raped twice by a police officer seeking revenge because the girl's mother—his landlord—had given him notice on the apartment he was renting from her. She didn't say a word to anyone other than her mom about the rape. Together they decided there was nothing they could do other than avoid this man, and so the young girl stayed close to home. But after weeks of seclusion, she started to get restless, and one afternoon went to the police station to visit another officer with whom she was friendly, thinking the station was as safe an arena as she would find. But the first person she saw was her assailant, who was working the reception area. As soon as he saw her, he called a security guard and had her thrown out.

Eventually, she ran into the officer she'd gone to visit, who was a higher-ranking official than the man who raped her. "Don't worry," he told her. "I'll handle this." He did, by transferring his colleague off reception-desk duty so that the girl could visit him whenever she wanted.

Another woman described watching men break into her home in search of her father-in-law, an outspoken Aristide supporter. This woman was short and matronly; she had innocent eyes and a clear complexion, but turned inward when she described the attack. "There was a bunch of them. They pushed their way in, knocking down the door as they fired random shots, up, down, past me, over me, in the room where I was sleeping and the bedroom where my kids were. Then they turned everything upside down just because they could. For no reason. Just to terrorize us. They slashed the chairs and curtains. They dumped dishes on the floor. They even went into the small *boutik* (grocery store) we have at the side of the house and dumped the contents of our fifty-pound bags of rice and flour."

Tears welled in her eyes and she stopped for a moment. "Only after they left did I discover that they had killed my infant daughter, covering her with a sheet to make it look as though she were still sleeping."

The woman recognized one of the thugs. "He was my neighbor, a regular customer at the *boutik*," she said. "I've known him since he was little. He joined the police corps a few years ago." She and her family went into hiding after the incident and never returned to live in that home again.

Whenever I was offered a job, I recommended hiring Sergo as the driver. With the shortage of gasoline and the dangers on the road and off, it was not only reassuring but prudent to have someone else worry about navigation. I had grown so attached to Sergo that I couldn't remember a time when he wasn't a part of my life. He was like a brother to me, a best friend to Jean Raymond, and an uncle to Kadja, just as Jean Raymond was like an uncle to Vanessa and Valerie, Sergo's daughters. His wife, Botine, was a shy, sensitive woman who would have preferred Sergo to work quietly as a mechanic at the garage they'd set up in the front yard of Sergo's parents' home next door to where they lived, but she was savvy enough to appreciate the economic advantages of working for foreign media.

Botine was a typical Haitian housewife for someone from the middle class. She had just enough money to have people work for her, go to the market, and wash clothes. She wasn't independent or industrious, like many Haitian women; she relied on Sergo for transportation if she needed to go somewhere, but she was more comfortable in her own neighborhood among her sisters, brother, and cousins than anywhere else. The farthest she wanted to venture was the countryside, where she still had family. My foreign female friends, like me, were the opposite. We hiked, explored, pushed ourselves in new directions. Fortunately, Botine and I could joke about our differences.

I hadn't needed a driver with LaShawn, which in the end was probably better because it gave us a chance to get to know each other—and I felt that we both grew from our working relationship—but after she left, the BBC hired Sergo and me to work with them on a news piece on Clinton's foreign policy. The crew stayed at the posh Hotel Montana, halfway up the hill between Port-au-Prince and Pétionville, where the International Civilian Mission had taken over an entire floor for their offices, and several U.S. networks had another.

It was weird to leave the classy five-star hotel and drive home through the darkness of Port-au-Prince at the end of the day. It was like going underground, into a cave where there was no hint of the luxury of light or fresh air. Sergo and I stayed a little later than usual the last night of the job; it was about 9:15 when we pulled out of the Montana parking lot. Normally I tried to be home by dark—in part for security, but mostly because I wanted to spend some time with Kadja before he went to sleep. It was lonely out there in the dark, even with the stars, and I tried to avoid traveling after the sun went down.

As we took the first curve down the winding road leading to the highway, we were wrapped in darkness. We heard a gunshot, but were unable to identify where it came from. It sounded close, but in the mountains, with the windows up, it was impossible to tell just how close. "Stay alert," Sergo said nervously. I tightened my seat belt out of habit, knowing even as I did it that a strap wouldn't be much protection against a bullet.

At the intersection of the Pan-American Highway, we pointed the nose of the car downhill, ready to make the turn east. Suddenly Sergo rammed on the brakes and brought the car to a full stop as our headlights illuminated a man in dark clothing pushing a motorcycle down the road. A second man—a uniformed soldier—stood in the middle of the street with a rifle. He was as startled as a deer caught in headlights. For a fraction of a second, we all froze, like a still in a movie. Then the soldier took off on foot at lightning speed down the hill in the direction we were headed.

Sergo and I hesitated, unsure what to do next. Without saying a word, Sergo mashed his foot to the accelerator and put out his right hand to brace me as we took off down the hill. "*Ann ale;* let's go," he shouted, adrenaline pumping. I barely had time to react, but managed to duck as we quickly passed the man trying to start the motorcycle. By now the soldier was in the middle of the street, running full speed. As our headlights flashed on him a second time, he became skittish, weaving back and forth, unsure whether we were going after him or trying to avoid him.

We were as uncertain of his intentions as he was of ours. But I trusted Sergo's instincts, and he slowed down to avoid hitting him. At that very instance the soldier lowered his arm toward his side. "*Atansyon,*" I squeaked in a voice that no longer sounded like mine. "*Lap rale ʒanm li an:* Watch out, he's pulling out his gun."

I ducked lower than before. Sergo floored the gas pedal and left tire marks on the road as we peeled past the soldier and raced down the hill.

Just minutes later, the two men passed us on the back of the motorcycle at what must have been in excess of 100 mph. It was hard to know who was more freaked out, us or them. We didn't dare speculate what it was they were up to.

I stayed home the next morning—Sergo drove to the hotel to pick up the BBC crew and take them to the airport. He noticed a crowd at the intersection of the Pan-American Highway and the Hotel Montana at the exact spot we'd stopped less than twelve hours earlier. Through the opening of elbows and hips and ankles he spotted a slumped body in a small pool of dried blood. Something we hadn't noticed the night before.

Reports were that the victim, a Haitian naturalized as American, was involved in drugs. And that his Haitian wife had hired hit men to get rid of him so she could make off with the $30,000 later found in their home. Another rumor circulated that the Mafia hired the hit men and the money was drug related. It could have been either of these rumors or another explanation entirely. There was no way to know, and I wasn't going to inquire. Sergo and I discreetly told the International Civilian Mission what we saw, just for the record, but asked that our names be listed anonymously. I shuddered to think what might have happened if we had come upon the soldier at that intersection just one minute earlier. There was a reason I didn't go out at night, and this was it.

A few weeks earlier, a friend of mine had been coming out of a parking lot after a binge of night gambling when he heard distressed cries of a woman. Instinctually he headed toward the shouts, but stopped cold in his tracks when he saw a group of men, some in uniform, gang-raping a woman in the back of a station wagon. Alone and unarmed, he returned to his car quietly, and, with an overwhelming sense of helplessness, got inside and drove away.

The feeling he described mirrored that which had unconsciously become part of my own daily repertoire of emotions. At times the highs were so great that it felt orgasmic, thrilling, intoxicating. It was also deeply troubling. For now, I had only to accept that I was no longer a foreign journalist reporting on a story, but a person recounting a history, for better or for worse, that was as much a part of my own as it was the country's. The impact of these feelings, like the history I was living through, wasn't clear. Only over time could I, like Haiti, know and understand its importance.

Chapter IX

Field Producer

Evite, pinga ak atansyon pa kapab anpeche jou malè dwe fèt.
Being on guard and paying careful attention can't stop misfortune from
taking place if that's your destiny.

By the summer of 1994, the tensions engulfing the country seeped into
my relationship with Jean Raymond. Just as the United States and
Haiti engaged in a series of chess moves—including a ban on all
commercial flights and most financial transactions between the two
countries, which triggered the Jonassaint government to declare a
state of emergency, Jean Raymond and I skirted around each other,
misinterpreting and overreacting to each other's comments. Everything we said to each other seemed laced with another meaning, inten-
tional or otherwise. It didn't matter that my Creole was as good as it
was going to get. It didn't even matter that Jean Raymond was still
resisting learning English—language wasn't the problem.

"I'm going out, the band is practicing," he said, and I heard: "I have to get out of here and be with my friends."

"Can we talk about this after my deadline?" I said, which he took to mean: "Don't bother me."

"Who's going to watch Kadja?" he asked, and I was sure he intended to say: "What kind of a mother are you, going off to work again?"

"We need to spend some time together," I said, and he imagined I was complaining: "You're never around; your friends and music are more important than Kadja and me."

It was hard to know if the difficulties were a result of the stress we were living with or the different direction our careers were taking— mine busier and more successful, albeit at Haiti's expense, Jean Raymond's plummeting because of Haiti's economic, political, and social situation. The most positive thing he had going on was a tentative offer by a New York producer to record an album, which required him to travel there with the band. And with the newly imposed ban on flights, that meant he would be stuck out of the country when it went into effect.

American Airlines monopolized 60 percent of air traffic through Haiti. These days their flights were full of the nonessential U.S. personnel the American government was evacuating—about 600 of the 2,000 American citizens living here had already left. In keeping with the increased sanctions, the airline announced it would fly its last plane on June 24—on June 25, the only way to reach the United States was on a connecting Air France or ALM flight to a neighboring island, and even those flights weren't expected to continue much longer.

"I don't have to go to New York," Jean Raymond said as we sat at the small table we'd set up on our patio. It was late afternoon, but still the air was stifling; the lack of breeze made it hard to concentrate.

"I wouldn't ask you to do that," I said, my facial expression belying my true feeling. But Jean Raymond, intentionally or otherwise, looked away. I remained silent because I understood the importance of pursuing a career—it was, after all, an important factor in my wanting to come back to Haiti. That he needed to go to New York now, to be with his band, wasn't something he planned, nor was it something he should give up.

"Maybe it won't be for very long," I added, but my tone implied that it would.

"Maybe," he said as he closed his suitcase.

I wanted to tell him that I was worried about our relationship, worried how the separation would affect us, but I couldn't find the right words. Instead, my attempt at support came out like an accusation. "Music is your life. I can't ask you to stay here while your band is in New York any more than you could ask me to leave."

"*Wi*," he said noncommittally.

I opened my mouth to ask if he was at all concerned how I'd manage with the logistical issues—conserving electricity so a lamp could stay on at night, making sure there was gasoline in the car and a surplus stock of contraband gas in a fifty-gallon drum, but I said nothing. This stuff was pretty evident. Without refrigeration we had to make sure there was a propane tank for the stove so we could always cook the dried grains and beans we kept as staples. We had to keep extra buckets of water around in case there was no electricity to turn on the water pump; otherwise we couldn't use the toilets or wash our clothes. Those things he understood, but I wondered if he knew what I meant when I talked about providing Kadja with the "normal" life I grew up with. Not a day went by that I didn't feel guilty that Kadja wasn't getting the attention he deserved because of the long hours I worked and the prolonged absence of his dad. I spent hours debating internally about the tightrope act of wanting to be a good mother and wife and succeeding as a reputable, respected journalist. Both required attention and concentration, and I feared that I wasn't balanced, that I was spending more time with my colleagues than with my son.

"What about Kadja?" Jean Raymond asked, as if he were reading my mind.

"Don't worry, I'll manage," I said. "I've already talked to Rose Andrée, and she said she'd spend the night anytime I had to work late." He nodded, relieved.

I talked about my personal struggle of being a good mom and a journalist with Sophie, a relatively new journalist friend, before she left for her sister's wedding in France. Like me, Sophie was living in Haiti; she'd moved to Haiti after the coup with her partner, a doctor with a nongovernmental health agency. Having a friend who was also a colleague made my days so much more enjoyable because we covered events together. Being French, she had different contacts—we shared resources and bounced ideas off each other. But on this subject of motherhood, I wasn't sure she could understand how hard it was for me to strike a balance because she didn't have children of her own.

I spoke about it with Martine and with Françoise, who understood because she was also a professional and a mother, and Gisele, because she just seemed wise about absolutely everything. Having good friends as a sounding board helped keep everything in perspective and allowed me to blow off steam I might otherwise have directed at Jean Raymond. Apart from Sophie, the other foreign correspondents that I'd become friends with had only one objective when they flew to Haiti, which was to cover the news. They didn't have the emotional tug of creating meaningful "playtime" or the logistical concerns about marketing and laundry. It wasn't that I considered myself precious in any way—I had full-time help and a good support network, but still it was draining. There were nights I couldn't sleep, trying to juggle my dual role, but taking care of Kadja was the only thing that kept me grounded and held everything else in its proper perspective.

"I'll be fine," I said to Jean Raymond, as he wrapped his arms around Kadja and me for the last time. Silently I prayed that I would be. The drive to the airport was tense. While I was sorry to see him go, part of me was relieved that it would be easier because the constant bickering about nothing that seemed to be our life together the last few months exhausted me. My days were already so full and required so much energy that the last thing I wanted to do was deplete the tiny bit of reserve I had left haggling with him over something trivial. The big things we had a process for hashing out. It was the small, annoying things that were killing us—keeping the car full of gas, the water tank full, the batteries charged.

"Well, this is it," he said, feeling my ambivalence.

I refused to read anything into that statement. "I'll wait to hear from you," I said as we embraced. We were in the airport's upstairs restaurant that overlooked the departure line—there were hundreds of people leaving that afternoon, and the bustle of activity gave the false impression that the economy was prospering. But outside the airport grounds the streets were deserted; even the street *machann* who were as much a part of the landscape as the mango and citrus trees were cutting back on their hours. There were just no customers, no business, and far less capital to work with.

Clinton's ban on financial transactions had the potential to affect tens of thousands of people. Looking around at the poor conditions, the rising cost of food in the supermarket, the devaluation of the gourde, I wondered how the economy could survive one more blow— but here it was. No one knew for sure how many Haitians lived abroad or how much they sent home, but there were estimates of 600,000

Haitian Diaspora in the States; between 200,000 and 400,000 Haitians in New York alone, and another 300,000 in Canada. Officials speculated that money sent from the States ranged between $200 and $300 million annually; Clinton's new policy restricted transfers to $50 per month, per person. Economists said that the top 1 percent of the population, estimated to control 49 percent of the country's income, remained well insulated from these measures. I was sure I knew who many of the people in that category were—they were the ones supporting the coup and who had ties to the military.

"How am I going to get by?" asked one of my friends, whose brother in Brooklyn religiously sent him a check every month. "There's absolutely no chance of finding a job now—there wasn't any work before the coup, and there's been even less of a possibility since. Then the Americans slap this embargo on us. Who is it hurting? Not the military or the bourgeoisie, just us poor people."

Meanwhile I had more work than I could handle. I added NBC to my list of regular freelancing. Someone from the network had approached me in May about helping out with a special three-minute piece on rape. That job segued into another, and pretty soon I was employed full time. My official title was field producer, but I also translated, set up interviews, facilitated navigation, and directed shots in the field. Never had I felt so stimulated. I started early in the day with NBC and after a final edit for the evening news, if there was nothing to prepare for early the next morning, I came home, played with Kadja, and then wrote a piece for the *Monitor*. Sometimes I was too exhausted to concentrate, so instead I went to sleep and set the alarm for 3:00 A.M., in time to write the article and file by my 6:00 A.M. deadline. Kadja was often awake just after that so I had a chance to enjoy his company before heading off again for NBC.

In the beginning I found working for the network overwhelming. I had always worked independently, with nothing more than a pad and pen, occasionally a tape recorder. For a television crew to work together effectively and produce a tight, solid piece, there had to be close coordination between the cameraman, the soundman, the field producer, and the correspondent. Unexpected glitches were part of the process, so we had to be prepared for anything, not the least of which was personality conflict. Plus the logistical hassles of the equipment—the lights, the accoutrements that went with the lighting, the tripods, the cords, etc. No decision was unilateral—the cameraman often had a different approach to the story than the correspondent, and what was shot in the field was never exactly what the producer back in the tech lab (in our case, hotel rooms that were transformed into makeshift studios, complete with editing machines and sound booths) expected. I had the benefit of an experienced, qualified staff—NBC flew people in from bureaus all over the world—our bureau chief in the beginning was an American who had been living in the former Soviet Union; our cameramen were from Mexico, South Africa, Miami, and our correspondents from London, Atlanta, New York, even the Middle East. As NBC expanded their crews, they needed more drivers—Sergo joined on and was given a four-door, four-wheel drive Montero. He was thrilled to be part of the crew, earning more than he ever had in his life, and I felt more at ease having a soulmate nearby.

Just a few days after Jean Raymond left, I was back at the airport with a camera crew filming American Airlines' final flight. Inside the hot halls of the long, narrow airport were long lines, overweight suitcases, and random confusion. Like all the other flights that week, this last one was overbooked. Harried airline employees tried to accommodate nervous mothers, distracted children, protective fathers, and emotional lovers but in the end it was a free-for-all.

The crew filmed the last check-in, the final baggage loading, the lone plane on the runway and, finally, the ultimate departure. Afterward, they filmed the silence. Gone were the porters, vendors, and money changers. No more suitcases, employees, luggage carts, or passengers. Everything was locked up, put inside desks, cabinets, and behind closed doors. Everything was deadly quiet. Only the sound of my sandals echoed in the hollow halls.

I stood quietly on the runway and watched the plane's back wheels lift off. I experienced the same pang of insecurity I felt when my parents left me at summer camp. Or later, when I was in college and awoke alone in my bed, deserted by a boyfriend. I was still that person, but I was also a mother now, struck by the reality that this was the last plane for the United States that I would see for what could be a very long time. The blue sky overhead, the hills in the background, everything was still the same—but so much had changed. That there were still European flights did little to ease the twinge of irresponsibility I felt. I knew that the chance of Kadja needing emergency medical care was minuscule, but still I didn't know what I would do if something did happen. I trusted the medical care in Haiti as much as I trusted the de facto government's will to do right by its people. Although I didn't make the decision to stay in Haiti impulsively, I still wondered if I was doing the right thing. Was it this sense of entrapment that drove Haitians to flee on the proverbial unseaworthy, rickety boats that crowded the waterways around the island nation?

The U.S. Coast Guard was picking up an average of 600 people a day. American officials were desperate to reopen the base in Guantanamo Bay, Cuba, a facility of 12,500 beds that had closed in May 1992. Boat people were an ongoing story, and the television crews increased their staff to make sure they had enough coverage for this as well as all the other events unfolding. By now ABC, NBC, and CNN had taken over all the available rooms at the Hotel Montana—they were spending tens of thousands of dollars a week, to say nothing of the $450 a day the hotel demanded from each station as rent for their satellite dishes to remain on the hotel roof. And I knew that the story was reaching the States because my sisters, none of whom watched the news, were now turning on their sets to find out what was happening. We spoke infrequently because I was rarely at home, but it helped to hear their voices and be reminded there was a world outside the crisis in Haiti.

Just in the nick of time, Haitians got a break from the chaos of their lives when, for a short two-week period, politics, violence, international maneuvering, and boat people took a backseat to the World Cup soccer games. Downtown, the only sign of life centered around a radio broadcasting a match; large groups of animated men dressed in yellow and green to root for Brazil, a team Haiti had historically adopted as its own; whenever World Cup was played, street vendors stocked up on Brazilian jerseys and people waved the Brazilian flag in support of Pelé or whoever else was the soccer superstar of the day. In middle-class neighborhoods fans watched the games on television, and the elite had parties complete with full bar and betting pool. I experienced the excitement in the lobby of the Hotel Montana, where the management shrewdly installed a full-sized screen. Television crews defied producers' requests to go out in the field to shoot footage if it conflicted with a home-team match. Technicians rescheduled "feeds" (sending the story through a satellite connection) to the United States so that they could reserve their satellite dishes for the *foutbòl* frenzy. Our Mexican cameraman got into heated arguments with his European counterparts—at one point a fistfight broke out between crew members from the same network. Sergo hid in the back, not up to the merciless needling he got from the other Haitian drivers who fanatically supported Brazil while he was a rare Argentinean fan. During the games, I took the opportunity to go home and get Kadja, and bring him to the Montana to enjoy uninterrupted electricity, play with the turtles in the pond in the hotel lobby, and be pampered by the Montana staff who declared him the most handsome boy they'd ever seen. Part of his appeal was the color of his skin, toffee bronze topped by fine, delicate, but abundant corkscrew curls. His eyes were a deep brown, proportioned perfectly above his small nose and full little lips. He inherited his dad's charm and used it indiscriminately, winning over even the most hard-core soccer fans, who during halftime showed him how their camera equipment worked.

Télévision Nationale d'Haiti, Haitian National Television, provided great comic relief from the spectator testosterone fests by running commercials of burning buildings and corpses from the 1915–1934 U.S. military occupation of Haiti, with an echoing "NO" flashing from the middle of the screen. Designed to win support for the de facto government and incite anti-American sentiment, a strip ran at the bottom of the screen with the words: "Intervention no, Democracy, yes." And: "Haiti is small but won't be trampled."

On the streets, another sort of propaganda was unfolding. The United Nations sanctioned a multinational force of up to 15,000 members, led by the United States, to be followed by a deployment of up to 6,000 UN member troops. The objective was to establish political stability and train a new army and police force. I headed downtown with a crew to film Haiti's response to the threat of an invasion. Men of all ages had gathered on the grassy Champs de Mars in front of the National Palace to train; hundreds of mostly thin, middle-aged men, though a few were conspicuously past their prime. The majority appeared to have no idea what they were supposed to be doing. An elite group of men known as "Ninjas" because of their black dress—

black shirts, black pants, black boots, black ski caps over their faces—snarled orders that the "soldiers" couldn't understand, let alone follow. The Ninjas appeared to be young and fit—their muscles rippled through their cotton shirts, and their calves were the size of melons. Some of them even spoke English—I immediately thought of the School of the Americas, where Police Chief Michel François had trained, and wondered if they were peers. "*Adwat, agosh, tou dwat,* (right, left, straight)," the Ninjas barked with utter disdain as the recruits trampled on their own feet, the heels of the men in front of them, and the toes of the men behind them.

I focused on an elderly man who couldn't have weighed more than 100 pounds. His eyes were buried behind flaps of skin and wrinkles; his thin arms stuck out from his tattered shirt like twigs. The weight of his ancient, poorly maintained rifle nearly knocked him over. He gasped for breath with every turn, struggling to keep up with the others. Just when it seemed that he couldn't stand one second longer, one of the drill sergeants approached him. The old man, aware that he was about to get attention he didn't want, made a genuine attempt to stand erect but his thin legs trembled like stalks in the wind.

"Ready," the officer snapped. The old man tottered as he lifted his rifle onto his shoulder.

"Aim," the officer snarled. The old man looked around, confused. The officer roughly lifted the man's hands from the butt of his rifle and placed them squarely in shooting position. "*Fèmen youn je*: shut one eye." The old man didn't understand and shut the wrong eye on the target.

"*Fèmen youn je,*" the officer growled again, his pale skin puffing out with anger. The rest of the group, sweat rolling down their sun-streaked faces, remained in position. The old man continued to squint through his left eye instead of his right, his legs wobbling back and forth, up and down, soft as feathers. Finally, his patience exhausted, the officer grabbed the old man's eyelid and with a harsh tug forced it shut, sending the weak, scared, and incompetent recruit to the ground.

Without Jean Raymond, the nights were long and lonely. Even when we weren't getting along, it was comforting to have him there, so I occasionally stayed at the Montana after work to sip a rum sour. But never for very long; I wanted to spend some time with Kadja before he went to sleep. I never would have been able to get by if it weren't for Rose Andrée. With her long legs, thin arms, and toothy smile, she became an institution in the house, knowing all our moods better than we knew them ourselves. She was playful and yet stern with Kadja, able to coax him to do things he would never do for me, like eat fruits and vegetables. She was a great cook, and I looked forward, after a long day, to whatever it was that she prepared because I knew it would be better than anything I made.

One night, after a particularly long, hot and sweaty day, I peeled off my sweat-stained dress to step into the shower as Sergo pulled back into my driveway, having just dropped me off five minutes earlier.

"Jonassaint just announced a press conference!" he shouted up at me through the open window. "At the National Palace. Says it's very important, all foreign press should come. Headquarters radioed me that they want you to cover it."

"Why me?" I shouted back, fed up with the demands NBC made on my time.

"Come on, Kathie," Sergo laughed. "You love this stuff. I'll bring you home afterward."

"And buy me dinner, too!" I yelled. "I'll be right down."

I begged Rose Andrée to spend the night and then, slipping on a fresh skirt and blouse, flew down the stairs to join Sergo. By 9:00 P.M.

all of us journalists, numbering about fifty, were giddy with hunger and short of patience. There were pockets of conversations in English, French, Spanish, Italian, Creole—everyone complaining in their native language, but no one wanting to leave for fear of missing an important announcement. The only comic relief came with the late entrance of Linda, a Dutch radio journalist, who, known for her nylon pedal pushers and plastic flip-flops, pranced in wearing high heels. The National Palace had implemented a dress code recently, prohibiting shorts and flip-flops.

"They denied me access at the palace door because of my shoes," she said with a wily grin. "So I went back out on the street and down rue Pavée. I found just my kind of gal standing there on the street corner. I got her for a bargain. Well, not her exactly. She rented me her shoes for just $25 for the night."

Jonassaint made us wait nearly two more hours before his grand appearance, which lasted less than five minutes. He read a prepared text, denouncing threats by the international community and confirming his commitment to hold legislative elections in December "followed by presidential elections after a relatively short delay." He left the room without responding to a single question, and I went to sleep that night hungry and fed up with everything.

I couldn't imagine another six months of this. It was like rowing upstream in a drought, trying to figure out where all this was headed, and how long anyone could maintain the pace. NBC rotated staff in and out, but those of us who were local were expected to sustain the same level of energy, commitment, and performance day after day. I wasn't sure I had it in me.

At the end of another particularly stressful day chasing an interview I never got, I awoke to a deafening and unfamiliar noise, one that was so loud I thought the roof had fallen in. I sat up with a start, panicked and unable to think straight. It wasn't raining so I knew it wasn't thunder, but I couldn't imagine what it was. With my pulse pounding in my eyelids I was paralyzed with fear and unable to move. Then my thoughts turned to Kadja, and I raced to his room, sure that my thumping heart would wake him if the noise hadn't already. Only then did I realize that it was a plane flying low overhead, and I screamed out in a state of shock: "They've done it. They've invaded with no warning. The Americans. They've fucking done it. Holy shit! They've invaded Haiti!"

Kadja was fast asleep with all the innocence he deserved. I had trouble catching my breath, and was so startled by own revelation that I didn't recognize the sound of the phone ringing until the plane faded off in the distance. I kept waiting for a bomb to drop but it didn't, just the ring, ring, ring of the phone.

"Kathie, you won't believe it," my Haitian journalist friend told me. "The Americans—"

"They've invaded, they've fucking invaded!" I interrupted him, my voice so high it was unfamiliar even to me.

He laughed. "No they haven't, Kathie, calm down, there's no invasion. Yet. They're dropping leaflets with Aristide's picture all over the city. There are pictures of Aristide all over the streets."

"Wait a minute. Come again? Who's doing what?" I asked, calmer and more alert than I'd been a few moments ago.

"The Americans," he said, still chuckling. "The Americans are littering photos of Aristide all over the city. Maybe they are finally serious about helping him return."

Even though I heard what he said, it didn't make sense. What was the purpose of dropping photos of Aristide? Bewildered, I called the Montana and startled my favorite NBC cameraman, Tony, from a deep slumber. A big, strapping Zimbabwean with short blond hair, Tony was known for his after-work partying as much as he was for his daring photography. After hours, he and Tom, an equally crafty NBC correspondent from New Zealand, consumed more than the sum total of everyone else in the bar. They always asked for assignments together that allowed them to be as far away from the main office as possible. That way they could take off and go to the beach. And they always requested that I be their field producer—I visited the beach more in the short time I worked with them than I did the previous three years combined. Tom was as quirky as Tony was brash, wearing only shorts and a T-shirt when they went out on a shoot, but he kept a fresh dress shirt in the vehicle just in case the producer radioed in for a stand-up (when the correspondent is filmed from some site out in the field). Tony made sure to aim the camera from the shoulders up.

I could almost see Tony's eyes grow wide across the phone line when I explained why I called. "No need to wake Tom for this, eh?" he said in his charming accent. "But let's be on the street before dawn." No planes had passed in the area around his hotel, and the thought of a scoop excited him. "No one here seems to know anything about this plane—it must only have flown over certain neighborhoods. Sergo should have his walkie-talkie with him, right? Radio him to pick you up—I'll be waiting downstairs for you by 5:00 A.M."

As daylight broke the neighborhoods where the plane passed overhead resembled Wall Street during a ticker-tape parade. Three-by-six-inch photos of Aristide were everywhere, like a white blanket of fresh snow. As people woke up and made their way outside, they stopped in their tracks, unsure what to do. We filmed a few people who, after they realized what they were holding, dropped the picture quickly. "They kill people just for saying his name," an older woman whispered to me off camera. "Think what they would do to me if they found me with his picture." Others looked around nervously before putting the small white papers in their pockets. Still others smiled and grabbed fistfuls.

We raced back to the hotel with the footage and were able to feed it to New York in time for the morning show. I had time to call my sisters and tell them to turn on the news. My mom was thrilled to watch something that she knew I'd helped film. Later that day we heard stories about FRAPH, the paramilitary group vehemently opposed to Aristide's return, beating people for having these photos in their possession. A military source told me that some of his peers in the Haitian army had stripped down to their civvies and bailed out of their barracks in the middle of the night thinking, as I had, that the planes were part of a U.S. military invasion. "There is no loyalty there," he said. "These guys may look like they're tough, but a lot of them are ready to desert at the first sign of an attack."

Things were heating up so quickly that it seemed as though there were as many journalists in the country as there were pictures of Aristide. Sophie, who after her sister's wedding returned to Haiti overland with dozens of other journalists who had camped out at the Dominican Republic border, waiting for the right time to cross over, accepted my offer to temporarily move in to my place. She and her partner lived a long thirty-minute trek up the mountain and her phone was always out of order, making it hard for her to work. Her partner, who was often in the countryside, had a harder time commuting because of how tenuous the situation was, so for her, too, the nights were lonely and, at times, frightening.

With the escalation of political maneuverings, NBC headquarters in New York sent even more people—we had several crews of cameramen, technical support, and reporters—more than 60 all told. ABC and CNN had more than 100 employees each. One evening after a particular long day at work, just as I was putting my papers in my backpack to go home, I stopped midsentence because I couldn't hear myself think. The noise that interrupted me was piercing, bombastic, and immediately placed me back in my bedroom the night the American plane flew over my home. Our walkie-talkies came alive with the voice of one of our technicians.

"I see them, the planes, they are flying overhead, real close," he crackled over the airwaves. "There are these things that are falling out. They look like parachutes. Shit, they are dropping parachutes from the plane."

Our producer catapulted into action. "You, call New York," he said to one of the cameramen who happened to be in the office watching American reruns on the satellite television. Looking around, he pointed his finger at another technician. "You, call Washington, and get Jeff to listen to the scanner. Kathie, make some local calls and find out what the hell is going on."

"Parachutes, what kind of parachutes?" the producer radioed back to the technician, his normally calm voice betraying anxiety. "You mean they are dropping people from the sky? Talk to me. Tell me what you see."

"Parachutes. You know, parachutes. It's dark out here, man, I mean I can't see anything other than these white things, little, what, umbrellalike things, parachutes, falling. All over. They can't be people, they're too small—but hell, I don't know what's going on. Wait, shit, hold on a second. Don't go away."

The producer and I looked at each other, unsure what to do next. I was on the phone with my Haitian radio journalist contact, who was also trying to find out what was happening. He was as clueless as the rest of us. Then our technician came back on the airwaves. "One landed in a tree—it's over there, in a tree."

"Where are you, what are you looking at?" the producer asked.

Over the Montana, the plane had left, but we were in an inside room and no one had come back to report any unusual parachute activity outside. "I'm on Delmas 31, on a side street. They're still falling, these little parachutes," he said, as we heard the sound of a plane fading away in the background of his transmission. We didn't know whether to be amused or frightened. It didn't appear to be an invasion and, according to the NBC desk in New York, the White House hadn't authorized anything unusual. Another technician who was monitoring the radio scanner said that everyone appeared to be as confused as we were about what was going on.

Our technician in the field radioed us again. "I'm going over to see what it is. Stay with me, guys. There's one of these things in a tree. I'm going to try to climb it to find out what it is."

"Okay, I'm at the base of the tree. Hold on, I got to put this walkie-talkie in my pants while I try climbing the tree. It's a few branches up. Hang with me, I'm hauling myself up. I knew I shouldn't have had that last beer. Okay, here I go. I can see the thing—it's not very large, just about the size of my hand with the parachute hanging over it. Just a little farther. Okay, I can grab it now."

Silence.

"What, what do you have?" the producer shouted.

"A radio," the technician chuckled. "A transistor radio. I'll be damned, the Americans are dropping radios!"

After years of not speaking Aristide's name on the street, suddenly people were speculating out loud about his return. The idea of the radios was to provide an illiterate population the chance to hear news, which was tentatively starting to be reported more freely than it had in years. Rather than run away from our cameras, people were running toward them to express their joy at the possibility of the crisis coming to an end and their president returning to the National Palace. First-time foreign journalists who didn't know Haiti before the coup were finally seeing the vibrancy that had enticed me to fall in love with it in the first place because people were expressing themselves. Like bears waking from hibernation, they were able to open their eyes and smile at a world they'd been closed off from for three years. Even I felt as if we were climbing out of the dark bowels of a black tunnel. We could see the rays of light ahead, but we weren't there yet.

"What do you think?" Jean Raymond asked during one of our infrequent conversations. I wasn't calling him as much as I had when he first left and when he called, more often than not I was working. We were estranged. He was stuck in New York, without his family and with no work—Foula's contract hadn't come through. I was busier than I'd ever been in my whole life, working eighteen-hour days, six and a half days a week—Sunday afternoon I reserved just for Kadja, when we often went to a friend's pool with Françoise and her daughter. There was danger, drudgery, excitement, and emotion in my daily life, so much of it that I didn't know how to begin to convey that to Jean Raymond, so rather than try I said almost nothing. That pushed us farther apart—Jean Raymond felt my reserve and resented it, but still I was unable to work through it. It was easier to share the trials and advances, disappointments and confusion, with my peers, with Sergo, with the staff at NBC who had become family, than it was with Jean Raymond. I felt both guilty and sad about that.

"You'd be happy at the change," I said. "You'd be proud that people are starting to resurface after years of being underground. It's not yet the Haiti you want it to be, but it's getting there."

"And when it does," he said, "will things be back to normal for everyone, including us?"

"I hope so," I said, but I wasn't sure.

In an effort to avoid a military invasion, President Clinton sent a diplomatic delegation to hold last-minute negotiations. He drew on the experience of former President Jimmy Carter, Senator Sam Nunn of Georgia, and the strategic advice of former Armed Services Commander Colin Powell. The delegation alternated between the National Palace and military headquarters, where promilitary supporters spent most of the day demonstrating—*attachés*, paid informers, friends who had a personal investment in making sure democracy wasn't restored. Hundreds of journalists camped out on the Champs de Mars. NBC drivers, like their colleagues from ABC, CBS, CNN, CBC, BBC, and others, shuffled crews back and forth to their hotels. They delivered food, filled water bottles and coolers, and speculated about what was happening inside, as did we during the long, boring hours of the stakeout.

When an agreement was finally reached, the official announcement came not from the National Palace, but the Oval Office in Washington. I rushed to the Montana to watch it broadcast live in English via NBC's satellite dish. Whatever I heard would be in English with an American slant. Sophie installed herself in front of my television, radio propped at her side; she would be listening to the French and Haitian reports, which presented the news from a different perspective.

The Montana was frenetic with activity. NBC headquarters was jammed with local and foreign staff and I had to jockey for a position in front of the screen. Clinton stood alone as he delivered his speech, solemn and emphatic. He announced that a military invasion has been prevented by a razor-thin margin after thirty-two hours of negotiation. General Cédras and Chief of Staff General Philippe Biamby agreed to step down—prompted, I'm sure, by the news that Clinton had already deployed sixty-one airplanes filled with U.S. military troops.

While the accord wasn't perfect, it instantly turned a "combat mission" into a "peacekeeping mission." Suddenly the very men the United States was planning to attack had become their allies.

Within twelve hours, Haiti's skyline was thick with U.S. military helicopters and surveillance planes. Daylight exposed a sea crowded with a variety of aircraft carriers, warships with large, flat decks for planes to land and take off. After just a few hours' sleep, I was back at the Montana by 5:00 A.M. to help with the live feed for the *Today Show*, so I missed Kadja lying on his back and counting the "noisy whirlybirds," but he told me all about them when I got home. Rose Andrée said he'd been busy inventing war games to go with the helicopters, even after she tried to explain that it was a peaceful intervention. "*Solda Ameriken yo vini*," he shouted with glee: The American soldiers are here.

Four days later, the U.S. Senate approved a resolution supporting a "prompt and orderly withdrawal of U.S. troops and the lifting of American and U.N. economic sanctions." By the end of the week, 10,000 American troops were in place in Port-au-Prince, Cap Haitien in the north and Jérémie in the south, even though Cédras had not yet agreed to leave.

Port-au-Prince was a Who's Who of the news world. Correspondents from all over the world swarmed to Haiti like ants to sugar; the networks sent in their top anchors, though many stayed less than twenty-four hours: Tom Brokaw, Brian Williams, Dan Rather, Peter Jennings, Peter Arnett, and Christiane Amanpour. Bryant Gumbel spent two frustrating days at the Dominican Republic border, unable to get the documents he needed to cross over. Reluctantly and rather bitterly, he and his crew flew back to New York.

The next few weeks were a blur. I worked harder than before, which I didn't think was possible. For the first time since I'd started reporting for them six years earlier, the *Christian Science Monitor* sent in a reporter to supplement the articles I was sending because the intervention was such big news. All the reporters were trying to come up with a story that was more interesting and original than their competitors. I used a contact to rent a sixty-foot boat so that Tony was able to get a reverse shot of the American warships with the Port-au-Prince skyline in the background. An ABC crew rowed along in a smaller boat—as we zipped past, they gave us the finger.

With the protection of American troops, the balance of power shifted.

"You wouldn't believe it," I said to Jean Raymond. "All these people who have been in hiding—thousands of them—they're all out on the street now. You should see the seaport at Cité Soleil—they're there every day shouting: *Nou Vle Aristide* (we want Aristide), *Fòk Cédras Ale* (Cédras has to go) and Disarm the Death Squads."

"I'm so happy," he said, but he sounded sad. I knew it was hard for him to be so far away, when life had returned to Haiti—real life, where normal people were doing normal things like taking walks and chatting freely on the street.

"If you were here, you would be able to hang out with your friends like you used to," I said and then wanted to swallow the words, which he might take as a dig that he was too often with his friends. "I mean, people aren't scared like they used to be—they're even starting to stay out after dark."

"Mmm," he said wistfully. "When is American Airlines going to start flying again?"

"Don't know," I answered. "There's still a lot of turmoil. Just yesterday—you probably saw it on television—there were these demonstrations downtown, and a Haitian policeman beat a coconut vendor to death."

"Yeah, it was all over the news," he said. "There's a killing, and suddenly the international community is making a fuss that there's human-rights violations in Haiti? Where have they been for the last three years? They don't care about the other 3,000 who died?"

As a result of this single incident, captured live by a television crew, the United States deployed 1,000 military to curb street violence. It did help, but in the process the Americans created its own news when a group of U.S. soldiers killed nine armed Haitian policemen outside the Cap Haitien police station in the north, where just under 2,000 U.S. Marines were stationed.

I was asked to cover that story with Tony and an NBC technician—we left Port-au-Prince at 3:00 A.M. to ensure that we arrived at Cap Haitien by dawn. We drove so fast through the mountain ranges that I vomited twice. Once we reached Cap, we discovered that 800 police, soldiers, and *attachés* connected to that police station had deserted their post. Marines recovered about 150 M-1 assault rifles and numerous handguns from the police station. Local residents burst in and took everything else. It reminded me of the *dechoukaj* of Claude Raymond's home back in 1989. It was hard to believe how integrated I'd become in just five years—my initial innocence and naïveté felt like a lifetime ago.

I left the crew and flew back to the capital on one of the U.S. Nighthawk helicopters later that afternoon so that our technicians would have time to feed the tape to New York for *Nightly News*. My eyes teared from the dust and the noise was deafening, but I was so excited I didn't notice. I was also struck by the sight of the never-ending, barren hillsides—the pilot flew low enough that we saw, up close, the vast impact of decades of deforestation. Still, scattered through the driest areas of the mountains were bright green and salmon houses, blue and orange huts, rose and kelly green cottages. Peasants lived on the highest peaks and in the deepest valleys. It was stunning to see Haiti from this aerial perspective and realize just how isolated 90 percent of the population was, away from roads, water, electricity, modernization. I pulled my scarf from my pocket to tie back my hair, and the money I'd secured went flying out the window. I smiled, imagining what the peasants below would say when the bills landed in their fields.

When I described my travels to Kadja, he pointed his finger to a passing helicopter. "Go again, Mommy," he said. "Wave. And this time, drop money over our house, too."

Aristide supporters planned a demonstration for the third anniversary of the coup. U.S. officials announced that there would be sufficient security for the thousands expected to march. On September 30 I woke up early to make sure I arrived at the Port-au-Prince cathedral by the time the marchers gathered. On the way I passed a dozen armored tanks filled with American troops. Helicopters flew low overhead.

After the memorial mass, the demonstrators headed toward the cemetery. Cameraman Tony and I broke off to see what was happening at the headquarters of the notorious Front for the Advancement and Progress of Haiti (FRAPH), one block parallel to the route of the march. If there was going to be any trouble, this is where it was likely to happen, because this lawless group was violently opposed to Aristide's return under any condition. But there was no sign of American security anywhere—not a single Humvee, tank, or helicopter. Meanwhile, FRAPH headquarters was swarming with men and women brandishing weapons the way a child swings a baseball bat— only these were guns, machetes, clubs spiked with nails, and large rocks. Seeing Tony's camera, they rushed toward us aggressively— not to attack, but rather to capitalize on the publicity. They peered into the lens and shouted death threats to anyone who supported Aristide's return. They strutted around like fighting cocks, waving their weapons and making lewd and derogatory gestures in the direction of the approaching marchers.

Another NBC cameraman was filming the march from the cathedral—Maurice, a tall, thin guy from southern California, laid-back, easygoing, and genial. We radioed back and forth to keep abreast of each other's position and the movement of the march. "Watch out for the area around FRAPH," I warned. "Crowd's unpredictable."

"The marchers are just about there already," he said. We could hear them chanting and singing, but we couldn't see them. What we could see, as we put down the radio, were dozens of FRAPH members taking off at top speed in the direction of the noise, hurling rocks and firing shots in the air. They advanced, then retreated as the demonstrators advanced and retreated, a seesaw battle that was undoubtedly going to escalate. There were fewer FRAPH members than demonstrators but the demonstrators were unarmed.

"Watch yourself!" Tony said to me as I stood in an alcove of a small house. I had no plans to go anywhere, and started to tell Tony to stay put, but he was already off, despite the onslaught of rocks and bullets flying overhead. I was terrified but lucid, unsure what to do next. Tony made it halfway down the block before he was grazed on the forehead by a stone. He retreated quickly, a lump already visible on his brow.

Enraged because the demonstrators were picking up the rocks and slinging them back, FRAPH became more aggressive, moving closer with each round of gunfire and stones.

"Maurice, where are you?" I radioed while Tony collected himself. "Tony just tried to come to you, but the street was too hard to navigate."

"At the corner," he said, but it was difficult to hear because of the tremendous amount of noise in the background. It was chaotic, with the demonstrators still singing and chanting while slinging stones and FRAPH shouting with anger as they moved forward and attacked.

Suddenly Maurice's voice rose sharply, panic and pain shooting over the airwaves. "I've been hit. I've fallen. I need help. Help, I need help!" Then silence.

"Maurice, Maurice, are you there?" Tony shouted as loudly as he could into the radio. "Maurice, man, what's happened?"

Maurice never responded. We raced frantically up and down our side of the street, in between houses and porches, trying to figure out how to get from where we were to where he was, but sporadic gunfire was flying in all directions. We were on parallel streets and the long block between us was filled with people behaving like maniacs.

I was really scared. Not a pitter-patter scared, where my heart raced faster than normal, but a deep, throbbing scare that went *ba-boom, ba-boom, ba-boom* and vibrated all the way to my toes. My head was pounding from the fear and the adrenaline raced through my blood like fire. I tried to stay focused but the commotion around me was overwhelming. In all my time in Haiti, even from that very first moment in front of the Palace during the 1988 coup, this was something different because people I cared about were directly involved.

"We should stay put, but—" Tony started to say before I cut him off.

"Not an option. We can do this. You lead, I'll follow."

I don't know where I got the courage to run out into the street, but I followed Tony as closely as a shadow. An inner resource I would never have known existed but for the years in Haiti nudged, prompted, and pushed me forward. Every few yards we ducked into doorways, between houses and behind poles to dodge the random danger flying overhead. When we got to the street where the demonstrators had been, they seemed to have evaporated, but sporadic bullets whirled overhead like a meteor shower. It was impossible to determine where the shots were originating from—but worse, Maurice was nowhere in sight.

As we huddled in a tiny alley carved between two houses we heard a series of shots, then silence, then a scuffle as rocks flew by. A few more shots were fired, followed by a long period of silence. We had our radio turned down to not draw attention to ourselves, but every chance I got, I tried to reach Maurice. He never answered. We tried to reach headquarters at the Montana to see if they knew anything but all we got was static. Frustrating static.

As we assessed the situation, we spotted another television crew huddled in an alcove farther down the street. We nodded at each other; then Tony and I signaled that we would make our way to them. We waited a few minutes to see if the rock throwing and shooting were going to resume, and when it didn't, we zigzagged our way over to them.

The cameraman had been filming behind Maurice. He explained quickly: "Maurice was filming, so his attention was on what was happening in front of him. All of a sudden this group of demonstrators started chasing this young guy, someone people had denounced as FRAPH. The crowd went nuts. They were vicious, man, beating and kicking him like a wild dog. He was absolutely terrified—you should have seen the look in his eyes, it was raw fear. Anyway, when he saw Maurice—I don't know, maybe it was like he thought because he was a white guy, he could save him. So he grabbed onto him, and Maurice—instinctively, I guess—reached out with his free arm to shield the man while he was filming the madness with the other. Just as he's doing this, someone from behind raises a large wooden stick and wham!—instead of hitting the Haitian guy, he clubs Maurice right on the head. Poor Maurice just collapsed."

"Where is he now?" Tony and I asked simultaneously.

"An ABC crew that was at the scene picked him up right away and shuffled him off in one of their vehicles. I guess they went to get him medical help."

CNN had also been on the scene when Maurice got hit—the rest of the world, tens of thousands of miles away, had known what happened to Maurice sooner than Tony and I had. Maurice's blood splattered the CNN camera lens, footage that ran throughout the day. Later that afternoon, American troops flew Maurice to their medical facility, where he was treated for a concussion and other injuries, none of which turned out to be serious.

Knowing that Maurice was getting help meant that Tony and I could now get the hell out of there. We worked our way back to our vehicle. Two blocks away—two short blocks away—we passed several Humvees filled with U.S. troops. There was also no shortage of American security as we drove up the Pan-American Highway to the Montana. The only place the Americans didn't seem to be was downtown, where they were needed. It didn't make any sense to me, and in an impulsive rage, I got in my car and drove to the U.S. Consulate, where I barged into the office of the spokesperson, Stan Schrager, and collapsed in tears at the injustice. Kindly, without a bit of irony, he offered me a handkerchief rather than an explanation.

Back in the safety and quiet of my home, away from the journalists and the crowds, I gave into the depth of emotion I'd been holding in check for what seemed like eternity. My tears spilled out with an intensity I thought was reserved for mourning. I shook uncontrollably—I had to sit before my wobbly legs gave out. I couldn't stop the gunfire in my head or the pounding in my gut. I allowed the fear to wash over my body and out of my system as I stared at the deceptively quiet city below and wondered what would come next.

▲   ▲   ▲

A few weeks before President Aristide's scheduled October 15 return, Police Chief Michel François fled to the Dominican Republic under the cover of darkness. Haitians were furious that he escaped like a cowardly shadow in the night and that they were unable to extract revenge on the man the country hated as much as General Raoul Cédras. Journalists were furious that they weren't able to snap just one, fleeing shot of the infamous torturer. To ensure that the situation wasn't repeated with Cédras, journalists camped out at his home twenty-four hours a day.

While NBC, like all the other networks, had a crew holding vigil in front of his house, we also befriended airport security, which allowed us to post a rotating crew in the control tower, too. We were prepared when Panama agreed to grant Cédras and his family political asylum, so they, along with Brigadier General Philippe Biamby, boarded a charter aircraft to Panama early in the morning of October 13. A second charter took twenty-three relatives to Miami. And with that, Cédras and the men who had terrorized the country for more than three years, were gone, paving the way for the October 15 return of Jean-Bertrand Aristide.

On Friday, October 14, I told my NBC producer that I had something personal to attend to. I slipped out of the office, wanting some time away from the crews, the cameramen, the other journalists. I wanted to roam the streets, anonymously and without any objective. I wanted to hear what people were saying, get a pulse on their mood, and see how the country was preparing for the return of their president.

For just a few hours I needed to shed my role as a journalist. For the past six years, but particularly the last two, I'd been living, breathing, and sleeping the country's crises. My world revolved around the current events in front of me—those that were newsworthy and dramatic, if not sensationalized, those that attracted the attention of some editor in some newsroom thousands of miles away, and those that had influenced me enough to want to stay in Haiti despite all.

I expected things to change with Aristide's return, and I knew that my life was going to change along with it. The crews were going to pack up and head off to the next world crisis, and Haiti was going to fade from the top story on the nightly news, dissolve from the front page to an inside story, then disappear all together.

But I had no plans to leave Haiti, so I knew I needed to brace myself for a major lifestyle adjustment. I expected commercial flights to resume shortly, which meant that Jean Raymond was going to come back. Without the pressures of reporting the news, we would have a chance to reacquaint ourselves with each other and, I hoped, have a sort of second honeymoon, fall back in love. I craved the intimacy and fantasized that this time our love would be deeper and more intense than the first time. For the first time in months, I also thought about traveling to Miami. I wanted to take Kadja to the beach, to the zoo, to museums and the library. I wanted to take long walks and short bicycle rides with him, play baseball, kickball, and football, and just be a mom, twenty-four hours a day.

But I also wanted to reconnect with my old life in Haiti, with friends who had suffered through the coup, and were going to have to prop the country back up. I wasn't surprised to see that they'd already started. Just as the population had done when Aristide won the presidential election nearly four years ago, people were already giving the city a face-lift. Groups were painting street curbs, lampposts, tree trunks, and city walls red and blue. Red-and-blue banners and flags hung from all corners of the streets, their tails curling in the wind. Buckets and wheelbarrows rolled through the filth, hauling away mounds of garbage and unwanted debris that had, for months, become as much a part of daily life as morning bread and coffee.

Out of nowhere murals adorned walls—the Champs de Mars, the national highway and Cité Soleil, welcoming Aristide back. People used rocks, branches and leaves, cornstalks and cloth, pebbles and bottles to line the streets with welcome shrines. They erected altars in the alleys between their homes, in their yards and on their porches. Everyone was ready; everyone was waiting.

On October 15, security around the palace and the Champs de Mars was tight. U.S. Marines, military police, and soldiers surrounded the perimeter of the palace with large trucks and Humvees. Some units were deployed to the rooftops of nearby buildings; others lined the top of the Palace. Sophie, Andrew, Harold, and I joined hundreds of journalists from all over the world in a long line that eventually admitted us to the palace grounds. No one wanted to miss the historic event of a deposed elected leader returning to office. After standing in a second line and enduring another search, we were released like cattle to graze on the palace lawn to await Aristide's arrival. It was beastly hot—there was no shade and too much time to kill. We instinctually gravitated to the fence separating the lawn from the street, where vendors peddling cold drinks tried to squeeze their bottles through the links to parched journalists. American security, tight and authoritarian, intervened. "Take those and you're out of here!" they barked at us.

"Yeah, right," said one guy, who before he could take his first sip was summarily escorted from the palace grounds.

The square on the other side of the fence was full with curious spectators, but not as full as it had been for the demonstrations I'd attended in 1988, or the presidential elections in 1990, or Aristide's inauguration in 1991. There was a crowd, but it lacked size, force—even conviction.

"Why do you think that is?" I asked Sophie as we waited in the hot sun for Aristide to appear.

"The people just may not want another disappointment," she said. "Maybe they don't really believe Aristide is coming back. It's not like they haven't been deceived before."

But when the helicopters started arriving, the reality started to sink in. Stands that had been erected on either side of the hundred and fifty or so international dignitaries who had been invited to the ceremony started to fill in as guests descended from the helicopters that landed on the left side of the palace lawn. Aristide eventually arrived in a swirl of dust—I was too far away to get a close look at him, and I wished that there were large screens projecting his image so I could have read the emotion in his face. As it was, he appeared like a dot, his image further distorted by the bulletproof shield in front of him, and the inadequate sound system muffled his short speech. The crowd in the square left even before he finished speaking.

"See, they just wanted to make sure he came back," Andrew said. "Seeing him was good enough for them. Now they just want to go home and get on with their lives."

Aristide retreated inside for a private celebration while NBC packed up. I felt displaced. Suddenly it didn't seem right to sit one more time with the group of foreign journalists who had become as much a part of my life as my morning cup of coffee because mentally they were already separating, thinking about the next job, this one completed, another country checked off in their laundry list of adventures, another notch in their belt of stories to boast of and parlay.

That night was particularly quiet. There were no parties on the street, no public display of celebration. There was a sense that the nation was at a new crossroads, more delicate than at any other time in the past.

It wasn't long before NBC, CBS, ABC, and CNN pulled out of Haiti, one after the other. Commercial flights resumed and the airport sprang alive with activity again as the networks' trademark silver footlockers with thousands of dollars of gear disappeared on the luggage conveyor belt. Local NBC staff fought over the goods left behind. I was rewarded with a Le Robert & Collins French-English dictionary, several reams of paper, and a cash retainer in case something else happened.

I hoped nothing would. The country deserved a respite, and I knew I needed one. I felt the impact of the coup, the long hours of work, the accumulated months of pressure to report accurately and on deadline. I wanted some downtime for myself and my family. Jean Raymond returned, thinner and more handsome than I remembered. He was wearing blue jeans and a white T-shirt; his dark eyes bore a hole in my heart.

"*Bonjou,*" he said, his arms wide open to receive me.

"*Bonjou,*" I said bursting into tears, burying my face in his chest.

"*Pa kriye, cheri kè*: Don't cry, sweetheart," he said, tears rolling down his cheek.

For the moment, we were able to put aside the tension we'd felt before, but like the country, we still had tremendous challenges ahead, and we knew it wasn't going to be easy.

"Guess we've got some catching up to do," I said, and smiled.

"No better time to start than right now," Jean Raymond said as Kadja came running down the hall and leapt wildly into his father's arms. "No better time than now."

Chapter X

Full Circle

Se pa tout je ki wè klè.
Not all eyes see clearly.

In the summer of 1998, Jean Raymond, Kadja, and I flew to Israel to visit a close childhood friend. Kadja played with her sons, Jean Raymond and her boyfriend played music, and she and I went off, by ourselves, for a three-day visit to Jordan.

To get from the northern Israeli border to the magnificent 2000-year-old Nabatean ruins of Petra in the south, we drove along King's Highway, the scenic route. It traverses the vast desert that dominates the country's geography. The desert seemed endless. We traveled for hours through rich red rock, past layers of dry, deserted land inhaling hundreds of thousands of years of history stored in the crevasses and canyons. I gained a new appreciation of time that was only underscored in Petra, where we crawled around temples, amphitheaters, and mountains carved from the bedrock millennia before I was born.

On the return drive to the Israeli border, through another stretch of limitless desert on the appropriately named Desert Highway, I was overwhelmed by the panorama of time and change and evolution. It hit me in the chest, a sharp blow that caused me to cough as I swallowed. I closed my eyes and shook my head to juggle everything back in place, and in that single instant I realized that there was another reason I had come to Jordan—to help me see my own evolution. It was time to leave Haiti.

In that very second, it was absolutely clear that I was ready to experience something else. I have no idea why this thought crystallized, but once it did, I knew it was the right one. Through osmosis, from the enormity of the desert and the cosmic history that created it, this innate sense of change grabbed on to me. It was like the Vodou spirits, something too powerful to ignore. Though I had no idea what the next step was going to be, I knew it was time to take it.

Much of what initially attracted me to Haiti had been slowly disappearing. I watched Port-au-Prince decline from a charming, manageable town to a sprawling, polluted, congested, and crime-filled city. During the coup, I stopped taking walks after dark, and then I stopped walking altogether. Even with the return of democracy, things were hardly safe and hadn't improved as I had hoped. My fear of the evils of the night after so many years of living with Haitian "insecurity" was so great that it was hard to adjust even when I wasn't in Haiti. When it got dark, I wanted to be in the safety of my own home.

I was also concerned about the impact the country's degradation was having on Kadja and Adjaline, Jean Raymond's eleven-year-old daughter from a previous relationship who was now living with us. Adjaline, a tall, spindly girl with long brown legs, moved in with us in

1996. I first met Adjaline shortly after I began to date Jean Raymond, and helped her get her United States residency after he and I married. Even before I returned to Haiti with Kadja, Adjaline had moved with her godmother to New York. I didn't get to know her well until she returned to Haiti two years later; by then she was fluent in English and had embraced the American culture with more zest than her native one. Adjaline was independent; her strong will was an asset and a challenge, and we circled around each other trying to find common ground.

While I felt confident that I was imparting important values to Kadja and Adjaline, other things I wanted them to grow up with were missing—the freedom and safety of playing in our neighborhood, competing in team sports, going to museums, libraries, parks. I felt the tug-of-war—Haiti's culture had won my heart, but now I wanted to return to the culture I'd grown up with. I didn't know if it was because I wanted to reproduce for my kids the childhood I had, or whether it was that the situation in Haiti had become too difficult to extract the things I loved about it. Either way, I was ready for a change.

I also had serious concerns about my own career; I no longer felt challenged or stimulated, academically or intellectually. The world that had intrigued me, the ever-changing political front that promised Haiti something new, better, and more democratic, wasn't materializing. I wasn't meeting as many interesting people because so many professionals and tourists alike were now avoiding Haiti because of its volatility, hardship conditions, and instability. I was also not getting as much work as I had had in the past—it dropped off drastically after the 1994 U.S. intervention, which I had expected, but it never really picked up again in any significant way. When I did write, it felt as though it was the same story I had been writing over the past ten years, only the names, dates, and places were different. I was sick of the corruption and lost my temper with the bureaucratic idiocy that went along with getting the most minor things done; renewing a license, paying an electrical bill. Little by little I shut myself off in order to avoid this nonsense as well as the endless traffic jams that suffocated most streets in the capital.

I waited until Jean Raymond came home from one of his rehearsals before I brought up the subject of moving. Autumn was just around the corner and the days were shorter—I'd been reading Don DeLillo's novel, *White Noise*, and put it aside when I heard Jean Raymond pull up. I was lying on the most comfortable piece of furniture in the house—a chair that looked like half a doughnut—wooden slabs joined together in a U shape that rocked back and forth. The year before I had cushions made for all the furniture—the floral pattern hadn't held up as well as I'd expected, but already I was thinking it wouldn't matter, now that we were going to move. I made room for Jean Raymond to lie on the chair next to me, and as we rocked back and forth I shared with him my thinking.

"So?" I asked after my long-winded explanation of why I thought it was time to leave.

"If you want to move, I can't stop you, but what about our life here?" Jean Raymond's hand drummed my thigh to a rhythm I was sure was in his head. "What do I do about my band?"

It wasn't leaving his band as much as his whole life in Haiti that was the real issue. I saw a hint of fear in his face. I reached across his chest and held his right hand. "We've got a lot of things to work out," I said, "but in theory would you support the idea of us moving?"

"I suppose." He refused to look at me.

"And we don't have to move back to San Francisco—it's far and there's no way I could go back to those foggy summers. How about starting in Miami and see what happens?"

"Hmmm." His ambiguous, maddening response was impossible to interpret.

We'd bought a condo in Miami a few years back—the commute to San Francisco was too long for short trips, and the real-estate market there had been ripe for selling. Jean Raymond stopped tapping with his left hand, flexing his fingers in a fist, in and out, in and out and I started to massage his right hand. "How about if we take the next few months to plan, and think about moving either at the end of this year or the end of the school year?"

"Hmmm," Jean Raymond said again. I leaned across to put my arms around him to see if I could get a straight answer, but he'd already disengaged. I picked up my book, but found after a few minutes that I wasn't concentrating, and followed him into the bedroom. In just those few minutes, he'd fallen asleep, shoes and all.

September was relatively quiet until Hurricane George blew through. We taped sheets over the open metal slats that served as windows but the wind was like a blender on high speed, whipping everything that got in its way. Branches fell, rain poured in, and mudslides *Wreaked* ~~reaped~~ havoc in the countryside. More than a quarter of a million people lost their homes in Haiti, and several hundred died. Journalists flew in for a two-week period to cover the story. I went with an NBC crew to film houses that had slid down embankments, rivers that flooded and destroyed homes, bridges that collapsed. I was as busy as I had been in four years—not enough to make me change my mind about leaving Haiti, but enough to remind me how much I enjoyed working as a journalist. And watching how a destitute population reacted with resilience and humor where none was readily visible renewed my faith that despite all, Haiti was going to survive.

In October an NBC *Dateline* crew hired me to assist them on a story investigating United Nations international peacekeepers who, in their host country, broke the law but paid no penalty. Although there were several components to the story, *Dateline* chose Haiti as the keystone because it was accessible and economical. They were focusing on several Pakistani soldiers who had been accused of beating and raping a Haitian in January 1998, just days before the United Nations peacekeepers were scheduled to leave.

After an interview at the United Nations Mission headquarters, we piled the equipment—lights, screens, filters, tripods—in a blue Mitsubishi pickup driven by Pato, a friend of Jean Raymond's; Sergo had stayed back at the hotel with the producer. I told Pato I'd follow with the crew in my car—the correspondent got into the passenger seat of my Honda Passport—the cameraman and soundman got in the backseat, their gear piled high behind them, and we took off for our next interview at Police Headquarters.

Unfamiliar with the new road we were on, I kept my eyes trained on the Mitsubishi. Just a hundred feet from the busy intersection with Delmas, I slowed down because of bumps in the road, and suddenly a white utility van cut me off, forcing me to a complete stop. Doors from the back of the van flew open and a group of brawny, well-dressed men charged out. When they started to pull handguns from their pants, I exclaimed: "Goddamn Haitian police. I'm sure they're going to cite me for some traffic violation I haven't broken."

One of the men pointed his gun at my head and yelled, "*Desann, desann,* get out, get out." He reached over and grabbed my arm, as if to pull me from the car. Furious, I took his hand and threw it off me. "*Pa manyen mwen,*" I said angrily: "Don't touch me." He waved his gun and continued to yell at me to get out of the vehicle. I did, but continued to curse him for being so rude.

I thought he was going to ask me for my license, then search me, a harassment that had become so routine I knew the drill; so I was surprised when he pushed past me and slipped into the driver's seat. It was only then that I realized that I had miscalculated what was going on. These were not plainclothes policemen, or if they were, they were off duty, and this was not a routine police check but a carjacking. So quietly, ever so quietly, I backed up, one step at a time, horrified at how close I had come to getting shot for my belligerence. I had another flash of panic that this man was going to drive away with the entire NBC crew, gear and all, until I realized that the other armed men had each taken a door and were simultaneously forcing my colleagues out of the car. Seconds later, the men spun my car around in the same direction from which we had come. The tires left skid marks as they peeled off, followed by the utility vehicle from which they had emerged—the only thing left behind was a dust bowl of dirt, and me and the crew, stranded in the middle of the street. Dozens of people, including a policeman at the nearby intersection who had watched the entire scene, stared at us for a few minutes, then shrugged and continued on.

I took a moment to catch my breath and assess the situation before I remembered that I knew someone who worked at the car dealership at the corner of the street we were standing on. My friend graciously gave us his office to call the American Embassy, the Haitian National Police, and the United Nations Civilian Police. My car was recovered about 2:00 A.M. the next morning, damaged, outside the same police station where we had filed our report after the carjacking. Our interpretation of the incident was that this had been a simple car robbery, but recovery of the car aroused speculation that this was an inside job by someone who knew what the NBC crew was doing in Haiti and didn't want the story covered, because the hijackers had gone through everything in the car. They went through our purses and backpacks and briefcases—all our personal things were littered throughout the car, but the important things, like passports and wallets and watches and other things of value, including the $100,000 camera, were gone.

The justice of the peace issued a summons for me because the car was registered in my name; he had "examined the evidence" and found ample cause to open an investigation.

"Three pieces of evidence that you have to explain," the round, dark-skinned judge said in French. His stomach folded over his pants, his fat fingers flipped a pencil back and forth as he spoke. I knew he was enjoying every minute of making me squirm, but I said nothing, sitting quietly even though I was smoldering inside. "Very incriminating."

"*Mwen pa pale franse,*" I said: I don't speak French. I knew that my speaking Creole would irritate him; he was the type who would consider the language of the population beneath him, which is exactly why I spoke it. "*Kisa ou vle mwen ekplikew*: And just what is it that you want me to explain?"

"Photographs of torture, pornography, and drugs," he continued in French, with an accent specific to a certain class of Haitians. The photos were ones the correspondent had in her briefcase on an internationally publicized killing by Canadian peacekeepers in Somalia in 1993. The justice of the peace thought he'd stumbled on evidence NBC was going to use in exposing Haitian police brutality. I wanted to point out to this pompous ass that he wasn't as smart as he thought he was if he couldn't recognize the difference between Haitian and Somalian police, but I'd not regained my sense of humor after losing it when the carjacker held the gun to my head a few days earlier. The "drug" the justice of the peace was referring to was the correspondent's anti-bee-sting kit.

The pornography was a personal photo I carried with me in my wallet. It was of Jean Raymond and Kadja cuddled on a couch, naked, their hands covering their private parts, each smiling at the camera. When I'd gotten out of the car during the hijacking, I'd left my pack behind; in thrashing through my things, the thieves had come upon this photo and maliciously torn it in two. The idea that others had shared this private, intimate photo made me wild with fury, and I struggled not to let my tears spill over.

I turned my chair to the side and looked out the dirty windowpanes toward the even dirtier side of the building next to it, refusing to make eye contact with the judge. I also refused to answer any more of his questions, singing Simon and Garfunkel's "Homeward Bound" in my head. The only time I responded was when he demanded that the correspondent and the man in the picture—Jean Raymond—come to see him.

"Why?"

"Because."

It was late in the afternoon, and I was emotionally spent. "When would you like them to come in?" I asked, still looking out the window. "From going through our papers, you probably know that the NBC crew was scheduled to have left Haiti today."

"I saw the itinerary," he said. "But there were no tickets, so maybe they weren't really scheduled to leave today."

"Right," I said, my anger now showing. "They put a false itinerary in their bag because they knew the car was going to get hijacked and they wanted to mess with you?"

Now it was the judge who ignored me. "There's nothing I can do today to get your car back. There are a few people who have to be taken care of before that happens, you understand?

"No," I said, knowing perfectly well that he was trying to extract a bribe. "What exactly do you mean by that?"

He stopped flipping his pencil for a second, just long enough to let me know that he still had the upper hand. "I'm busy tomorrow, and then it's the weekend. So have them come in next week. Monday morning. Not too early. Ten or eleven? Come with them and we can talk about your car."

I nodded and walked out without closing the door behind me. Sergo was waiting outside, his concern a comfort. He took one look at my face and put his arm around me.

"He's an asshole, Kathie," he said. "Whatever he said, forget it. There are other ways to settle this."

I shook my head, rattled by the chain of events and how, instead of getting resolved, everything was becoming increasingly more complicated—with the drugs and the pictures and the extortion for my car. "Just take me home, Sergo," I said. "I can't handle any of this."

As soon as I got inside, I called the one person in the government I trusted and explained the entire story. An hour later, I got a call back to say that I should return to the justice of the peace's office the following morning, that he suddenly wasn't busy anymore and would be expecting me.

When I arrived, the justice of the peace received me as as if I were his best friend. Whatever he'd been told, he understood that I was not to be harassed or extorted.

"No one needs to come in to see me anymore," he said with a big smile. "All that's been cleared up. But I couldn't get your car for you—that's another department. Go speak to Louis at *Circulation* on Delmas; he's expecting you."

In the end, it took another few days before the police released my car—the following week they recovered some of the stolen material, including the camera and videocassette tapes of the interviews we had done with the United Nations, removing any suspicions that this was more than a simple robbery. The more logical explanation was that we were victims of a gang who tracked people traveling that road because it was a main artery from the airport. "Bad timing," I said to the NBC crew when they left. "But still we were lucky. Other people on this road had been robbed and killed."

While I was grateful that only material things were lost, I was permanently unnerved and routine things began to traumatize me. When he was available, Sergo accompanied me places during the day. Jean Raymond tried to coax me to go out at night, but I didn't want to leave home. I felt marked by the police, the gangs, even the corrupt judiciary. It affected my work and made me an edgy mom and a bitchy wife. I didn't see how I could wait until the following June to leave Haiti, so with Jean Raymond's support, I advanced our departure date and within a week I packed up ten years of my life and left, telling almost no one that I was going.

Two days after we landed in Miami, Kadja started second grade in a private French-American school so that he could continue with his French; Adjaline enrolled as a sixth grader at the local middle school. I found myself lost, utterly and completely, even though this was my country, my language, my culture. Despite the fact that I had been the one to decide to leave, I felt alone and abandoned. Jean Raymond stayed behind to close up the apartment and figure out what to do with our stuff, as well as decide what direction his music and career should take. Every morning I dragged myself out of bed, got the kids off to school, and then stared at myself in the mirror, trying to figure out what I needed to do to reintegrate. After ten years of being away, certain things in the States seemed as foreign as those I had encountered in Haiti a decade ago.

Walking down the aisles of the supermarket, I was overwhelmed with the choices for any one item—low-salt crackers, low-fat crackers, crackers with wheat, wheatless crackers, cracked-wheat crackers. In Haiti there were only soda crackers. Going into a Star-bucks now made the simple process of ordering a cup of coffee an ordeal: coffee with cream, coffee with steamed milk, coffee with steamed low-fat or fat-free milk, Frappuccinos, cappuccinos, mochac-cinos. I walked out without ordering anything.

After I got my driver's license replaced, I went to the Budget car-rental office located at the back of the Sears in Coral Gables. The man behind the counter pointed to a form I needed to fill out. When I handed it back to him he looked it over, then asked: "What's your address and phone number, ma'am?"

I looked down and realized that I'd left those lines blank. I hesitated, confused. I had trained myself to avoid telling strangers in Haiti any-thing personal about myself, particularly intimate details like my address and phone number, and it had become such a reflex that I'd automatically omitted it from the car-rental form. Only when the clerk repeated the question did I realize my paranoia. "Without the infor-mation, ma'am, we can't rent you a car," he said, chiding me the way an adult does a negligent child.

Before I got a school car-pool together, I spent my days driving. Kadja's school was less than 20 miles from where we lived but traffic was so heavy that it sometimes took me an hour and a half roundtrip, twice a day. Adjaline's school was a ten-minute walk, but it took her an hour because she always had a book in front of her face—she was an avid reader, but hadn't figured out there were certain times when it wasn't appropriate.

I fixed up the house and created a daily schedule. I was much more successful with my exercise routine than the kids were with their homework routine. After school we went to the park or the beach or the library—whatever we did, I always made sure we were in by dark. I still was uncomfortable going out after the sun set. It was coming on winter, and by 6:00 the sun had disappeared—after we turned back the clocks, it was dark by 5:00, and once it was dark, I knew I was in for the evening. We played games, did homework, watched movies, and read books. It was quiet and comforting, and because we were in a safe neighborhood I went to sleep at night without worrying about gunshots or coups.

One evening we were invited by some Haitian friends to see a Creole play in Little Haiti, an area north of where we lived. I had never driven to this section of town before, and the darkness made it more difficult to find the streets. The kids sat in the back as I navigated the directions, but I got lost and increasingly more anxious with each wrong turn. When I finally stopped at a red light, two big, tall black guys in their twenties, approached the car. I broke out in a full sweat that dripped from my brow before I'd finished exhaling. My clammy hands slipped from the wheel and my heart pumped furiously. "Get down!" I shouted to the kids in the backseat, only to realize that these men were walking by my car just to cross the road.

"What's wrong, Mom?" Kadja said, shaken by my outburst.

"Nothing, sweetheart, just me being silly," I said, wanting to believe it was no more than that.

I wanted Jean Raymond by my side during this period of adjustment, but he was going through his own adjustment in Haiti. Although he said that he supported the move and wanted to be with us, he had some legitimate reservations about leaving behind everything that was familiar to him. The area where we had moved to in Miami, while ideal for the kids' safety and schooling, was hardly diverse. There were mostly wealthy white and upper-class Hispanics—Colombians, Venezuelans, some Cubans. I knew of only one other black guy in our neighborhood, who also had dreadlocks, and stereotypically everyone thought that he and Jean Raymond were brothers.

I was impatient to start building a new life as a family and when I asked Jean Raymond what was taking so long for him to finish up whatever it was he was doing, he got defensive.

"I can't just leave like that," he said.

"Yes, you can," I answered. "We need you here, with us."

"Don't make this so personal," he shot back. "I have a lot of responsibilities here—don't forget, you were the one who decided to leave so quickly. I have to close up the house. I have to find a place to store our things. I have to figure out what to do with the band, with my instruments. You knew when you moved up the date that I was going to stay behind to get this stuff taken care of."

"But how long can that possibly take?

"Why are you pressuring me?"

"Why aren't you pressuring yourself?" But I already knew the answer. My reality, schedules, time frames, expectations were foreign to him and, although he never admitted it, these things also intimidated him. My transition to his world wasn't seamless, but it was far less threatening than the transition I was asking him to make. He didn't see himself as being irresponsible, but rather very responsible.

I knew that he loved the kids and me, and it wasn't that he didn't want to be with us, but that didn't make me any more understanding. I wanted him to jump into my world with all the gusto I'd shown for Haiti. I wanted him to tackle English, take some classes at the local university, even join another a band. I was certain that the longer he spent away from us, the harder it was going to be for him to integrate not only into an American lifestyle, but a rhythm and familiarity that the kids and I were creating as we went along.

Underlying this was my own old question about his fidelity and if he was in Haiti with someone else. I knew it was futile to ask the question directly, and short of spying on him, I had no way of knowing if he was being faithful or not. He might have had the same question of me, but I doubted it. I didn't think he was ever going to leave me, but in my absence, given what I'd come to learn was so inherent in Haitian culture, it would hardly have been a surprise. Accepting that I would never know for sure, I focused instead on trying to see if we could salvage what we did have if and when we returned to living in the same house together. Through it all, Jean Raymond continued to say and do the right things one expects in a marriage, except the one thing that would have made the most difference; moving to Miami.

He did come, eventually, and we were happy to be reunited. Kadja and Jean Raymond went to the local park and played soccer. We all went fishing, to the movies, and took walks on the beach. But within a relatively short period of time, the concerns I had surfaced, and most of the problems boiled down to language. While Jean Raymond got by with rudimentary skills, his lack of confidence in speaking English held him back socially and professionally. "Call the community college for me," he said, "to see what kind of classes they're giving." Or "I got this number off the community board at the Winn-Dixie for guitar lessons. Will you call this guy to set up something for me?" Wherever we went, he stuck close to my side, not willing to have independent conversations without me to translate. With each favor, I was increasingly more resistant and resentful. I hated my lack of patience, but hated his lack of independence even more. It was hard for me to understand because I so wanted to be independent in Haiti, but Jean Raymond didn't seem the least bit interested in being independent in Miami. He refused to drive in the States because he was terrified of being picked up for being black. By now his dreadlocks were to his waist, and he often wore them in a tall woven hat, so he stuck out in a crowd, in a car, in the community where we lived.

Working on the relationship and being a mom in the States with no family or friends in the same city was hard. I knew almost no one in Miami and didn't have an immediate context for meeting people. My mom, who had a condominium as a second home just seconds from our home, came down for a few weeks and helped me get settled. Her support was as important emotionally as it was logistically. She babysat when I needed a break, advised me on where to get things, even how to get some things done—things I should have known, having been born and raised an American. I took great comfort in having her objective yet sympathetic ear as I made the cultural adjustment to an American lifestyle.

I was glad that I didn't have to look for work right away. But I knew that eventually I would, and was troubled because I didn't know what I wanted or could do. For the last decade, I'd built an expertise on Haiti, and now I wanted a break from it. I wasn't sure about journalism, either—I couldn't imagine applying to the *Miami Herald* and working on the metro desk—Haiti had spoiled me with coups and political intrigue. I did, however, make an appointment at the *Herald* to see about being a copyeditor, but halfway through their laborious exam I realized what a bad match that would be and left the test unfinished on the desk.

Slowly, as time went on and I became more involved in the community and picked up some interesting freelance work, things fell into place. Jean Raymond learned English and became more independent, if not more accepting of my culture and the benefits of being in the United States. Adjaline stopped reading when walking down the street and turned her passion for words into writing; her poems were insightful and wise and reflective of the two cultures she bridged. She learned to ride a bicycle and played softball on the local team. Although she still sucked her thumb and was a victim of her own raging hormones, she was developing into a smart, perceptive, and funny young lady. Kadja was growing up quickly, too. Because of his French instructors, he now sounded like a Parisian. He continued with the violin—something he'd started in Haiti—but soon gave it up for football, soccer, baseball, and swimming. His hair was no longer in tight curls, but long locks that he kept tied back at the base of his neck. As if overnight, he transformed from an affectionate, innocent toddler into a charming, self-assured adolescent with all the spitfire and confidence I had hoped for him.

It took more than a year to get back to Haiti, but when I was asked to work for the *Lehrer NewsHour* on a ten-day shoot in Haiti in December of 1999, I jumped at the chance. Sergo picked me up at the airport, a slimmed-down, jollier version of his old self, and in his presence I felt as if I had never left. On the drive to his house, we barely had a chance to catch up before his wife and his daughters scooped me up and plopped me down on the wooden rocker on their porch, where I'd sat for hours and hours and hours over the years. Within minutes everyone in the neighborhood knew I was back, and they all came by to ask me about Jean Raymond, Kadja, Adjaline, and my life in the States.

"How can I complain?" I said. "We live in a lovely neighborhood where the kids ride their bikes, walk to the beach, Rollerblade, and play sports. Adjaline's at the library 24/7. There's no insecurity, no political problems, electricity and hot water and telephones twenty-four hours a day."

"But," I added, "I don't have this—a community. I don't have any really good friends; I mean, not the kind I left behind here. And no one there knows anything about my life in Haiti or how important this country and you all have been in shaping who I am."

Gisele, my closest Haitian friend, who had watched my evolution as a naïve American to a wife and mother and accomplished journalist, grinned when I said I missed Haiti. She had known that I wouldn't stay in my anti-Haiti stage for very long. "You're just going to have to come more often," she said over a meal of rice and beans and veg-etable *graten*.

"And if you don't bring Kadja next time, you may as well stay home," said her father, who was as close to a grandfather as Kadja was ever going to have.

With the exception of Françoise, most of my foreign friends had left Haiti: Mike was working for the United Nations in Guatemala, Sophie had moved to Vietnam and was now the proud mother of a little girl, Andrew had moved first to Mexico, then to Brazil, where he was freelancing, and Martine had moved back to Montreal with her boyfriend and their two-year-old son. Another good friend of mine, Anne, was, like me, back and forth between Haiti and the United States, but our paths crossed infrequently. Despite their absence I still felt like I had a large community in Haiti—a larger community than anywhere else I'd ever lived as an adult. Every day I met someone with whom I had some sort of history, and every day I was pulled in closer to the life I'd never left very far behind.

There were no great changes in Haiti since I'd left the year before. There was still a lot of insecurity, political upheaval, and poverty. But the creative energy, lively conversations, artistry, and humor pulled me right back in, and I fell in love with the country all over again, wanting to reconnect to my old life even though I was no longer the same person. My time away from Haiti had given me a perspective on the value of how I'd grown that I couldn't have seen when I was there. The com-munity, the lifestyle, the immediacy, and the ability to discern my core values from the choices I made were things I had yet to find easily in Miami. When I had a free hour, I left the crew to walk downtown. As I sidestepped the perennial garbage, I heard my name and looked over to see Wawa, a much larger version of the little boy I'd first met eleven years ago in the courtyard of St. Jean Bosco Church. He towered over me by nearly a foot now—under his gray T-shirt his muscles rippled like those of a professional body sculptor. His hair was cropped short and he looked good, healthy, and happy. He swooped me up in his arms and swung me around, screaming, "Kati, Kati!"

"Put me down." I laughed and embraced him, my arms barely making it around his thick body. "How are you? What are you doing these days?"

Wawa smiled and the dimple I remembered as a little boy was still there. "Same business—not as good as before because things aren't as good as they used to be, but I get by." As a pickpocket, if I remembered correctly.

"And the rest of the gang?" I had attended Ayiti's funeral before I left—he'd died from a long battle with tuberculosis. There I'd run into Ti David, the soccer player, who later developed an undiagnosed illness that caused his leg to swell to the size of an elephant's before it eventually killed him. Eril had also been at Ayiti's funeral—he was thin and wobbly and also suffered from tuberculosis, but refused treatment.

"David's girlfriend and baby live in Tokyo," he said, referring to a neighborhood inside Cité Soleil. "But Fatil, well, Kathie, I hate to be the one to tell you, but he's dead."

I gasped. Fatil, Eril's older brother, had been smart, clever, someone I'd marked as a survivor.

"They say he was a member of the *Lame Wouj*, Red Army." No one was sure that there really was a Red Army, but it was blamed for a lot of clandestine activity in Cité Soleil, the former Aristide stronghold. Best guess was that the Red Army started out as a local slum gang that was then manipulated for political purposes, but eventually got out of hand. Whereas other countries successfully disposed of such gangs when they were of no more use, this was Haiti, and it was believed that the Red Army took on a mystical life of its own. Still, with the deterioration of the political situation in Haiti, nothing was clear; maybe Fatil was part of the Red Army, maybe he wasn't. But he was gone. I wasn't sure I wanted to hear any more news, but I couldn't stop myself from asking about Eril.

"*Mwen pa kache di-w, li nan dwòg. Dwòg ap touyel:* I'm not going to cover for him; he's still taking drugs. Drugs are going to kill him. I've tried, but there's nothing I can do to stop him."

Wawa paused, then looked me straight in the eye. "I sell drugs, but I don't do them. Not me. I'm not stupid. Don't be mad, Kathie, it's not my fault. It's the only way I can get by. Aristide came back and never did a thing to help us. Shit, half of our original group is dead, the other half dying. Nothing's easy."

"*Atansyon,*" I said to him: Be careful. "Please, please, Wawa, take care of yourself. You are the only one left I can count on."

"*Map konte souw, tou,*" he said: I count on you, too.

I didn't say good-bye because I'd said it too many times before. I handed him a 500-gourde note, and he pocketed it gratefully, promising to keep in touch.

I hoped he would, in his own time, if death didn't intervene first.

In 2002 Jean Raymond built a house in Port-au-Prince. He bought a plot of land just down the street from where he was born, across from the cemetery where I'd had my first Vodou experience with Maggie the photographer. He designed it after our Miami home, with big picture windows and a wide, generous porch with columns and inlaid sculptures. He built the house at the back of the lot, landscaping the long rectangle in front with grass and trees and scattered zinnias along the border. He put up a wall on either side of the property and a big metal gate in the front, full of sculptures and colors—it was a unique contribution to the neighborhood and one Jean Raymond was proud of.

It was an oasis in the midst of chaos, and as soon as I saw it I fell deeper in love with Jean Raymond. All the time he'd spent away from us he'd poured into building something that would draw us back, and he did. Even before the house was finished, we started to spend holidays there, and now we go as often as possible. We consider it as much our home as we do our house in Miami.

Despite the country's inconveniences, frustrations, even dangers, when I return, I put them all aside. I don't pretend they aren't there, but after all these years they are just part of the Haiti that I fell in love with, a country full of unpredictable flaws and wonders. We've done what we can to limit the inconveniences; Jean Raymond installed a powerful generator so we always have electricity, and we have a large reservoir that can adequately supply our needs. The installation of antennas allows for cellular phones, which makes communication easier, and since I don't have any deadlines to meet when I go, my only agenda is to spend time with family and friends, sip coffee in the morning, nurse an occasional rum sour at night, and be seduced by the magic unique to Haiti. I'm enchanted anew each time I step off the airplane and breathe in the tropical winds, feel the Caribbean sun hit my face as I walk across the tarmac and listen to the excitement of Diaspora returning home. I feel like one of them. My days in Haiti are never boring and the emotions they evoke twist and torque me, stretching me to be a better person. I am infinitely more tolerant, calmer, and not as quick to judge. Haiti has taught me that there is not only one way to look at a situation, but infinite ways to create a solution, with humor and devotion, heart and determination as key ingredients.

Haiti brings out the best in me; the gentler, softer side, the part of me that allows circumstances, rather than my predetermined ideas, to dictate. It strips away all the trivialities to uncover that one kernel of truth I need to guide me in my decision making. It fosters community while opening up the door to be an individual. I step off the plane, inhale the earthy mountains, and my entire body relaxes. I leave my impatience behind and mold myself to the looser lifestyle like an old pair of shoes.

Adjaline doesn't bother to unpack, she's immediately out the door to walk her old neighborhood, catch up with friends, eat *paté* and *fritay* and drink Haitian cola. Kadja reverts to Creole even before we've stepped off the plane. "*Men nou, manmi, nou rive,*" he shouts gleefully: Here we are, Mom, we've arrived, and he immediately begins to plan for a trip to the countryside so he can sit with his grandmother on her porch and dunk fresh bread in the sugary coffee she always offers him, climb the trees on her farm, ride the horses, and hang out with his cousins.

Jean Raymond radiates beauty and goodwill, thriving with his family and friends and culture surrounding him. He navigates the country's difficulties with an expertise and confidence he has yet to find in the States, and seeing him so peaceful reminds me of the things that made me fall in love with him.

As a couple, we melt into a rhythm that we never quite get right in the States. "What is it that we do differently here that we can't figure out in the States?" I ask as we watched the sunset from a spot near our house.

"You just answered your own question," Jean Raymond replies. "It's not what we do differently. It's Haiti. That's the difference."

I nod my head. Silently, we watch the yellow ball sink below the horizon, and the rainbow of pink and orange fade into blue and the darkness of the night. This is the same sunset we see in Miami but there's an aura about it in Haiti that is intangible, like the allure of the country. We don't try to analyze it or even understand it anymore, we just accept it. When it's too dark to see, we turn together, arm in arm, and head for home.

Epilogue

In the summer of 2004, my British friend Mike, who by a circuitous route was now living in Spain, flew to Haiti for a two-week vacation after having left the country three and a half years earlier. On his return, he came through Miami and stayed with me for a few days. He hadn't changed much in the sixteen years I'd known him—a bit balder, perhaps, and slightly more conscious of his waistline—but his curiosity about the world and interest in Haiti were as keen as ever.

"So, how was Haiti?" I asked as I wheeled his suitcase around my Honda Accord and placed it in the trunk. The congestion at the airport was as thick as the air—August was my least-favorite month in Miami, but it didn't seem to affect the steady stream of people coming through customs.

"Beautiful." His loud voice resonated with real emotion. "I'd forgotten how beautiful it was."

I nodded, acknowledging that we both had a love of Haiti that was at times hard to explain. Still, I wasn't expecting his reply. Beautiful? In its own way, but not a word commonly used to describe Haiti, even though the country has picturesque beaches and vast, rolling mountains. The valleys and some of the hillsides turn a rich, verdant green during the rainy season, despite the rampant deforestation, and set against the backdrop of an unobstructed skyline and large bodies of water the panoramic vistas are eye stoppers. But even during my first visit to Hispaniola in 1986, I would have used other words to describe the country: quixotic, exotic, intriguing, charming, frustrating, fascinating, alluring, difficult. And today, with nearly two more decades of devastation, deforestation, economic decline, and overpopulation—to say nothing of continued political instability—even some of those adjectives were a stretch.

Being with Mike again took me back to my first days in Haiti. Listening to his descriptions of his hikes in the mountains, trips to the beach, and reunion with old friends, made me nostalgic for a period of my life that would be impossible to replicate.

"I'm thinking of moving back," he said, as if he were reading my mind. Then the shock of what he said sank in. Happy reunions are one thing, but returning to live was another. "Of course it depends on a lot of things, but. . . ."

"Taina?" I asked, referring to his ten-year-old daughter, who after a bumpy start was thriving in Spain, speaking Spanish in addition to French, English, and Creole. "And work, Mike. What will you do?"

"Depends," he said. "I'm just looking into it."

On the one hand, I understood the impulse to return—Haiti's infectious charm wasn't something that waned with time. I didn't want to discourage him, but I had my doubts. My last few visits there had been difficult—more difficult than usual—and I wondered if he would be thinking of moving if he'd experienced the same things there that I had during the last eight months.

For the 2004 New Year, Kadja, Adjaline, and I flew to Port-au-Prince. Jean Raymond had been working hard to complete the second floor of our house so that it would be ready for our visit, and we were looking forward to relaxing and visiting with friends. But the addition was nowhere near completion. There were so many boxes of tiles on the dining-room table that the table legs eventually buckled under the weight, truckloads of dirt blocked access to the driveway, and there were more workmen than mosquitoes.

Like so many Haitians and Haiti lovers, we had been talking about spending the New Year there since 2002. January 1, 2004, marked the bicentennial of Haiti's independence, an act that was symbolic for many reasons, not the least of which was that the leader of the movement that eventually overthrew the French army was former slave Toussaint-Louverture. Although Napoleon captured Louverture and sent him to a remote prison in France where he eventually died, the battle at home raged on. Jean-Jacques Dessalines, Toussaint's lieutenant, led the slave army to independence and gave Haiti the right to boast of being the first and only black country in the world to overthrow its white colonizer. This commemorative occasion presented Aristide with the perfect opportunity to showcase his nation to the rest of the world, and the government had been talking—if not planning—an elaborate, expensive celebration for several years. The problem was that the festivities were targeted at foreign dignitaries and diplomats, not the Haitian people.

As the date approached, many of my friends canceled their plans. In part it was a response to the general state of the country, and reluctance to "celebrate" amidst renewed political instability. There was also concern about the crime, inflation, and the growing animosity toward Aristide. When, exactly, the tide turned against Aristide was hard to pinpoint, but there had been growing animosity for quite some time. The indisputable truth was that for the vast majority of the poor—the very people Aristide had promised to help—things hadn't improved. There was still no reliable electricity, no decent health care, education, or government services. The police as an institution had failed to provide protection and cronyism lived on. Aristide's advocates argued it wasn't lack of will but rather lack of resources and an antagonistic United States that was to blame for the mess. His critics claimed he not only did nothing to dismantle the corruption, but that he himself had become a part of it. I thought the truth was somewhere in between, but it was hard to know anything for sure. But that things were out of control was evident. In early December government supporters had stormed the university during a student protest, beating students savagely and breaking both of the dean's legs. At that point I was already asking myself whether or not things had spun so far out of control that Aristide was unable to rein them back in, even if he wanted to.

The situation had settled down a bit by Christmas, but there was enough bad press to scare away a lot of people. I'd already bought our tickets and Kadja and Adjaline, who hadn't seen their dad in more than a month, were eager to go. Once there I advocated going to the countryside to avoid the hoopla in the capital, but Jean Raymond wanted to stay close to home. In the end, we decided to throw a party at the house for our friends and people in the neighborhood with Jean Raymond's band providing the music. He spent the day preparing and cleaning the street, which, like most of the other roads in the capital, suffered months of neglect. I went to the market to buy some cake mixes, an American touch to an otherwise-typical Haitian menu: fried goat, fried chicken, fried plantains.

Our house was just about ten blocks from the rear of the palace. The government's priority had been to landscape and decorate the front and only the front, as that was the officially scripted route for those attending the festivities. I hoped that the media, however, would be savvy enough to venture just a few blocks away to see the knee-deep sewage and heaps of garbage that lined the roads and created an obstacle course for buses, pedestrians, and schoolchildren. These were not little piles of trash, but huge mounds accumulated over the months, sometimes six feet high, sometimes trodden down into foot-paths, carpets of plastic discards, rotten food, and soiled goods. The mound of garbage opposite our house ran the entire length of the block and then wound around the side of the cemetery. Every evening some unknown person set it on fire, which meant that we spent most of the time inhaling smoky plumes or ashen remains. Finally we paid some guys to haul away the pile with wheelbarrows, even though we knew it would be replaced before we had a chance to fill our lungs with fresh air.

Late in the afternoon of December 31, as we were preparing for the party, I received a phone call from Michelle Karshan, President Aristide's foreign-press liaison. Although I had said I wasn't in Haiti to report, when she told me that Aristide had scheduled a last-minute press conference, I couldn't pass up the opportunity to visit the palace again, and see for myself what Aristide had to say. I had felt conflicted for several days now, wanting to report because it was part of my routine in Haiti, but not wanting to because of my disgust with the government's sham celebration.

Separating my personal feelings from my professional ones was complicated. I hadn't reported on Haiti in more than a year, and I was feeling remiss that I hadn't made any effort to contact news agencies before I left to get a pulse on their interest for stories. I said I was in

Haiti on vacation, which I was, but I'd always been involved in the events of the day—in Haiti it was hard to be anything but. It would be like going to a bookstore and not reading. My response to whatever it was that happened in Haiti was always on two levels: the professional, and the personal. My personal reaction to the January first festivities was disgust. Rather than squander money on a fancy reception with specially made china, Aristide should have allocated his resources to collecting garbage. But in the end my curiosity won out and I threw on a skirt, grabbed a notebook, and headed to the palace to hear firsthand what he had to say.

I hadn't seen Aristide in three years, and the last time had been a fiasco. By then I was working for *Time* magazine and traveled with *Time*'s bureau chief, the intrepid Tim Padgett, from Miami to Port-au-Prince for an exclusive interview with Aristide. But once we got to the presidential residence, Aristide's wife Mildred stopped me from entering because, she explained as if I were some rookie, "Only Padgett's name is on the list." I was both insulted and annoyed. When the interview was over, she shuffled me into the president's office to say hello, a concession that was hardly worth the two seconds he spared to greet me. As was his habit, he said nothing clear or precise in the interview with Padgett, and thereafter I'd lost all interest in reporting what Aristide had to say.

But I followed Haiti like a mother hen, and among Jean Raymond, Gisele, and Françoise there was never a lack of insight. Sergo, who had continued to work with journalists as a driver and fixer, had accumulated a great résumé and a bevy of interesting stories. For the January 2004 celebration a television crew from South Africa hired him—when I got the news of the press conference I called him right away but he was in the countryside. We promised to trade stories later that night.

As I stood in the security line to gain access to the palace, there were a few faces I recognized, but more that I didn't know. Over the ten years that I'd reported there, I'd grown friendly with quite a few Haitian journalists, but there'd been a big turnover in my five-year absence, at least at the reporting-in-the-field level. Many serious journalists I'd known had either opened their own radio stations or were in managerial positions at someone else's station, or they'd left the country. I called the ones still there on occasion from the States just to check in, and when they came to the States, they looked me up. But unfortunately the beat reporters were by and large new faces, still dominated by men. And equally as unfamiliar were the foreign reporters; those I'd grown to know from our days of reporting during the coup years had also moved on. Sophie was in France, Andrew in Brazil, Howard somewhere in Asia, Harold in New York. It was bizarre to feel so at ease, and yet so alone with this group.

As we shuffled through the courtyard and into the palace proper, I was overwhelmed by its makeover. The majestic staircase hugging the right and left corners of the palace's main lobby was embellished by a red ribbon woven through its beams. A gigantic floral arrangement of bird-of-paradise and other exotic Caribbean flowers graced the first landing. At the top of the staircase on the bright red carpet was an enormous Christmas tree—the only live one I'd ever seen in Haiti in sixteen years. It was decorated with red and blue balls, the colors of Haiti's flag. I'd never seen the palace look better, not even when Aristide was installed in 1991.

The press conference was held in a long, rectangular room on the second floor. On one side were portraits of important Haitian figures—Aristide, Catherine Flon—Haiti's Betsy Ross—and Jean-Jacques Dessalines, their George Washington. Opposite the paintings were large windows overlooking the presidential lawn. I'd stood before those windows numerous times before and had always been awed. This feeling came not only from being inside a building where so many important historic events, conversations, coups, and ceremonies had taken place, but at the privilege of being part of Haiti's history even as it was happening. In just the short time that I began my journey in Haiti power in the palace had changed hands nearly a dozen times. And each government represented a different stage in my own development, from naïve reporter with no experience to a self-confident and competent one. Each time I was in that room, and each time I looked out that window onto the park below, I saw something different, whether it was a pro- or antigovernmental demonstration, Haitian tanks or American troops. On the eve of Haiti's bicentennial, with the stands below and the lights illuminating the freshly scrubbed plaza, I should have been happy. But I felt a sadness that tugged at my middle and made me slouch. Whereas I had grown, Haiti had regressed. I saw no bright future on its horizon.

I stood with the rest of the press corps at the back end of the room, separated from the president by a large boardroom table with twenty-two microphones that were unused. Aristide looked slightly older, his droopy left eye more pronounced. Like the palace grounds, he was well groomed but seemed misplaced. When his eyes scanned the crowd, they passed over me as if I were invisible. I didn't flinch at the slight, but bristled at the softball questions. This press corps was pretty green. When someone asked him if he was at all threatened by the growing discontent, and whether he would be able to fulfill his five-year term, he gave a rare smile.

"Yes, I'll be here on February 7, 2006," he said. "We will use it as an example of how democracy works."

Eventually, the press coordinator handed me the microphone and I pushed myself toward the front of the pack so that he could get a clear view of me. I asked my question in English: "What is the government's position regarding the Haitian refugees who are deported from the United States?" Aristide stared at me without acknowledgment. I matched his poker face as I pushed on, not expecting that I was going to get a straight answer. If Aristide admitted that there were refugees seeking political asylum in the United States, he'd have to admit there was civil unrest, a lack of security, a malfunctioning judicial system in Haiti. "Is there an agreement between the two countries about deportation? What happens to the refugees when they return? Are they routinely jailed, as some human-rights groups claim?"

"We need to use the law to protect the rights of citizens." As usual, he sidestepped the question. "One way we can help Haitians stay in Haiti is through economic achievement. But we have to dialogue to see what can be done."

Economic achievement, I thought cynically as I walked down the palace steps out into the fresh air. How about paying them to pick up the garbage? How about the millions of Haitians who will be celebrating this New Year's Eve in the dark, without electricity, food, or water? With each step away from the palace, I grew more irritated as the stench of the sewage-flooded streets grew stronger. By the time I reached our front door, my shoes were thick with gook, I smelled nasty, and I was in a foul mood for our New Year's party.

In contrast to the foreigners who had a great time at the palace party, as one of the few foreigners at our party, I didn't have a very good time. It wasn't that I was a foreigner—I knew many of the people there, but I wasn't in a party mood. The band was loud and Jean Raymond was far more interested in his music than he was in spending time with me. The kids were distracted with their own friends, and the few friends that I had invited decided instead to go to the beach. Kadja and I rose early to join them the next day, leaving

Adjaline and Jean Raymond to sleep. I was only too happy to stay away from the palace festivities, where tens of thousands of supporters—or hundreds of thousands, according to some reports—gathered to hear Aristide speak amidst tight security, as protestors set up burning tires and flaming cars in other neighborhoods in the capital. Following his speech, the president took a helicopter to the northwestern town of Gonaives, the City of Independence, where a far smaller crowd had gathered. Two hundred years earlier, Gonaives was ground zero for Independence Day, when the country that had been called Saint-Domingue, was restored to its Taino name, Haiti, (Mountainous Land) by Dessalines. But unlike Dessalines, who basked in victory, Aristide was met with protests and gunfire and had to cut short his Gonaives trip; and the president of South Africa, one of the few high-ranking foreign dignitaries who had come to Haiti for the New Year celebration, stayed behind in the capital.

"It was terrible," Sergo said later that day. "There were a dozen busloads of people who'd been brought in from the capital, but they were the only ones there. Most of Gonaives stayed away. There were protestors who got beaten by the police, and burning tires everywhere. And when rocks started to fly, the police panicked and began to shoot into the air. You should have been there, Kathie!"

Kadja and I, however, had a wonderful day with our friends, sunning, surfing, playing Scrabble and enjoying pumpkin soup, the traditional New Year's Day dish. I was sorry to say good-bye because with everything going on in Haiti I wasn't sure when I would be back, and I truly loved these people. Despite the time and distance, they remained my family.

In the end, I returned just a few weeks later, as it became increasingly clear in January 2004 that the situation was about to explode. Demonstrations for Aristide's departure were not only becoming more frequent, but swelling in numbers. The Group of 184, an alliance of businessmen, civil leaders, trade unionists, and students organized most of the marches. Meanwhile, Aristide supporters were holding their own demonstrations, and the inevitable clashes were making international, not just local news. My journalist juices kicked in. Padgett and I spoke every day, and he gave me carte blanche to go to Haiti the minute I thought the story was going to break.

By Tuesday, February 10, it was clear to me that I should be in Haiti witnessing events, not obsessing over them on the Internet and through television and radio reports. I was nervous about the trip, more so than I had ever been before. The previous week, a rebel group from the north calling for Aristide's departure had taken over Gonaives and nearby St. Marc, burning buildings, killing local police, and creating panic. The government had sent in Special Forces to retake St. Marc, but the situation was dicey. The rebels still controlled Gonaives and both sides were heavily armed.

But I booked myself a flight because I couldn't stay away. I felt an inexplicable draw to be a part of what I knew was going to be a new chapter of Haiti's history. Instinctually, I felt that something big was going to happen and whatever it was, I wanted to be there. I'd missed Aristide's forced departure in the 1991 coup d'état when I was giving birth to Kadja in California, and if there was even the slightest chance of something like that happening again, I wanted to be there. I was sorry that Padgett was in Brazil on assignment, but was relieved when I was able to reach Sergo. "I can't do this without you," I said, giving him my flight details. "Can you work with me for the next few days?"

"Of course," he assured me. He'd been urging me to come for weeks, and I could feel his smile across the phone line. He knew, maybe more than anyone else besides Jean Raymond, how much I depended on his eyes and ears and common sense. "What's the game plan?"

"I leave here on the 6:30 A.M. flight. Can you meet me at the airport? Come prepared to head north right away. Let's see if we can get through the roadblocks at St. Marc and make it all the way to Gonaives."

"I'll be there, Kathie," he said. "I'll get a four-wheel-drive and fill up. But don't be disappointed if we are turned back along the way."

"Let's see how far we get."

At 4:00 A.M. I was already on I-95 headed north to the airport, my stomach churning in anticipation. The normally long check-in line with Haitians and their oversized suitcases were as absent as the cars had been on the freeway that morning. No one, it seemed, was interested in going to Haiti. I saw one other group of foreigners who I guessed to be a television crew because of their luggage—the proverbial silver steel cases—but otherwise I just gazed out the window, knowing the only thing I could count on when I got there was that Sergo would be waiting for me.

And, of course, he was, with a four-wheel-drive vehicle and a full tank of gas. Jean Raymond was also there with a warm kiss and a thermos of hot coffee that he handed off to me in exchange for my luggage and computer, taking my things back to the house for safekeeping.

We didn't encounter any problems on the road as we headed toward St. Marc, a ninety-minute drive on the northern highway; but just a few miles before town, a blue pickup screeched out onto the highway from a bushy area of grass and headed in our direction at high speed. As we drove past the point where the pickup had emerged, we saw a group of agitated peasants. Sergo knew immediately that something was wrong and doubled back to find out what was happening.

On the grassy knoll just feet from the highway we saw the corpse of a young man, who probably had been in his twenties. The entire back portion of his head was ripped open. I retched. The man's teeth were shattered and his eyes were wide open. His T-shirt was pulled up, exposing his stomach, which was covered with blood. His pants were pulled down to his knees, his white boxers a muddled dirt color. He wore just one lone flip-flop, unsoiled in the midst of blood everywhere else on his body—his legs, his arms, and what was left of his skull.

"*Sak pase la?*" Sergo asked, wanting to know what had happened.

"*Nou pa konnen,*" a young man said, wringing his hands: We don't know. "We saw the pickup pull out and so we walked over. Think they dumped the poor guy's body just here on the other side of the *kandelab* (cactus barrier)."

The man had been dead long enough for his body to become stiff, but not so long that it had started to decompose. After discussing among themselves what to do, the men in the group decided to dig a hole and bury him before decomposition started. Sergo kept shaking his head, as if he was having trouble processing the whole thing. That upset me further because I so completely depended on Sergo's clear and level head. The coffee jiggled in my stomach, and I felt slightly nauseous as we got back into the car. We kept the windows rolled tight, continuing cautiously toward St. Marc.

But we couldn't have gone quickly even if we'd wanted to. The remains of the previous week's turmoil littered the road leading up to the town's center—everything from rocks to burned tires to the chassis of charred vehicles were strewn across the highway. A unit of Special Forces stood guard at the entrance to the town. We explained what we had just seen but they were uninterested.

"Tell the justice of the peace," said one of the strapping guys who sported an Uzi, flak jacket, and steel-tipped boots.

"You don't need a justice of the peace to confirm that he's dead. He's dead. Half his brain is gone," I insisted. "Doesn't anyone want to go there to investigate or talk to people about what happened, find out who he is?"

"No," said an even larger man with an equally menacing weapon and the same accoutrements. He readjusted his Uzi in front of his chest.

Chastened, Sergo and I nodded, rolled the window back up and inched forward, though my thoughts remained back at the checkpoint. Were those Special Forces men really heartless, or just so desensitized from all the political corrosion that they couldn't show emotion? They must have known that even though they were heavily armed they had no real authority, and the dead man down the road was yet one more example of their ineffectiveness.

St. Marc was lifeless save for an occasional cluster of young men along the side of the road. About a quarter of a mile farther in to town, across from one of the buildings that had been burned in the clashes one week earlier, we found some members of *Bale Wouze*—Clean Sweep, a local "popular" organization whose actions so mirrored those of a gang's that it was hard to tell the difference. *Bale Wouze* had regained control once the Special Forces kicked out the rebels. Rumor had it that they were well armed and ready to retaliate against anyone who didn't support their president.

I put my reporter's notebook in the pocket of my cargo pants, not knowing how receptive they'd be to a journalist. I approached them with a smile and extended my hand, saying I'd just flown in from the States and wanted to get a sense of what was happening in their town. No one wanted to say very much until one guy, wearing a white tank top and pink flip-flops, pushed back the metal chair he was sitting on and walked over.

"We're defending ourselves against the opposition with our goodwill," he said, identifying himself as Figaro Desir, self-appointed spokesman for the group. I asked him if it was okay to take notes because I wanted the people in the United States to hear firsthand what was going on. Warming up to this white woman who spoke Creole, he agreed.

The butt of some sort of metal weapon stuck out from the pocket of his tan shorts, which he fondled while he spoke. When pressed, he wouldn't tell me where *Bale Wouze* got its financing, although it was clear the members were heavily armed and drove expensive four-wheel-drive vehicles parked nearby. Figaro dripped bravado. We stayed only as long as I needed to get my quotes, then I excused myself by saying we had more distance to travel.

The farther along the main road we went, the more deserted the town became. "*Blanch, blanch, blanch,*" Sergo said: completely bare. The graffiti on the walls seemed to have come alive: "*Sourit pa janbe la ri*: Even the mice don't cross the street."

Just before the far edge of town, we noticed a plume of dark smoke off to the right. We turned down a side street and drove less than a few hundred yards until we came across two new four-wheel-drive vehicles aflame. The bodies of the cars were still intact. "Whoever did this can't be far from here," Sergo said, not taking his eyes off the street.

But no one was in sight. We backed up, sweating. I could feel the back of my pants sticking to my legs as fear worked its way down my body. Sergo stayed cool, ever mindful of our surroundings but a bead of sweat stopped on the side of his cheek just below his earlobe. In the shadows between two houses, a young man beckoned us over, motioning toward a house behind him that was also on fire.

"They killed two people and dumped their bodies in that house," he said, afraid to identify himself other than that he lived in the neighborhood. "Then they set the house on fire to make sure no one discovered who the victims were."

"*Kiles yo?*" I asked: Who are they?

"*Yo?*" he said. "The ones who want to destroy anyone who doesn't support Aristide."

We drove on, only later learning that an alleged massacre took place that afternoon. In Gonaives the atmosphere was equally tense but in a different way. This town was under the "protection" of the rebels, many of whom were part of a makeshift gang called the Cannibal Army. Just days before, they'd burned down the police station, attacked and driven out all government representatives (specifically targeting police officers) and emptied the prison. Former soldiers and military officers who had lost their jobs when Aristide disbanded the army were now on the warpath to take over the country.

Men with black ski masks and Uzis, some on motorcycles, many more on foot, amassed at the entrance into town. The road was splattered with rocks, broken glass, car parts, burned tires, and other, unidentifiable items. Everything was the color of pasty dust. Young kids washed their bicycles at the roadside while men stood in line to check their lottery tickets against the day's winners at the small booths.

The Cannibal Army's power base was the Gonaives seaside slum of Raboteau. They were joining forces with other gangs, and their name was morphing from the Artibonite Front to the National Resistance Front to the Front. Their spokesman, Winter Etienne, was hanging out on the street corner by their makeshift headquarters, a run-down building with wooden chairs and chipped tables. Despite the 90-degree weather, he had on black boots and a blue ski cap. Amiot Metayer, who headed up the Cannibal Army, was one of his closest friends, he told us. At one time Metayer and Aristide were allies but after a series of disputes, Metayer was murdered in September 2003. Etienne blamed Aristide, and said that was the start of the slow rebellious process that eventually led to the gang's taking control of Gonaives.

"After Gonaives, we will take the other towns in the north. Then," he said, as if he were planning a road trip, "we will march into the capital and take the rest of the country."

Metayer's tomb was at the intersection of the street, beneath a bust adorned with bottles of orange soda, a wicker tray, plastic containers, candles, and a photo of his mutilated body, from which the eyes and heart were cut out after he was killed. Even though I was familiar with the incidents leading up to Metayer's death, seeing the photo of his corpse made me gag. The wave of nausea I'd felt outside St. Marc just a few hours earlier returned. My legs felt wobbly as I got back into the car, where I rolled up the windows and asked Sergo to crank up the air conditioning, as if the cold air would blast away the images we'd just seen.

It was impossible to collect my thoughts as we headed out of town and back toward Port-au-Prince. And surreal to know that just twelve hours earlier, I'd gotten out of my nice, comfortable, safe bed in Miami. That world was as far from this as a rain forest is to a desert. This day required complete and utter attentiveness; all my senses were engaged. From past experiences, I knew that a wrong word or a wrong move could have been fatal. I was aware of our vulnerability, but at the same time I felt strangely confident. This wasn't a new situation. Though the names and place were different, I'd been through such hell before. This time I was in complete command of the language and had no trepidation about maneuvering the terrain. That gave me energy for what I knew was going to be a very long week.

The need for being so alert, so observant, and so sharp energized me. It was what made me feel alive in Haiti, where everything was profound, unpredictable, and ultimately fascinating. The closest thing I came to being pulled into reporting in the States had been the 2000 presidential election, but that didn't begin to compare with the intrigue, impulsiveness, and volatility of Haiti's political world and its capricious actors.

"I wonder," I said to Sergo as we bounced along the potholed highway, "how long this can go on. You know, when I got here this morning, I firmly believed that no matter how bad the situation, Aristide had to stay, that he had every right to serve out his five-year term. He was elected, after all. Christ, it's time Haiti broke this ridiculous cycle of kicking out its leaders every time there's a problem."

"But can Haiti take another two years of this?"

"Yeah, that's what I'm asking myself, too. The problem is that there's no process in place for voicing complaints. It's not like the people can turn to the legislature to take action—it hasn't really been functioning for what, months—years?"

"You remember there was that dispute following the 2000 parliamentary elections when the opposition pulled out because they said the voting was rigged?" Sergo asked.

"Right. And then there were some senators who resigned, and four left in January when their terms expired, just like the entire eighty-three-member Chamber of Deputies. So clearly there's no way the legislature can do anything. And, if I remember correctly, the constitution has no provision for impeaching and removing the president, does it?

"Not that I know of."

"So what options are there?"

"I don't know, Kathie, but I know that weapons are going to play a role in whatever happens. When I was in Gonaives a few weeks ago, these guys showed me their stockpile—they have a shitload of weapons—all kinds—grenades, pistols, guns, rifles, a full arsenal."

"And they're not the only ones, right? Isn't that part of the problem? This group of rebels has arms, but so do Aristide's people. We saw that in St. Marc."

"And there are a whole lot more in Cap Haitien and in Port-au-Prince. I think it's going to get a lot uglier before it gets better."

Sergo's prediction played out over the next few days. We took a puddle jumper to Cap Haitien, which was cut off from the rest of the country because of roadblocks north of Gonaives. In theory the government still controlled the country's second-largest city but the police were at best lackadaisical, if not incompetent. We found an amiable young man with some gas in his car, Willy, who agreed to a flat rate to take us around for the day. We paid him half the cash up front.

Almost immediately we felt the tension in the streets and saw it on the faces of merchants who, instead of their normal frenetic movement, seemed to move with a rabid urgency. There were far fewer people in the markets in Cap than in Gonaives even though Cap was a larger city. Willy told us that at night absolutely everything shut down because there was no electricity. "*Epi tout moun pe,*" he said: Everyone is scared. "They're waiting for the rebels."

We asked Willy to go along the northern road toward the eastern border with the Dominican Republic. We knew we wouldn't make it all the way, but we wanted to see just how far we'd get. After less than an hour, we hit a roadblock where all vehicles were being turned back, including buses full of people who'd traveled from the Dominican border that morning. We sidestepped the problem by having Willy wait for us while we hired a couple of guys with little motorcycles who were obviously in financial cahoots with those responsible for the roadblock.

I held on tight as we headed toward Trou de Nord, a small town less than five minutes away. Anti-Aristide people had attacked it recently. We toured the police station, the government buildings, the school. We talked to a few men in the town, then asked our motorcycle chauffeurs to continue further east to visit some of the other towns where the government had been forced out. Sergo's driver refused.

"*Nou fè yon deal,*" said Djonni, a rotund guy with fat lips and fat eyelids.

"Yes, to take us around," Sergo answered. "You've only taken us to Trou de Nord."

"We're not going any further," he said.

"What do you mean, you're not going any further?" I asked, immediately pissed off at the apparent move to take advantage of us. I got off the back of my motorcycle, sensing that this could get ugly but unable to control myself. If I had to, I was determined to walk back to Willy's car rather than be exploited by these guys.

"Just what I said. We're going back."

"Hold on," Sergo said to me in English, and had a muted conversation with his driver. I knew that at least my driver had a pistol in his pocket that I had felt when I put my hands on his hips during the ride, and that thought quieted me down. I saw money exchange hands and Sergo motioned for me to get back on my motorcycle. I didn't say a word the entire ride back, afraid that my driver might just dump me on purpose. He went faster than he had on the way out and I was forced to hold on tighter, my hands pressing on the pistol butt. I started to think that with our luck Willy wasn't going to be there when we got back but not only was he waiting for us, he'd gone out and purchased a round of *kasav* for me because I'd remarked earlier that I wanted to take home some of the manioc-flour bread. His thoughtfulness made me forget the motorcycle guys and remind me what I loved about Haiti, the kind gestures in the oddest of places and most unexpected of times.

Before flying back to Port-au-Prince we stopped at the police station, where despite the chaos in the town the mood was as calm as a warm Caribbean breeze. The only officers we could find were sitting on overturned buckets playing *lido* (Haiti's version of Parcheesi) and eating greasy chicken. They refused to talk to us because, they said licking their fingers, that wasn't in their job description.

We caught our flight back to the capital without incident. The last two days of my trip were largely devoted to edits for my *Time* article. It was my first foreign solo assignment for them and the editors were scrupulous with their fact checking. Each time they made a change I had to drive back to the Oloffson Hotel and try to log on to the complimentary computers they had for guests, since there was no Internet access at Jean Raymond's house. By the tenth trip there, I was reeling with exhaustion. And for a brief second, self-doubt, because of the sheer number of questions they asked. But then I reminded myself how far I'd come and the nagging voice of incompetence faded away. Unlike my panic in the early years of reporting, when I wasn't sure that I was going to get the story right or embarrassed that I didn't understand the language or know the players, I knew what the story was now. I'd stretched myself as far as I could to make sense of the country's intricacies, complexities, confoundedness. I was not going to let a word or phrase in an article trip me up, not after the distance I'd come personally and professionally.

My article was on the escalating power struggle between those who supported Aristide and the rebels based in Gonaives. The final sticking point was the translation of *chimères,* the term popularly used to describe the rowdy, erratic, and violent gang of Aristide supporters. The literal translation was "chimera," but *Time* wanted to use "Monster" so they could title my piece "Monsters Versus Cannibals." In the end, they won, but the article was an entire page long, and I had a monster-size grin on my face when I saw my solo byline. Back in Miami, I bought lots of copies. Kadja took one to school, and I took extra delight in knowing that made him proud.

Returning to Miami was an adjustment, even though I'd been gone only five days. Adjaline was away, but Kadja needed and deserved my attention. I found that I was focused more on the news than I was on him and even though I knew I should slow down and redirect myself, I couldn't. I listened to the Haitian radio stations each morning, and combed the news for the most up-to-date information I could find all day long, logging on just one last time before turning out the light each night. There were frequent developments, and I found them taking up the time I would have otherwise spent doing laundry, going grocery shopping, or cooking dinner.

Within a few days of my return to Miami, the rebels took over Cap Haitien, destroying the airport and police station in the process. I knew I needed to return to Haiti.

"Do you mind, Kadja?" I asked, praying that he would absolve me of my guilt by saying no.

"If I stay with Frankie," he said, referring to his friend, "what am I going to eat?"

The innocence of the question brought me back to earth. It wasn't that he didn't care about Haiti, but his needs were typical of a young boy's, and I responded with a hug and an assurance that I would keep the house stocked with his favorite things so that he could always come home and grab something if he didn't like what they served at Frankie's house. He regarded me skeptically when I promised to be back in a week, but I promised to rent a cell phone and call him every day. "As long as it's not Iraq, you can go," he said.

This time I went with Padgett, a *Time* photographer, and his assistant. On the morning of February 24 we piled into a four-wheel-drive and took off toward Gonaives, hoping to find Etienne and some of the other rebel leaders I'd met the previous week. More than ever the rebels seemed on course to take over the country, one city at a time. We got as far as St. Marc. This time it was the government, not the rebels, who had set up the roadblocks; the Special Forces were determined to keep the rebels from advancing toward the capital. They were all enormous men who wore ski masks and flak jackets and camouflage uniforms and had piled up massive buses and four-wheel-drive vehicles to block the road, leaving only a tiny space for pedestrians to squeeze through. The men were imposing and unfriendly and told us to turn around. "Maybe you can get through tomorrow if you get here early," one of them said, his deep voice ominous. "But there are no guarantees."

Disappointed, we had no choice but to turn around, only to be caught in the unanticipated transformation that had taken place in Port-au-Prince during our three-hour absence. It was as though a tsunami passed over the city and spread fear everywhere. Roads that had no traffic on our trip out of town were now cordoned off with mobs of crazed, well-armed youths, some still in their teens, brandishing weapons as if they were hockey sticks. The roadblocks were sporadic—as might be expected in such an anarchic country—popping up like gophers without any pattern or reason. It was the chaotic nature and careless manner in which the armed, roving *chimères* handled the weapons that sent a shiver of fear from my shoulders to my toes. I found myself clenching my fingers, as if squeezing my hand would make them hold their guns with more care. These guys were far more dangerous than the rebels, many of whom were former soldiers with weapons training. These were merely unemployed youths drunk with power, unfettered by any ideology, and free to behave so recklessly because there was no one to stop them.

We had to negotiate nearly a dozen roadblocks to make it back into town; it took twice as long to cover the last ten miles as it had traveling to St. Marc and back. I decided not to stay at our house with Jean Raymond on this trip, but with Padgett and dozens of other journalists at the Villa Creole Hotel in Pétionville, where we had computer access, a restaurant, and guaranteed electricity. Although I desperately wanted to be with Jean Raymond, sleep in our bed, and wake up to the pulse of our neighborhood, it wasn't prudent to stay at our house. The situation was too precarious and the house too close to the palace. That meant, however, that unless Jean Raymond drove up the hill before sunset, we wouldn't be spending our nights together. Neither of us wanted to risk the danger of darkness.

On Wednesday, February 25, Padgett, the two photographers and I, along with four other journalists, negotiated our way onto a small plane to take us to Cap Haitien. We had tried for hours to make the fifteen-minute drive to the airport from our hotel but because of roadblocks had been turned back so many times that we'd almost given up. When we did get there, none of us had anything more than the things on our back, but we jumped at the chance to go to Cap Haitien because that was where the rebel leaders were, and we felt it was impossible to tell the story properly without speaking with them.

By now flying to Cap Haitien was "illegal" because the airport, per se, no longer existed—the shells of the building were still there, but everything that had been inside them during my last trip was gone apart from the overturned file cabinets and papers, documents, manifests, and ticket stubs littering the ground like leaves in autumn. The town was still without electricity and there was no telephone communication. Our pilot dropped us off on the tarmac and pointed to a spot several yards away. "Wait for me tomorrow morning, around 7:30," he said. "I'll try to come back for you then."

Try, I said to myself, then pushed the thought away, not wanting to go down that road. If he didn't come back, we'd figure out something, though I had no idea what since the roads were blocked and we had no vehicle. Kadja, I thought, would be quite unhappy with that uncertainty.

Jean Raymond knew better than to tell me that I never should have gotten on the plane in the first place, though he'd have wanted to, and my mother—well, I hoped that she might never have to know.

We took a taxi to the Mont Joli, ironically, a lovely hillside hotel with views overlooking the Atlantic Ocean, where the rebels were camped out. Men in military uniforms, their weapons strapped to their chests, roamed the reception area as we checked in. There were more such men in the bar area, a Graham Greene moment that took me back ten years to when the FAd'H (Armed Forces of Haiti) ruled. Even more uniformed men lay on broken chaise longues among the bougainvillea by the pool, some with drinks in hand, others snoring with their Uzis nestling in their arms like steel lovers. Below the pool deck, by the restaurant patio, we spotted the ringleader, Guy Philippe, who agreed to speak with us as soon as he finished lunch.

He was younger than I expected, and though I wasn't predisposed to like him, I found him charming and congenial. He spoke fluent English with just a trace of an accent. A boyish grin masked the ambition and destructiveness that I suspected was inherent to him, and he sported a gold chain over his camouflage uniform. He was self-effacing at times but I had no doubt he could be ruthless. When we asked him why he'd come back from the Dominican Republic to lead the rebellion, he said, "I'm not the leader of the people—the people are the leaders and we're just following them.

Déjà vu. That is exactly what Aristide said when he announced his presidential candidacy in 1990, that he hadn't chosen to run, rather it was the people who had chosen him and he would just follow their lead.

Philippe and Aristide, the two men now battling for control of the country, both had supersized egos. They were both multilingual, well educated, and highly motivated. Each believed he was the Messiah and would bring transformation to their country. Aristide had failed miserably. Philippe was still green, but I suspected he had the tacit approval of at least some in the U.S. government who would be only too happy to see Aristide go, and would therefore assist him in getting the job done. But that hardly made him a capable leader.

Philippe had figured out that part of gaining power had not to do with popularity but with the appearance of popularity, and for that he needed the press. He'd stationed himself in the best hotel in Cap Haitien and made himself available to the flow of reporters who were crafty enough to get there. I felt completely safe, as bizarre as that sounded, much more so than in Port-au-Prince, where there were dozens, if not a hundred or so journalists. Philippe rewarded those reporters that made their way to Cap Haitien by schmoozing with them and cultivating personal relationships with the photographers to make sure his picture was in all the major publications. He also spent time each morning cruising the Internet, getting news from different countries and sources so he'd know how to play his cards most effectively.

His sidekick, Gilbert Dragon, was equally savvy, though the intense gaze from his dark eyes made me ill at ease and I suspected he was quite capable of violence. Equally fluent in English, he explained that he and Philippe had graduated from the Haitian military academy, trained in Ecuador, served as police officers, and then fled to the Dominican Republic shortly before Aristide was reelected in 2000 because of "false accusations" that they had been plotting a coup d'état. "This is war," Dragon stated. "It is my dream to bring Aristide to trial. And if I have to die in the process, so be it."

"But what do you expect to accomplish?" I asked, unable to get a hold on his logic. He was smart enough to know that taking over Port-au-Prince was one thing, but governing it was quite another.

"Education, food, health," he said, like any good politician. He boasted of how his men were already positioned in Port-au-Prince, just waiting for their orders to move in. And that those would be given soon.

I had no reason to doubt him. Philippe, Dragon, and a few others appeared to have the manpower and the organizational structure to take over the capital as they'd threatened. I suspected their financing came from drug trafficking, and perhaps well-placed backers in the Haitian elite, the United States, and even the Dominican Republic. I also believed that despite their disclaimers, they were coordinating on some level with the U.S. government and the Group of 184. It was creepy to be around them, around their groupies, around the weapons and uniforms and sheer machismo of the setting. I took a long shower, sorry that I didn't have a change of clothes and even sorrier that there were no females with whom I could commiserate.

I was also angry. Angry and disgusted with Aristide for messing things up so badly that it had come to this. For wasting unprecedented support, nationally and internationally, for not knowing how to use his popularity to at least take the country from, as he had promised, the most abject penury to poverty with dignity. For his mismanagement, his tolerance of corruption, and his authoritarianism. And for distributing weapons that he thought would help consolidate his power but in fact were now being used against him.

I was angry with the rebels, too, whom I trusted no more than Aristide. I didn't believe they had any more intention of helping their country than any other military leader had ever done in Haiti's tortured 200-year history.

But even more than that, I was sad for Haiti. Almost no one I knew was better off. Jean Raymond's mom, Agnes, had stopped planting her fields years ago, unable to compete with the local market and even lacking the money to buy the necessary seeds. Her youngest son, who had dreams of getting a college education, dropped out of high school because he couldn't afford the tuition—and public school was so ineffective that it wasn't even an option. At twenty-one he'd already had two kids. Another son had moved back to the countryside to live with Agnes because he couldn't support his wife and three kids in the city. Jobs were nonexistent, school was increasingly more expensive, and the police department, not even ten years old, was corrupt and politicized. I was frightened, but more for Haiti than I was for myself. This time Haiti had so much more to lose if things unraveled, not the least of which was the hope that at one time had been placed on Aristide to fix this broken country. That hope was gone, but I couldn't imagine Haiti with *no* hope, and that was where things seemed headed.

Philippe and his men hung out poolside that evening, and early the next morning many were asleep in the chairs scattered throughout the lobby. It was like walking through a movie set; camouflage uniforms bunched on beefy men with the ocean in the background of this resort hotel. I wasn't sorry to leave. Shortly after daybreak, as instructed, we returned to the tarmac and then just sat, waiting to see if the plane was going to show up. It was cool and there was a slight breeze. I wondered if Kadja had gotten up in time for school, and if he would be worried that I hadn't called since it was impossible to do so from Cap Haitien. I hoped he wasn't even thinking about me but I couldn't stop thinking of him; we were surrounded by a group of local children who, for lack of anything better to do, were playing with the debris from the ransacked airport offices when they should have been in school. One young girl had a two-ring notebook filled with hundreds of pages of documents. She meticulously lifted each sheet of paper off the rings, held it up in the air, and waited for the wind to catch it so she could watch it fly off. An image for the willful way that Haiti's meager achievements were being allowed to slip away.

After more than two hours of sitting in what was by then a broiling sun we heard the distant rumbling of an engine overhead and heaved a collective sigh of relief when the plane came into view. Back in Port-au-Prince, the palpitation of fear that had subsided when I was with the rebels returned with an even greater pulse. Our driver had been robbed on his way back from the airport the day before. Other journalists had had their vehicles stolen. Downtown was anarchy. Everyone—or rather no one—had authority. Police had deserted their posts, and Aristide's gangs, the *chimères,* armed with the weapons he had provided, were stopping traffic, demanding money, stealing vehicles, and patroling the streets yelling *Rat Pa Kaka*—even the rats must stop shitting—a warning to everyone that they must do nothing. In the hotel, we were one step removed from the danger, but not foolish enough to think it wasn't still lethal.

Schools, banks, and businesses closed. Gas stations dried up. Flights to and from Haiti discontinued, following American Airlines' lead. There were as many weapons on the street as there were piles of garbage. We passed dead bodies in the middle of the road and had to avoid roadblocks manned by drugged-out hoodlums. I went to sleep with random shooting, woke up to random shooting, heard random shooting even when it wasn't there. When I spoke with Kadja, I made sure to ask about his activities and meals, not wanting to give him any real information about how things were going. I asked Frankie's mom not to let him watch the news. But my mother watched, and listened to the radio, and read the paper. Nothing I said calmed the fear I knew she felt.

On two separate occasions, helicopters landed at the Dominican embassy next to our hotel to evacuate their staff; the journalists scrambled into action, thinking that it might be Aristide evacuating. It reminded me of how frightened I had been ten years earlier when the Americans had flown their helicopters overhead in the middle of the night, on one occasion dropping pro-Aristide leaflets, and on the other tiny transistor radios on parachutes. I was a wiser reporter now—more experienced, more confident, and professionally satisfied. I loved working on a story that was receiving world attention. I had the advantage of drawing on my previous personal experiences in Haiti to speak of current events with a unique perspective, and I was flattered to be considered a competent sounding board for those less familiar. This feeling of competence helped soothe the otherwise anxiety-filled days

Although I was there for *Time,* Padgett was flexible and allowed me to do additional writing for the *Christian Science Monitor,* some reporting for the *Houston Chronicle,* and many radio updates for local NPR stations as well as the Terri Gross show. I wished that my old reporting buddies—Andrew, Sophie, Harold were around, or lovely Maggie the photographer, but I was grateful that Gisele and Françoise were still around. We barely saw each other during the melee, but thanks to cell phones it was now much easier to keep in touch. And of course having Jean Raymond there was a supreme comfort, even though I was concerned that Kadja would feel lonely without the presence of at least one of his parents.

Around 9:30 P.M. on Saturday, February 28, I received an anonymous call on my cell phone. I was in my hotel room with Jean Raymond, lying on the bed in a stupor. I didn't recognize the voice, nor could I make out for sure what the man said, only something about "he's leaving tonight" before he clicked off. No one answered when I called the number listed on caller ID.

Reluctantly, I got dressed and went to the bar to find Padgett, who was hanging out with a few other journalists knocking back rum drinks. We called some of our best sources, but no one could confirm anything. Around midnight another group of journalists sped out of the hotel—we guessed they must have heard a similar rumor that

Aristide was leaving, but in the end we figured it was just that, a rumor, and eventually shuffled back to our respective rooms. Jean Raymond was sound asleep when I crawled into bed, but I snuggled close, needing his body to warm the chill in my soul.

My phone rang the morning of Sunday, February 29 at 6:30 A.M. It was Jeffrey, the ABC correspondent with whom I'd been working informally for the last three weeks. He had a confirmed interview with Aristide at the palace for the Sunday-morning talk show out of New York, and he'd been told to arrive at that time to set up.

"We've been honking the horn, but the gate's shut, Kathie, and there's a large padlock on it."

"Is there anyone around?" I asked. "Any of the Palace Guard visible?"

"Not a soul," he said. "And we confirmed this interview three times yesterday."

Jeffrey figured out how to do a conference call from his cell phone and was able to plug into my call to my best government contact, who seemed as perplexed by the locked gate as we were.

"Is Aristide still here?" I asked.

"Yes," my contact said.

"Well, can you confirm that?" Jeffrey asked, only to be interrupted by the sound of gunfire in the background. "Get out of here!" he yelled at Sergo, who was driving for them.

And then the line went dead.

Meanwhile Jean Raymond had turned on CNN to see if there was any news, and shortly thereafter CNN announced that Aristide, along with his wife Mildred and a small retinue, had left Haiti on a plane just a few hours before for an unknown destination (which turned out to be the Central African Republic).

The rest of the day was a blur, with Guy Philippe's men arriving in the capital and former army soldiers coming out of the woodwork.

Even a driver for one of the television crews ran home to put on his old military uniform. Mobs began to loot the deserted police stations before former soldiers came in to take charge. Aristide's gangs, which only twenty-four hours earlier had been ruling the streets, were now running for their lives. The official story was that Aristide had agreed to leave and signed a paper to that effect, but an alternative version began to circulate almost immediately that he'd been kidnapped by the United States and didn't even know where he was going until he had been in the air for twelve hours.

Padgett and I spent another five days following events, including Guy Philippe's arrival in Port-au-Prince, which was like the Second Coming. We were little worker bees in the swarm of journalists that hovered around him as he greeted people like the savior he imagined himself to be. He gave us a special acknowledgment, but we didn't pursue him, having gotten what we needed in Cap when none of the other journalists were around. Writing for a weekly that wasn't due out for another seven days, our challenge was to come up with an interesting angle that would capture the essence of what had happened while taking into account that it was going to be old news by the time of its publication.

As we worked on the elements of the story for the upcoming edition of the magazine, we worked desperately to find a way to get home. The border was still closed and flights hadn't resumed. Eventually we caught a small plane to Santo Domingo and then from there to Miami. When I was finally able to hug Kadja, I had a hard time letting go. The exhaustion I felt was close to general anesthesia, and it was about two weeks before I began to feel like myself.

In the past, however, when I'd experienced such intense events in Haiti, Haiti had been my home. This time, I felt a sense of relief that I was living in Miami. It was bittersweet, because I still loved Haiti and wished it only the best. I knew it had to change from the inside out, but I had no illusions that this new regime could make that possible.

I was comforted by knowing that I now had a community in Miami who cared about what I'd gone through and, because of that, cared just a little bit more than they might have otherwise about Haiti. I knew that none of this was going to change their lives, but it made a difference to me to know that in some way I'd helped people better understand a country I loved. And I continued to hope that by understanding how things happened there, or for that matter in any other part of the world, we could improve our own lives.

As the details emerged about what had happened in Haiti, it became apparent that the United States had left itself open to accusations of meddling, at the very least, if not the outright kidnapping of Aristide, who immediately cried foul play. He stayed in the Central African Republic for just a short time before flying back to the Caribbean, to Jamaica, on the pretext of reuniting with his kids. But I think he was testing the waters by getting close to Haiti to see if the temperature was right for him to try to return. It wasn't, and several months later he found asylum in South Africa, where he continues to dream of returning to Haiti for another attempt to lead his people to the promised land.

In the meantime the United States helped orchestrate the installation of an interim government led by Gerard Latortue, a Haitian who used to work for a UN agency and had been living in Boca Raton, Florida. He has been dubbed The Turtle (*la tortue* means "turtle" in French) but he lost no time in making some major blunders, such as embracing the rebels as freedom fighters, including former military and old Tonton Macoutes in his government and focusing on after the prosecution of only Aristide supporters rather than depoliticizing the justice system and running the country.

No one thought that change would be easy, and it certainly hasn't been. Aristide supporters believe they were robbed of their leader and as the new underdogs they laid low for about six months, but brought out their weapons on September 30, 2004, the thirteenth anniversary of Aristide's coup. Chilling, that his supporters were asking for his return yet again, but this time they used unprecedented violence by decapitating their victims. Meanwhile, the former Haitian military emerged from underground and have been waiting, none too patiently, to return to their old jobs in an official capacity. Then there are the heavily armed rebels who hope to sweep elections scheduled for the end of 2005. And finally, there is the hodgepodge coalition of businessmen, civil leaders, and washed-out politicians who are still trying to figure out how to get back into the game after being sidelined by the international community when Aristide left. UN troops, which do not include the Americans, have been at best unsuccessful in their efforts to bring peace to the population.

What will it take to fix Haiti? I have no answers. But I worry that the infrastructure is so fragile that it may not survive many more punches. It's been reduced to a country in name only. Some say that the international community has done nothing but mess up Haiti. Others say that it hasn't done enough. What's true is that nothing has worked. And nothing certainly will until there's disarmament, because Haiti will otherwise revert to the only system it knows, in which power lies in the weapon, not in the voice. For a brief period, Haitians were willing to try something new, and Aristide was it. But he failed miserably, and I don't know if during my lifetime new leadership will be able to overcome that failure and engage the population again. If enough money is pumped in that's not grafted, if enough jobs are created and enough schools and colleges are built, if enough of the professionals who have emigrated out of Haiti return home, then perhaps there could be some hope. But until then, I see more of the same. Just different names, with the same old pattern prevailing. Each political and natural disaster will eat away just a little bit more from Haiti's core.

That was made shamefully true when twice in just a matter of months storms devastated two separate areas of the country, the result of decades of deforestation and nonexistent environmental policies. In the south, a major flood along the border left more than 3000 dead in May; in September a tropical storm flooded Gonaives, wiping out most of the city. The government was not only incapable of responding, but couldn't protect the convoys of international aid earmarked for the flood victims. Some say the destruction was payback for the violence that gripped Gonaives in February 2004; others say it was the hand of Vodou, but that's just an easy way to deflect the necessary introspection that has to be done if the next generation hopes to live better.

Which brings me back to Mike, and his thoughts of moving back to Haiti, and my reluctance to encourage him. He spoke about it some more during the few weeks he was in Miami, but by the time he returned to Spain at the end of August, he was already having second thoughts, every day e-mailing me clips of military takeovers around the Haitian countryside, remarking on the increase in crime and the ineffectiveness of the UN forces that had come to restore order.

Like Mike, I will probably always consider Haiti home no matter where I am. It's as much a part of my life as any childhood memory. It helped shape and define me as an adult and I am eternally grateful for that. It transformed me from a relatively unexceptional middle-class Jewish girl with rote American experiences to a woman with an exceptional bond to a people and country with whom I shared no race, religion, culture, or frame of reference, and to a man whose life experiences were initially impenetrable. It forced me to rethink my preconceived ideas about the way things were supposed to be and experience them as they were. No part of me was left untouched— my spiritual boundaries were extended, the depth of my emotions expanded, and the range of my senses heightened. Because of Jean Raymond, I am wiser, more compassionate, and more passionate. Because of Haiti, I am more keenly aware that there are alternative ways of looking at the world and living life. I wouldn't be the person I am today if all the people I'd met in Haiti hadn't had such a strong and potent influence on me, and if I hadn't lived there—not as an American on vacation or in a fancy resort, but as a friend, neighbor, wife, mother, reporter. I only hope that someday my son will be able to experience the magic of Haiti that I did, all those years ago. Haiti gave me that hope, and it is only fitting that I now give it back to Haiti.